THE PLAYS OF
GEORGE CHAPMAN

THE TRAGEDIES
VOLUME I

THE PLAYS OF

GEORGE CHAPMAN

EDITED WITH INTRODUCTIONS
AND NOTES BY

THOMAS MARC PARROTT, Ph. D.

Professor of English Literature at Princeton University

THE TRAGEDIES

VOLUME I

NEW YORK

RUSSELL & RUSSELL · INC

1961

PUBLISHED 1961 BY RUSSELL & RUSSELL, INC.
BY ARRANGEMENT WITH ROUTLEDGE & KEGAN PAUL LTD.
L. C. CATALOG CARD NO: 61-13786

PRINTED IN THE UNITED STATES OF AMERICA

FREDERICK JAMES FURNIVALL

In Memoriam

PREFACE

THIS, the first volume of a new edition of the plays and poems of George Chapman, includes his tragedies, *Bussy D'Ambois*, *The Revenge of Bussy*, *The Conspiracy and Tragedy of Byron*, *Chabot*, and *Cæsar and Pompey*, together with the two tragedies ascribed to him by their first publishers, *Alphonsus Emperor of Germany*, and *Revenge for Honour*. The second volume will contain his comedies, and the third his poems, along with a general introduction, a glossary, and a bibliography.

The need of a complete edition of Chapman's plays and poems has long been felt by students of Elizabethan literature. It was not until more than two centuries after his death that the first collection of his plays, *The Comedies and Tragedies of George Chapman*, London, 1873, appeared. This collection was incomplete, omitting *Chabot* and *Eastward Ho*, and the text which professed to be an exact reprint of the old editions left much to be desired. In 1874–5 the first complete edition of his works appeared, edited by R. H. Shepherd, who is generally understood to have been the editor of the previous edition. This later edition, although remedying the omissions of the former, is satisfactory neither to the general reader nor to the student of the Elizabethan drama. There is no need to go into details here ; evidence of the careless manner in which the task was performed will be found in abundance in my Text Notes to the various plays. Since 1875 only selected plays of Chapman have been published, and of these the largest collection, that included in the *Mermaid Series*, rests upon the work of Mr. Shepherd. There is, I believe, ample room for a new and complete edition, which will at once satisfy the demand of scholars for an accurate text, and present the work of the noble old poet in a form suited to the general reading public.

Such, at least, is the opinion of the present editor, and it is at this goal that he has aimed in the preparation of the present edition.

The text has been the object of peculiar care. Founded in every case but[1] one upon the first edition of the play in question, it has been compared, wherever possible, with later editions in Chapman's own age, and with the work of modern editors.

The spelling has been modernized throughout, and for this, in a work offered to the general public, I believe that I need offer no apology. Exact reproductions of old books are for a limited circle of scholars. They are not editions in the true sense of the word, as I understand it, but merely material from which scholars who have not access to the originals may construct editions. Nothing is gained for the general reader, nor indeed for the average student, by reproducing with painful exactness the misprints, variants in spelling, often due to the old compositors rather than to the author, and the confusing punctuation of the old texts.

On the other hand, I have attempted to keep, so far as possible, the actual language of the author. I have made no attempt to correct his grammar in accordance with our modern notions of propriety. I have even retained the old spellings when they appeared to me to denote a true, though now obsolete form of the word, as, for example, *murther*, *shipwrack*, and *porcpisc*. Here I have in the main followed the guidance of the *New English Dictionary*, modernizing such forms as it includes under the mere variants of spelling, and retaining those to which it assigns an independent place. That I have been strictly consistent in dealing with the hundreds of cases on which I have had to pass judgment, I will not venture to assert. Compromises are rarely consistent, and this edition is a frank attempt to find a middle ground between a slavish retention of the errors of the old texts, and such a radical revision as would dispel the ancient flavour of the work.

In the matter of metre, I have gone perhaps to undue lengths in my desire to retain the old. Nothing, I think, is clearer than that Elizabethan blank verse, written for the stage and meant to be judged by the ear rather than the eye, differed very widely from our modern conception of the ten-syllable iambic line meant rather to be read than heard. What seem to us irregularities and even palpable errors, were licenses which were claimed and freely employed by the Elizabethan playwright. I have

---

[1] The one exception is *Bussy D'Ambois*, where the edition of 1641 presents Chapman's own revision of his text. See Notes, p. 541.

therefore seldom emended a line for the sake of rendering it more ' regular,' never, indeed, except when I have been persuaded that the ' irregularity ' was not due to the author, but had occurred at press.

One typographical matter I may be allowed to mention here. Chapman, it seems, was in the habit [1] of denoting the contracted pronunciation of the past tense and the past participle in -*ed* by using the apostrophe; where he wrote out the *e* he meant to indicate that the final syllable was to be pronounced. I have followed this usage throughout, even at the cost of reproducing forms that may seem uncouth to modern eyes; where I have altered it I have treated the alteration as a correction of the text and have noted it in the Text Notes.

Any additions that I have made either to the text or to the stage directions of the old editions I have included within square brackets. Where the alteration has involved the dropping of a word or part of a word, as in the change of *suspection* to *suspect*, on p. 362, l. 105, it has been impossible to indicate this in the text, but all such changes have been carefully recorded in the text notes. In regard to the text itself no comment is necessary on this customary practice, but a word may be in place in regard to the added stage directions.

It is a matter of common knowledge that the earliest editions of Elizabethan plays are, to our modern minds, extremely deficient in stage directions. So scanty are they, indeed, that often it is difficult to grasp the situation at a glance without adding, in imagination at least, the stage directions that a modern author would supply. To facilitate the reading, then, of Shakespeare or of Chapman, I believe that a modern editor is justified in introducing whatever stage directions may seem to him to conduce to this end. On the other hand, to omit to distinguish such additions from the original directions is at once to give a false impression of the old texts, and to render the edition quite unreliable for that study of the Elizabethan stage to which at present so much attention is being directed, and from which such valuable results are, we may well hope, shortly to be obtained. I have, therefore, added stage directions wherever I saw fit, knowing that all danger of confusing my additions with the original was prevented by the typographical device of including the new within square brackets.

---

[1] Instances of this usage may be found in the first lines of the first play of this volume, *Bussy*, I, i. 19 and 22. Cf. with these I, i, 44.

One addition alone is not so marked. Where the old texts gave us no list of the *dramatis personæ* I have supplied such a list, omitting on account of the awkward appearance of the device to include the whole list within square brackets, but calling attention to it in the Text Notes. Where the old text gives a list, but omits one or more of the personages, the additions are marked as usual.

For the convenience of the reader and for the purposes of reference I have divided the usually[2] unbroken acts of the original into scenes and have numbered each scene separately.

The notes, beginning on p. 541 of this volume, include a special introduction, illustrative and explanatory notes, and text notes on each play. The introduction attempts to give whatever is known as to the date of composition, the sources, the stage history, and so forth, of the play, together with a brief appreciation of its peculiar characteristics. In the case of collaboration or of disputed authorship I have tried to give a careful and, I hope, impartial survey of the facts on which I have based my conclusions. So far as possible I have tried to give an answer to the varied problems presented by these plays, but I do not presume to think that I have in any case ' settled Hoti's business.' I can only hope that my work has made the conditions of the problems clearer, and brought them some stages nearer to a final solution.

The notes in general are meant to elucidate and illustrate the text. Chapman is by no means easy reading. Swinburne ranks him along with Fulke Greville as ' of all English poets the most genuinely obscure in style.' I have tried to throw light upon his obscurities, sometimes by comment, sometimes by the method of paraphrase ; but I cannot pretend to have solved all the difficulties which the text presents. The definition of single words has as a rule been left to the Glossary, which will appear in the third volume. Special attention has been paid in these notes to Chapman's use of his sources, to his borrowings from the classics, to parallels with other Elizabethan writers, and to parallels with other passages in his own work illustrative of his trick of repetition.

The text notes give an account of the former editions, both

---

[1] This is the case, for example, with *Bussy, The Conspiracy and Tragedy of Byron,* and *Chabot.*

[2] *Revenge for Honour* alone of the plays in this volume presents the modern division into scenes.

contemporary and modern, and record the various readings of the old editions, where more than one exists, except in the case of mere variants of spelling. Even these latter are noted, however, when they may throw light upon any difficulty. The readings from the old texts are, of course, given *verbatim et literatim*, so that the reader may see how far the alterations proposed or adopted are justified. I have recorded also the most important emendations proposed by modern editors or commentators even when these have not been received into the text. In short, I have tried to make these notes full enough to enable the reader who is interested in such things to check my text, to restore, if he so pleases, the old, or perhaps to suggest a better reading than that which I have adopted.

Finally, my thanks are due to scholars on both sides of the Atlantic who have assisted me in my labours. First of all to the late Doctor Furnivall, to whom this volume is dedicated, as a slight token of gratitude for many instances of personal kindness and scholarly counsel; then to Dr. Bradley, Mr. P. A. Daniel, and Mr. Le Gay Brereton, from all of whom I have received valuable aid in the construction and annotation of the text. I owe Mr. Charles Crawford special thanks for placing at my disposal a series of parallel references in Chapman which have more than once availed to solve perplexing difficulties. I have made frequent use of Professor Koeppel's *Quellenstudien zu den Dramen Chapman's*, and take this opportunity to acknowledge my indebtedness to my friend, the author. To my colleague, Dr. Kennedy, of Princeton University, I owe a deep debt for hours of long and painstaking labour spent with me in the determination of the text and the correction of proof sheets. Nor must I omit to thank Mr. T. J. Wise, of London, and Mr. Armour, of Princeton, for their kindness in allowing me the use of their copies of old editions of Chapman. And finally along with hundreds of workers in the field of English letters my sincerest thanks are due to the authorities of the British Museum and the Bodleian for the courteous assistance which alone renders work like this possible.

The list of Errata, somewhat longer than I should like, is due, in part at least, to the circumstances under which I have been forced to read the proof. I dare not hope that it is complete, and will be grateful to all who will point out other errors in text or comment for future correction.

T. M. P.

OXFORD, *September*. 1910.

CONTENTS

ERRATA.

Page 15, l. 146, *for* a *read* o'.
  ,, 32, *in the headline, for* Act II *read* Act III.
  ,, 50, l. 183, *for* Chymæra *read* Chimæra.
  ,, 80, *for* ghost[s] *read* Ghost[s].
  ,, 84, *supply the marginal number* 150.
  ,, 109, l. 159, *for* Char. *read* [Char.].
  ,, 116, l. 96, *for* Casimir *read* Casimer.
  ,, 125, l. 38, *for* Bastile *read* Bastille.
  ,, 146, l. 170, *dele the comma after* mind.
  ,, 147, l. 210, *for* Char. *read* [Char.].
  ,, 174, l. 144 *and elsewhere, for* Fountaine Françoise *read* Fontaine
        Française.
  ,, 283, l. 68, *for* realities *read* realties.
  ,, 288, l. 46, *for* others *read* other.
  ,, 289, *in the stage direction omit* and.
  ,, 289, l. 77, *omit* the *before* favour.
  ,, 297, *the marginal number* 40 *should be one line lower.*
  ,, 297, *omit* and *in the stage direction after* l. 42.
  ,, 302, *in the stage direction after* l. 208 *for* Exit *read* Exeunt.
  ,, 318, ll. 313, 315, 316, 318, 329, 332, *include* Judge *in brackets.*
  ,, 320, l. 403, *for* home *read* [home].
  ,, 334, l. 141, *for* had *read* Had.
  ,, 353, l. 282, *for* lyncean *read* Lyncean.
  ,, 361, l. 68, *for* above *read* [a]bove.
  ,, 384, *in the headline for* Act V *read* Act IV.
  ,, 390, l. 120, *for* possess *read* profess.
  ,, 400, l. 200, *for* Oot *read* Out.
  ,, 408, l. 147, *for* ton *read* tun.
  ,, 411, l. 37, *for* Lorrain *read* Lorraine.
  ,, 416, l. 243, *for* conforted *read* comforted.
  ,, 423, l. 181, *for* art *read* part.
  ,, 430, l. 109, *for* schelm *read* schelm.
  ,, 432, l. 29, *for* Rheinpfal[z] *read* Reinfal.
  ,, 434, l. 100, *for* We'll *read* We['ll].
  ,, 435, l. 146, *for* spiel fresh up *read* spiel fresh up.
  ,, 436, l. 183, *for* Ric *read* Rich.
  ,, 441, l. 348, *for* Ate *read* Até.
  ,, 455, l. 78, *for* Lieve *read* Süsse.
  ,, 479, l. 124, *for* Abo[la]fi *read* Abo[la]ffi.
  ,, 485, l. 373, *dele the comma after* East.
  ,, 498, l. 4, *insert commas after* Do *and* affections.
  ,, 503, l. 113, *dele the comma after the parenthesis.*
  ,, 504, l. 136, *for* [Enter Mura] *read* (Enter Mura).
  ,, 506, l. 212, *for* befits *read* befit[s].
  ,, 508, l. 8, *for* ton *read* tun.
  ,, 500, l. 1, *for* [without] *read* [within].
  ,, 512, l. 149, *insert a dash after* her.
  ,, 515, l. 113, *for* 'Twere *read* ['Twere].
  ,, 517, l. 200, *for* [Cries without] *read* [Cries within].
  ,, 517, l. 209, *for* [Enter Simanthes] *read* (Enter Simanthes).
  ,, 520, l. 289, *for* starts *read* start[s].
  ,, 537, l. 336, *for* festivals *read* festival[s].
  ,, 560, l. 24, *for* prince *read* Prince.
  ,, 563, *column* 1, l. 45, *for* like *read* likely.
  ,, 614, l. 15, *for* 261-6 *read* 256-61.
  ,, 626, *column* 2, *for* 239 *read* 234.

BUSSY D'AMBOIS

A TRAGEDY

Bussy d'Ambois

A TRAGEDY

PROLOGUE

Not out of confidence that none but we
Are able to present this tragedy,
Nor out of envy at the grace of late
It did receive, nor yet to derogate
From their deserts, who give out boldly that   5
They move with equal feet on the same flat ;
Neither for all, nor any of such ends,
We offer it, gracious and noble friends,
To your review ; we, far from emulation
(And, charitably judge, from imitation)   10
With this work entertain you, a piece known,
And still believed in Court to be our own.
To quit our claim, doubting our right or merit,
Would argue in us poverty of spirit
Which we must not subscribe to : FIELD is gone,   15
Whose action first did give it name, and one
Who came the nearest to him, is denied
By his gray beard to show the height and pride
Of D'AMBOIS' youth and bravery ; yet to hold
Our title still a-foot, and not grow cold   20
By giving it o'er, a third man with his best
Of care and pains defends our interest ;
As RICHARD he was liked, nor do we fear
In personating D'AMBOIS he'll appear
To faint, or go less, so your free consent,   25
As heretofore, give him encouragement.

DRAMATIS PERSONAE

Henry III, *King of France*
Monsieur, *his brother*
The Duke of Guise
The Count of Montsurry
Bussy d'Ambois
Barrisor, ⎱ *Courtiers ;*
L'Anou, ⎬ *enemies of*
Pyrhot, ⎰ *Bussy*
Brisac, ⎱ *Courtiers ;*
Melynell, ⎰ *friends of Bussy*
Beaumond, *an attendant on the King*
Comolet, *a Friar*
Maffé, *steward to Monsieur*
Nuntius

Murderers
Behemoth, ⎱ *Spirits*
Cartophylax, ⎰
Umbra *of the Friar*

Elenor, *Duchess of Guise*
Tamyra, *Countess of Montsurry*
Beaupré, *niece to Elenor*
Annable, *maid to Elenor*
Pero, *maid to Tamyra*
Charlotte, *maid to Beaupré*
Pyra, *a court lady*

Courtiers, Ladies, Pages, Servants, Spirits, &c.

ACTUS PRIMI SCENA PRIMA

[*A Forest near Paris*]

Enter Bussy d'Ambois, *poor*

Bus. Fortune, not Reason, rules the state of things,
Reward goes backwards, Honour on his head ;
Who is not poor, is monstrous ; only Need
Gives form and worth to every human seed.
As cedars beaten with continual storms,   5
So great men flourish ; and do imitate
Unskilful statuaries, who suppose,
In forming a Colossus, if they make him
Straddle enough, strut, and look big, and gape,
Their work is goodly : so men merely great   10
In their affected gravity of voice,
Sourness of countenance, manners' cruelty,
Authority, wealth, and all the spawn of Fortune,
Think they bear all the kingdom's worth before them ;
Yet differ not from those colossic statues,   15
Which, with heroic forms without o'er-spread,
Within are nought but mortar, flint, and lead.
Man is a torch borne in the wind ; a dream
But of a shadow, summ'd with all his substance ;
And as great seamen, using all their wealth   20
And skills in Neptune's deep invisible paths,
In tall ships richly built and ribb'd with brass,
To put a girdle round about the world,
When they have done it, coming near their haven,
Are fain to give a warning-piece, and call   25
A poor, staid fisherman, that never pass'd
His country's sight, to waft and guide them in :
So when we wander furthest through the waves
Of glassy Glory, and the gulfs of State,
Topt with all titles, spreading all our reaches,   30
As if each private arm would sphere the earth,

We must to Virtue for her guide resort,
Or we shall shipwrack in our safest port.

Procumbit

Enter Monsieur *with two* Pages

   Mons.   There is no second place in numerous state
That holds more than a cipher ; in a king   35
All places are contain'd.   His words and looks
Are like the flashes and the bolts of Jove ;
His deeds inimitable, like the sea
That shuts still as it opes, and leaves no tracts
Nor prints of precedent for mean men's facts :   40
There's but a thread betwixt me and a crown,
I would not wish it cut, unless by nature ;
Yet to prepare me for that possible fortune,
'Tis good to get resolved spirits about me.
I follow'd D'Ambois to this green retreat,   45
A man of spirit beyond the reach of fear,
Who (discontent with his neglected worth)
Neglects the light, and loves obscure abodes ;
But he is young and haughty, apt to take
Fire at advancement, to bear state, and flourish ;   50
In his rise therefore shall my bounties shine :
None loathes the world so much, nor loves to scoff it,
But gold and grace will make him surfeit of it.

[*Approaching* Bussy.]

What, D'Ambois ?
   Bus.   He, sir.
   Mons.   Turn'd to earth, alive ?
Up, man ; the sun shines on thee.
   Bus.   Let it shine :   55
I am no mote to play in't, as great men are.
   Mons.   Callest thou men great in state, motes in the sun ?
They say so that would have thee freeze in shades,
That (like the gross Sicilian gourmandist)
Empty their noses in the cates they love,   60
That none may eat but they. Do thou but bring
Light to the banquet Fortune sets before thee,
And thou wilt loathe lean darkness like thy death.
Who would believe thy mettle could let sloth
Rust and consume it ? If Themistocles   65
Had liv'd obscur'd thus in th'Athenian state,
Xerxes had made both him and it his slaves.

If brave Camillus had lurk'd so in Rome,
He had not five times been Dictator there,
Nor four times triumph'd. If Epaminondas　　　　70
(Who liv'd twice twenty years obscur'd in Thebes)
Had liv'd so still, he had been still unnam'd,
And paid his country nor himself their right ;
But putting forth his strength, he rescu'd both
From imminent ruin ; and like burnish'd steel,　　　75
After long use he shin'd ; for as the light
Not only serves to show, but renders us
Mutually profitable, so our lives
In acts exemplary not only win
Ourselves good names, but do to others give　　　80
Matter for virtuous deeds, by which we live.
 Bus. What would you wish me ?
 Mons.　　　　　　　　　Leave the troubled streams,
And live, where thrivers do, at the well-head.
 Bus. At the well-head ? Alas, what should I do
With that enchanted glass ? See devils there ?　　　85
Or, like a strumpet, learn to set my looks
In an eternal brake, or practise juggling,
To keep my face still fast, my heart still loose ;
Or bear (like dame schoolmistresses their riddles)
Two tongues, and be good only for a shift ;　　　90
Flatter great lords, to put them still in mind
Why they were made lords ; or please humorous ladies
With a good carriage, tell them idle tales
To make their physic work ; spend a man's life
In sights and visitations that will make　　　95
His eyes as hollow as his mistress' heart ;
To do none good, but those that have no need ;
To gain being forward, though you break for haste
All the commandments ere you break your fast ;
But believe backwards, make your period　　　100
And creed's last article, ' I believe in God ' :
And (hearing villanies preach'd) t'unfold their art
Learn to commit them ? 'Tis a great man's part.
Shall I learn this there ?
 Mons.　　　　　　No, thou need'st not learn,
Thou hast the theory ; now go there and practise.　　　105
 Bus. Ay, in a threadbare suit ; when men come there,
They must have high naps, and go from thence bare :
A man may drown the parts of ten rich men

In one poor suit ; brave barks and outward gloss
Attract Court loves, be in-parts ne'er so gross.   110
    Mons.   Thou shalt have gloss enough, and all things fit
T'enchase in all show thy long-smother'd spirit :
Be rul'd by me then ? The old Scythians
Painted blind Fortune's powerful hands with wings
To show her gifts come swift and suddenly,   115
Which if her favourite be not swift to take,
He loses them for ever. Then be wise :
Stay but awhile here, and I'll send to thee.
                        Exit Monsieur [*with the* Pages]. *Manet* Bussy
    Bus.   What will he send ?   Some crowns ?   It is to sow
      them
Upon my spirit, and make them spring a crown   120
Worth millions of the seed-crowns he will send.
Like to disparking noble husbandmen,
He'll put his plow into me, plow me up ;
But his unsweating thrift is policy,
And learning-hating policy is ignorant   125
To fit his seed-land soil ; a smooth plain ground
Will never nourish any politic seed ;
I am for honest actions, not for great :
If I may bring up a new fashion,
And rise in Court for virtue, speed his plow !   130
The King hath known me long as well as he,
Yet could my fortune never fit the length
Of both their understandings till this hour.
There is a deep nick in Time's restless wheel
For each man's good, when which nick comes, it strikes ; 135
As rhetoric yet works not persuasion,
But only is a mean to make it work ;
So no man riseth by his real merit,
But when it cries clink in his raiser's spirit.
Many will say, that cannot rise at all,   140
Man's first hour's rise is first step to his fall.
I'll venture that ; men that fall low must die,
As well as men cast headlong from the sky.

                    Enter Maffé

    Maf.   Humour of princes ! Is this wretch indu'd
With any merit worth a thousand crowns ?   145
Will my lord have me be so ill a steward
Of his revenue, to dispose a sum

So great with so small cause as shows in him ?
I must examine this. [*To* Bussy.] Is your name D'Am-
    bois ?
  Bus. Sir ?
  Maf.   Is your name D'Ambois ?
  Bus.   Who have we here ? 150
Serve you the Monsieur ?
  Maf.   How ?
  Bus.   Serve you the Monsieur ?
  Maf. Sir, y'are very hot. I do serve the Monsieur,
But in such place as gives me the command
Of all his other servants. And because
His Grace's pleasure is to give your good   155
His pass through my command, methinks you might
Use me with more respect.
  Bus.   Cry you mercy !
Now you have open'd my dull eyes, I see you,
And would be glad to see the good you speak of ;
What might I call your name ?   160
  Maf.   Monsieur Maffé.
  Bus. Monsieur Maffé ? Then, good Monsieur Maffé,
Pray let me know you better.
  Maf.   Pray do so,
That you may use me better. For yourself,
By your no better outside, I would judge you
To be some poet ; have you given my lord   165
Some pamphlet ?
  Bus.   Pamphlet ?
  Maf.   Pamphlet, sir, I say.
  Bus. Did your great master's goodness leave the good,
That is to pass your charge to my poor use,
To your discretion ?
  Maf.   Though he did not, sir,
I hope 'tis no rude office to ask reason   170
How that his Grace gives me in charge, goes from me ?
  Bus. That's very perfect, sir.
  Maf.   Why, very good, sir ;
I pray, then, give me leave ; if for no pamphlet,
May I not know what other merit in you,
Makes his compunction willing to relieve you ?   175
  Bus. No merit in the world, sir.
  Maf.   That is strange.
Y'are a poor soldier, are you ?

Bus.   That I am, sir.
Maf.   And have commanded ?
Bus.   ' Ay, and gone without, sir.
Maf. [*aside*] I see the man ; a hundred crowns will
    make him
Swagger, and drink healths to his Grace's bounty,   180
And swear he could not be more bountiful ;
So there's nine hundred crowns sav'd.—Here, tall soldier,
His Grace hath sent you a whole hundred crowns.
  Bus.   A hundred, sir ? Nay, do his Highness right ;
I know his hand is larger, and perhaps   185
I may deserve more than my outside shows ;
I am a poet, as I am a soldier,
And I can poetise, and (being well encourag'd)
May sing his fame for giving, yours for delivering
(Like a most faithful steward) what he gives.   190
  Maf.   What shall your subject be ?
  Bus.   I care not much.
If to his bounteous Grace I sing the praise
Of fair great noses, and to you of long ones.
What qualities have you, sir, beside your chain
And velvet jacket ? Can your Worship dance ?   195
  Maf. [*aside*] A pleasant fellow, 'faith ; it seems my lord
Will have him for his jester ; and, by'rlady,
Such men are now no fools ; 'tis a knight's place.
If I (to save his Grace some crowns) should urge him
T'abate his bounty, I should not be heard ;   200
I would to heaven I were an errant ass,
For then I should be sure to have the ears
Of these great men, where now their jesters have them.
'Tis good to please him, yet I'll take no notice
Of his preferment, but in policy   205
Will still be grave and serious, lest he think
I fear his wooden dagger.—Here, Sir Ambo !
  Bus.   How, Ambo, sir ?
  Maf.   Ay, is not your name Ambo ?
  Bus.   You call'd me lately D'Ambois ; has your Worship
So short a head ?
  Maf.   I cry thee mercy, D'Ambois.   210
A thousand crowns I bring you from my lord :
Serve God, play the good husband ; you may make
This a good standing living : 'tis a bounty
His Highness might perhaps have bestow'd better.

Bus.   Go, y'are a rascal ; hence, away, you rogue !   215
Maf.   What mean you, sir ?
Bus.   Hence ! Prate no more,
Or, by thy villain's blood, thou prat'st thy last !
A barbarous groom grudge at his master's bounty !
But since I know he would as much abhor
His hind should argue what he gives his friend,   220
Take that, sir, [*striking him*] for your aptness to dispute.
                                                    Exit

Maf.   These crowns are set in blood ; blood be their
      fruit !   *Exit*

[SCENA SECUNDA

A Room in the Court]

[*The curtain is drawn disclosing*] Henry, Guise, Montsurry,
      Elenor, Tamyra, Beaupré, Pero, Charlotte, Pyra, An-
      nable. [Henry and the Guise are playing chess]

Hen.   Duchess of Guise, your Grace is much enrich'd
In the attendance of that English virgin,
That will initiate her prime of youth
(Dispos'd to Court conditions) under the hand
Of your preferr'd instructions and command,   5
Rather than any in the English Court,
Whose ladies are not match'd in Christendom
For graceful and confirm'd behaviours ;
More than the Court, where they are bred, is equall'd.
Guise.   I like not their Court fashion ; it is too crestfall'n 10
In all observance, making demigods
Of their great nobles, and of their old queen
An ever-young and most immortal goddess.
Mont.   No question she's the rarest queen in Europe.
Guise.   But what's that to her immortality ?   15
Hen.   Assure you, cousin Guise, so great a courtier,
So full of majesty and royal parts,
No queen in Christendom may vaunt herself.
Her Court approves it, that's a Court indeed,
Not mixt with clowneries us'd in common houses,   20
But, as Courts should be th' abstracts of their kingdoms
In all the beauty, state, and worth they hold,
So is hers, amply, and by her inform'd.

The world is not contracted in a man
With more proportion and expression,   25
Than in her Court, her kingdom.   Our French Court
Is a mere mirror of confusion to it :
The king and subject, lord and every slave,
Dance a continual hay ; our rooms of state
Kept like our stables ; no place more observ'd   30
Than a rude market-place : and though our custom
Keep this assur'd confusion from our eyes
'Tis ne'er the less essentially unsightly,
Which they would soon see would they change their form
To this of ours, and then compare them both ;   35
Which we must not affect, because in kingdoms
Where the king's change doth breed the subject's terror,
Pure innovation is more gross than error.
    Mont.   No question we shall see them imitate
(Though afar off) the fashions of our Courts,   40
As they have ever ap'd us in attire ;
Never were men so weary of their skins,
And apt to leap out of themselves as they,
Who, when they travel to bring forth rare men,
Come home, deliver'd of a fine French suit ;   45
Their brains lie with their tailors, and get babies
For their most complete issue ; he's sole heir
To all the moral virtues that first greets
The light with a new fashion, which becomes them
Like apes, disfigur'd with the attires of men.   50
    Hen.   No question they much wrong their real worth
In affectation of outlandish scum ;
But they have faults, and we more ; they foolish proud
To jet in others plumes so haughtily ;
We proud that they are proud of foolery,   55
Holding our worths more complete for their vaunts.

Enter Monsieur *and* D'Ambois

    Mons.   Come, mine own sweetheart, I will enter thee.
[*To the* King] Sir, I have brought a gentleman to Court,
And pray you would vouchsafe to do him grace.
    Hen.   D'Ambois, I think ?
    Bus.   That's still my name, my lord, 60
Though I be something alter'd in attire.
    Hen.   We like your alteration, and must tell you
We have expected th'offer of your service ;

For we (in fear to make mild virtue proud)
Use not to seek her out in any man.   65
  Bus. Nor doth she use to seek out any man :
They that will win must woo her.
  Mons. I urg'd her modesty in him, my lord,
And gave her those rites that he says she merits.
  Hen. If you have woo'd and won, then, brother, wear him.   70
  Mons. Th'art mine, sweetheart. See, here's the Guise's
    Duchess,
The Countess of Montsurreau, Beaupré.
Come, I'll enseam thee. Ladies, y'are too many
To be in council ; I have here a friend
That I would gladly enter in your graces.   75
  Bus. 'Save you, ladies.
  Duch. If you enter him in our graces, my lord, methinks
by his blunt behaviour he should come out of himself.
  Tam. Has he never been courtier, my lord ?
  Mons. Never, my lady.   80
  Beau. And why did the toy take him in th' head now ?
  Bus. 'Tis leap-year, lady, and therefore very good to
enter a courtier.
  Hen. Mark, Duchess of Guise, there is one is not bashful.
  Duch. No, my lord, he is much guilty of the bold extre-   85
mity.
  Tam. The man's a courtier at first sight.
  Bus. I can sing prick-song, lady, at first sight ; and why
not be a courtier as suddenly ?
  Beau. Here's a courtier rotten before he be ripe.   90
  Bus. Think me not impudent, lady ; I am yet no courtier :
I desire to be one, and would gladly take entrance, madam,
[*To the* Duchess] under your princely colours.

Enter Barrisor, L'Anou, *and* Pyrhot

  Duch. Soft, sir, you must rise by degrees, first being the
servant of some common lady, or knight's wife, then a little   95
higher to a lord's wife, next a little higher to a countess, yet
a little higher to a duchess, and then turn the ladder.
  Bus. Do you allow a man, then, four mistresses, when the
greatest mistress is allowed but three servants ?
  Duch. Where find you that statute, sir ?   100
  Bus. Why, be judged by the groom-porters.
  Duch. The groom-porters ?

Bus.   Ay, madam ; must not they judge of all gamings i'
th' Court ?

Duch.   You talk like a gamester.   105

Guise.   Sir, know you me ?

Bus.   My lord ?

Guise.   I know not you ; whom do you serve ?

Bus.   Serve, my lord !

Guise.   Go to, companion, your courtship's too saucy.   110

Bus.   [*Aside*] Saucy !   Companion !   'Tis the Guise, but
yet those terms might have been spared of the Guisard.   Companion !   He's jealous, by this light.   Are you blind of that
side, Duke ?   I'll to her again for that—Forth, princely mistress, for the honour of courtship.   Another riddle !   115

Guise.   Cease your courtship, or by heaven I'll cut your
throat.

Bus.   Cut my throat ? Cut a whetstone ! Young Accius
Nævius, do as much with your tongue, as he did with a razor :
cut my throat !   120

Bar.   What new-come gallant have we here, that dares
mate the Guise thus ?

L'An.   'Sfoot, 'tis D'Ambois.   The Duke mistakes him,
on my life, for some knight of the new edition.

Bus.   Cut my throat !   I would the King feared thy cut-   125
ting of his throat no more than I fear thy cutting of mine.

Guise.   I'll do 't, by this hand.

Bus.   That hand dares not do't.
Y'ave cut too many throats already, Guise,
And robb'd the realm of many thousand souls,   130
More precious than thine own.   Come, madam, talk on.
'Sfoot, can you not talk ?   Talk on, I say.
Another riddle !

Pyr.   Here's some strange distemper.

Bar.   Here's a sudden transmigration with D'Ambois—
out of the knights' ward into the duchess' bed.   135

L'An.   See what a metamorphosis a brave suit can work.

Pyr.   'Slight, step to the Guise and discover him.

Bar.   By no means ; let the new suit work ; we'll see the
issue.

Guise.   Leave your courting.   140

Bus.   I will not.—I say, mistress, and I will stand unto it,
that if a woman may have three servants, a man may have
threescore mistresses.

Guise. Sirrah, I'll have you whipped out of the Court for
this insolence.   145

Bus. Whipped ? Such another syllable out a th' presence,
if thou dar'st for thy dukedom.

Guise. Remember, poltroon.

Mons. [*To* Bussy.] Pray thee, forbear.

Bus. Passion of death ! Were not the King here, he 150
should strow the chamber like a rush.

Mons. But leave courting his wife, then.

Bus. I will not. I'll court her in despite of him. Not
court her !—Come, madam, talk on, fear me nothing.—
[*To* Guise] Well may'st thou drive thy master from the Court, 155
but never D'Ambois.

Mons. [*Aside*] His great heart will not down, 'tis like the
    sea,
That partly by his own internal heat,
Partly the stars' daily and nightly motion,
Their heat and light, and partly of the place   160
The divers frames, but chiefly by the moon,
Bristled with surges, never will be won,
(No, not when th' hearts of all those powers are burst)
To make retreat into his settled home,
Till he be crown'd with his own quiet foam.   165

Hen. You have the mate. Another ?

Guise. No more.   *Flourish short*
Exit Guise, *after him the* King [*and*] Monsieur *whispering*

Bar. Why, here's the lion, scared with the throat of a dung-
hill cock ; a fellow that has newly shaked off his shackles ;
now does he crow for that victory.   170

L'An. 'Tis one of the best jigs that ever was acted.

Pyr. Whom does the Guise suppose him to be, trow ?

L'An. Out of doubt, some new denizened lord, and thinks
that suit newly drawn out o' th' mercer's books.

Bar. I have heard of a fellow, that by a fixed imagination 175
looking upon a bull-baiting, had a visible pair of horns grew
out of his forehead, and I believe this gallant, overjoyed with
the conceit of Monsieur's cast suit, imagines himself to be the
Monsieur.

L'An. And why not ? as well as the ass, stalking in the lion's 180
case, bare himself like a lion, braying all the huger beasts out
of the forest ?

Pyr. Peace, he looks this way.

Bar. Marry, let him look, sir, what will you say now if
the Guise be gone to fetch a blanket for him?   185
L'An. Faith, I believe it for his honour sake.
Pyr. But, if D'Ambois carry it clean? *Exeunt* Ladies.
Bar. True, when he curvets in the blanket.
Pyr. Ay, marry, sir.
L'An. 'Sfoot, see how he stares on's.   190
Bar. Lord bless us, let's away.
Bus. [*To* Barrisor] Now, sir, take your full view, how
does the object please ye?
Bar. If you ask my opinion, sir, I think your suit fits as
well as if't had been made for you.   195
Bus. So, sir, and was that the subject of your ridiculous
jollity?
L'An. What's that to you, sir?
Bus. Sir, I have observed all your fleerings; and resolve
yourselves ye shall give a strict account for't.   200

Enter Brisac *and* Melynell

Bar. Oh, miraculous jealousy! Do you think yourself
such a singular subject for laughter that none can fall into the
matter of our merriment but you?
L'An. This jealousy of yours, sir, confesses some close
defect in yourself that we never dreamed of.   205
Pyr. We held discourse of a perfumed ass, that being disguised in a lion's case, imagined himself a lion: I hope that
touched not you.
Bus. So, sir; your descants do marvellous well fit this
ground; we shall meet where your buffoonly laughters will 210
cost ye the best blood in your bodies.
Bar. For life's sake let's be gone; he'll kill's outright else.
Bus. Go, at your pleasures, I'll be your ghost to haunt
you; and ye sleep on't, hang me.
L'An. Go, go, sir; court your mistress.   215
Pyr. And be advised; we shall have odds against you.
Bus. Tush, valour stands not in number! I'll maintain it,
that one man may beat three boys.
Bris. [*To the* Courtiers] Nay, you shall have no odds of him
in number, sir; he's a gentleman as good as the proudest of 220
you, and ye shall not wrong him.
Bar. Not, sir?
Mel. Not, sir: though he be not so rich, he's a better man
than the best of you; and I will not endure it.

L'An. Not you, sir ?   225
Bris. No, sir, nor I.
Bus. [*To* Brisac *and* Melynell] I should thank you for this
kindness, if I thought these perfumed musk-cats (being out of
this privilege) durst but once mew at us.
Bar. Does your confident spirit doubt that, sir ? Follow 230
us and try.
L'An. Come, sir, we'll lead you a dance.   *Exeunt*

FINIS ACTUS PRIMI.

ACTUS SECUNDI SCENA PRIMA

[*A Room in the Court*]

Henry, Guise, Montsurry, [Beaumond] *and* Attendants

Hen. This desperate quarrel sprung out of their envies
To D'Ambois' sudden bravery, and great spirit.
Guise. Neither is worth their envy.
Hen.   Less than either
Will make the gall of Envy overflow ;
She feeds on outcast entrails like a kite ;   5
In which foul heap, if any ill lies hid,
She sticks her beak into it, shakes it up,
And hurls it all abroad, that all may view it.
Corruption is her nutriment ; but touch her
With any precious ointment, and you kill her :   10
Where she finds any filth in men, she feasts,
And with her black throat bruits it through the world
Being sound and healthful ; but if she but taste
The slenderest pittance of commended virtue,
She surfeits of it, and is like a fly   15
That passes all the body's soundest parts,
And dwells upon the sores ; or if her squint eye
Have power to find none there, she forges some :
She makes that crooked ever which is straight ;
Calls valour giddiness, justice tyranny ;   20
A wise man may shun her, she not herself :
Whithersoever she flies from her harms,
She bears her foe still clasp'd in her own arms ;
And therefore, cousin Guise, let us avoid her.

Enter Nuntius

Nun.   What Atlas or Olympus lifts his head   25
So far past covert, that with air enough
My words may be inform'd, and from their height
I may be seen and heard through all the world ?
A tale so worthy, and so fraught with wonder
Sticks in my jaws, and labours with event.   30
   Hen.   Com'st thou from D'Ambois ?
   Nun.   From him, and the rest,
His friends and enemies ; whose stern fight I saw,
And heard their words before and in the fray.
   Hen.   Relate at large what thou hast seen and heard.
   Nun.   I saw fierce D'Ambois and his two brave friends   35
Enter the field, and at their heels their foes ;
Which were the famous soldiers, Barrisor,
L'Anou, and Pyrhot, great in deeds of arms :
All which arriv'd at the evenest piece of earth
The field afforded, the three challengers   40
Turn'd head, drew all their rapiers, and stood rank'd :
When face to face the three defendants met them,
Alike prepar'd, and resolute alike.
Like bonfires of contributory wood
Every man's look shew'd, fed with either's spirit ;   45
As one had been a mirror to another,
Like forms of life and death, each took from other ;
And so were life and death mix'd at their heights,
That you could see no fear of death, for life,
Nor love of life, for death ; but in their brows   50
Pyrrho's opinion in great letters shone ;
That life and death in all respects are one.
   Hen.   Pass'd there no sort of words at their encounter ?
   Nun.   As Hector, 'twixt the hosts of Greece and Troy,
(When Paris and the Spartan king should end   55
The nine years' war) held up his brazen lance
For signal that both hosts should cease from arms,
And hear him speak : so Barrisor (advis'd)
Advanc'd his naked rapier 'twixt both sides,
Ripp'd up the quarrel, and compar'd six lives   60
Then laid in balance with six idle words ;
Offer'd remission and contrition too ;
Or else that he and D'Ambois might conclude
The others' dangers.   D'Ambois lik'd the last ;

But Barrisor's friends (being equally engag'd　　　65
In the main quarrel) never would expose
His life alone to that they all deserv'd.
And (for the other offer of remission)
D'Ambois (that like a laurel put in fire
Sparkled and spit) did much much more than scorn,　　　70
That his wrong should incense him so like chaff,
To go so soon out, and like lighted paper
Approve his spirit at once both fire and ashes ;
So drew they lots, and in them Fates appointed
That Barrisor should fight with fiery D'Ambois,　　　75
Pyrhot with Melynell, with Brisac L'Anou :
And then like flame and powder they commix'd
So spritely that I wish'd they had been spirits,
That the ne'er-shutting wounds they needs must open
Might as they open'd, shut and never kill :　　　80
But D'Ambois' sword (that lighten'd as it flew)
Shot like a pointed comet at the face
Of manly Barrisor ; and there it stuck :
Thrice pluck'd he at it, and thrice drew on thrusts,
From him that of himself was free as fire ;　　　85
Who thrust still as he pluck'd, yet (past belief)
He with his subtle eye, hand, body, scap'd ;
At last, the deadly-bitten point tugg'd off,
On fell his yet undaunted foe so fiercely
That (only made more horrid with his wound)　　　90
Great D'Ambois shrunk, and gave a little ground ;
But soon return'd, redoubled in his danger,
And at the heart of Barrisor seal'd his anger :
Then, as in Arden I have seen an oak
Long shook with tempests, and his lofty top　　　95
Bent to his root, which being at length made loose
(Even groaning with his weight) he gan to nod
This way and that, as loath his curled brows
(Which he had oft wrapt in the sky with storms)
Should stoop ; and yet, his radical fibres burst,　　　100
Storm-like he fell, and hid the fear-cold earth :
So fell stout Barrisor, that had stood the shocks
Of ten set battles in your Highness' war,
Gainst the sole soldier of the world, Navarre.
　　Guise.　Oh, piteous and horrid murther !
　　Beau.　　　　　　　　　　　Such a life.　105
Methinks had metal in it to survive

An age of men.
   Hen.   Such often soonest end.
[*To the* Nuntius]   Thy felt report calls on ; we long to know
On what events the other have arriv'd.
   Nun.   Sorrow and fury, like two opposite fumes   110
Met in the upper region of a cloud,
At the report made by this worthy's fall
Brake from the earth, and with them rose Revenge,
Ent'ring with fresh powers his two noble friends ;
And under that odds fell surcharg'd Brisac,   115
The friend of D'Ambois, before fierce L'Anou ;
Which D'Ambois seeing, as I once did see,
In my young travels through Armenia,
An angry unicorn in his full career
Charge with too swift a foot a jeweller,   120
That watch'd him for the treasure of his brow,
And ere he could get shelter of a tree,
Nail him with his rich antler to the earth :
So D'Ambois ran upon reveng'd L'Anou,
Who eyeing th' eager point borne in his face,   125
And giving back, fell back, and in his fall
His foe's uncurbed sword stopp'd in his heart :
By which time all the life-strings of the tw'other
Were cut, and both fell, as their spirits flew
Upwards, and still hunt honour at the view :   130
And now, of all the six, sole D'Ambois stood
Untouch'd, save only with the others' hlood.
   Hen.   All slain outright but he ?
   Nun.   All slain outright but he,
Who kneeling in the warm life of his friends,
(All freckled with the blood his rapier rain'd)   135
He kiss'd their pale lips, and bade both farewell :
And see the bravest man the French earth bears.

Enter Monsieur *and* D'Ambois *bare*

   Bus.   Now is the time ; y'are princely vow'd, my friend ;
Perform it princely, and obtain my pardon.
   Mons.   Else heaven forgive not me ; come on, brave friend. 140
                     [*They kneel before* Henry.]
If ever Nature held herself her own,
When the great trial of a king and subject
Met in one blood, both from one belly springing,
Now prove her virtue and her greatness one,

Or make the t'one the greater with the t'other, 145
(As true kings should) and for your brother's love
(Which is a special species of true virtue)
Do that you could not do, not being a king.

Hen. Brother, I know your suit; these wilful murthers
Are ever past our pardon.

Mons. Manly slaughter 150
Should never bear th'account of wilful murther;
It being a spice of justice, where with life
Offending past law equal life is laid
In equal balance, to scourge that offence
By law of reputation, which to men 155
Exceeds all positive law, and what that leaves
To true men's valours (not prefixing rights
Of satisfaction, suited to their wrongs)
A free man's eminence may supply and take.

Hen. This would make every man that thinks him wrong'd 160
Or is offended, or in wrong or right,
Lay on this violence; and all vaunt themselves
Law-menders and suppliers, though mere butchers;
Should this fact (though of justice) be forgiven?

Mons. Oh, no, my lord; it would make cowards fear 165
To touch the reputations of true men;
When only they are left to imp the law,
Justice will soon distinguish murtherous minds
From just revengers: had my friend been slain,
His enemy surviving, he should die, 170
Since he had added to a murther'd fame
(Which was in his intent) a murther'd man;
And this had worthily been wilful murther;
But my friend only sav'd his fame's dear life,
Which is above life, taking th'under value, 175
Which, in the wrong it did, was forfeit to him;
And in this fact only preserves a man
In his uprightness, worthy to survive
Millions of such as murther men alive.

Hen. Well, brother, rise, and raise your friend withal 180
From death to life; and, D'Ambois, let your life
(Refin'd by passing through this merited death)
Be purg'd from more such foul pollution;
Nor on your scape, nor valour, more presuming
To be again so daring.

Bus. My lord, 185

I loathe as much a deed of unjust death,
As law itself doth ; and to tyrannize,
Because I have a little spirit to dare
And power to do, as to be tyranniz'd.
This is a grace that (on my knees redoubled),   190
I crave, to double this my short life's gift,
And shall your royal bounty centuple,
That I may so make good what God and Nature
Have given me for my good ; since I am free,
(Offending no just law), let no law make   195
By any wrong it does, my life her slave :
When I am wrong'd, and that law fails to right me,
Let me be king myself (as man was made),
And do a justice that exceeds the law ;
If my wrong pass the power of single valour   200
To right and expiate ; then be you my king,
And do a right, exceeding law and nature :
Who to himself is law, no law doth need,
Offends no law, and is a king indeed.
    Hen. Enjoy what thou entreat'st ; we give but ours.   205
    Bus. What you have given, my lord, is ever yours.
        Exit Rex *cum* Beau[mond, Attendants, Nuntius *and*
            Montsurry]
    Guise. Mort Dieu, who would have pardon'd such a
        murther ?   *Exit*
    Mons. Now vanish horrors into Court attractions
For which let this balm make thee fresh and fair.
And now forth with thy service to the Duchess,   210
As my long love will to Montsurry's Countess.   *Exit*
    Bus. To whom my love hath long been vow'd in heart,
Although in hand for shew I held the Duchess.
And now through blood and vengeance, deeds of height,
And hard to be achiev'd, 'tis fit I make   215
Attempt of her perfection ; I need fear
No check in his rivality, since her virtues
Are so renown'd, and he of all dames hated.   *Exit*

[SCENA SECUNDA

A Room in Montsurry's *House*]

Enter Monsieur, Tamyra *and* Pero *with a book*

    Mons. Pray thee regard thine own good, if not mine,
And cheer my love for that : you do not know

What you may be by me, nor what without me;
I may have power t'advance and pull down any.

    Tam. That's not my study; one way I am sure　　5
You shall not pull down me; my husband's height
Is crown to all my hopes; and his retiring
To any mean state, shall be my aspiring:
Mine honour's in mine own hands, spite of kings.

    Mons. Honour, what's that? Your second maidenhead: 10
And what is that? A word: the word is gone,
The thing remains: the rose is pluck'd, the stalk
Abides; an easy loss where no lack's found:
Believe it, there's as small lack in the loss
As there is pain i'th' losing; archers ever　　　15
Have two strings to a bow; and shall great Cupid
(Archer of archers both in men and women)
Be worse provided than a common archer?
A husband and a friend all wise wives have.

    Tam. Wise wives they are that on such strings depend, 20
With a firm husband joining a loose friend.

    Mons. Still you stand on your husband; so do all
The common sex of you, when y'are encounter'd
With one ye cannot fancy: all men know
You live in Court, here, by your own election,　　25
Frequenting all our common sports and triumphs,
All the most youthful company of men:
And wherefore do you this? To please your husband?
'Tis gross and fulsome: if your husband's pleasure
Be all your object, and you aim at honour　　　30
In living close to him, get you from Court;
You may have him at home; these common put-offs
For common women serve: 'My honour! Husband!'
Dames maritorious ne'er were meritorious:
Speak plain, and say 'I do not like you, sir;　　35
Y'are an ill-favour'd fellow in my eye';
And I am answer'd.

    Tam.　　　　　Then, I pray, be answer'd:
For, in good faith, my lord, I do not like you
In that sort you like.

    Mons.　　　　Then have at you here!
Take (with a politic hand) this rope of pearl,　　40
And though you be not amorous, yet be wise:
Take me for wisdom; he that you can love
Is ne'er the further from you.

Tam.   Now it comes
So ill prepar'd, that I may take a poison
Under a medicine as good cheap as it ;   45
I will not have it were it worth the world.
  Mons. Horror of death ! Could I but please your eye,
You would give me the like, ere you would loose me :
' Honour and husband ! '
  Tam.   By this light, my lord,
Y'are a vile fellow, and I'll tell the King   50
Your occupation of dishonouring ladies,
And of his Court : a lady cannot live
As she was born, and with that sort of pleasure
That fits her state, but she must be defam'd
With an infamous lord's detraction :   55
Who would endure the Court if these attempts
Of open and profess'd lust must be borne ?—
Who's there ? [*To* Pero] Come on, dame, you are at your
    book
When men are at your mistress ; have I taught you
Any such waiting-woman's quality ?   60
  Mons. Farewell, ' good husband ! '

                              Exit Monsieur
  Tam.   Farewell, wicked lord !

                Enter Montsurry

  Mont. Was not the Monsieur here ?
  Tam.   Yes, to good purpose ;
And your cause is as good to seek him too,
And haunt his company.
  Mont.   Why, what's the matter ?
  Tam. Matter of death, were I some husbands' wife :   65
I cannot live at quiet in my chamber
For opportunities almost to rapes
Offer'd me by him.
  Mont.   Pray thee bear with him :
Thou know'st he is a bachelor and a courtier,
Ay, and a prince ; and their prerogatives   70
Are to their laws, as to their pardons are
Their reservations, after Parliaments—
One quits another : form gives all their essence :
That prince doth high in virtue's reckoning stand
That will entreat a vice, and not command :   75
So far bear with him ; should another man

Trust to his privilege, he should trust to death :
Take comfort, then, my comfort, nay, triumph
And crown thyself ; thou part'st with victory :
My presence is so only dear to thee   80
That other men's appear worse than they be.
For this night yet, bear with my forced absence :
Thou know'st my business ; and with how much weight
My vow hath charg'd it.
 Tam.   True, my lord, and never
My fruitless love shall let your serious honour ;   85
Yet, sweet lord, do not stay ; you know my soul
Is so long time without me, and I dead,
As you are absent.
 Mont.   By this kiss, receive
My soul for hostage, till I see my love.
 Tam. The morn shall let me see you ?   90
 Mont.   With the sun
I'll visit thy more comfortable beauties.
 Tam. This is my comfort, that the sun hath left
The whole world's beauty ere my sun leaves me.
 Mont. 'Tis late night now, indeed ; farewell, my light !
              Exit

 Tam. Farewell, my light and life ! But not in him, 95
In mine own dark love and light bent to another.
Alas, that in the wane of our affections
We should supply it with a full dissembling,
In which each youngest maid is grown a mother.
Frailty is fruitful, one sin gets another :   100
Our loves like sparkles are, that brightest shine
When they go out ; most vice shows most divine.
[*To* Pero] Go, maid, to bed ; lend me your book, I pray :
Not, like yourself, for form ; I'll this night trouble
None of your services : make sure the doors,   105
And call your other fellows to their rest.
 Pero. I will. [*Aside.*] Yet I will watch to know why you
  watch.   *Exit*
 Tam. Now all ye peaceful regents of the night,
Silently-gliding exhalations,
Languishing winds, and murmuring falls of waters,   110
Sadness of heart and ominous secureness,
Enchantments, dead sleeps, all the friends of rest,
That ever wrought upon the life of man,

Extend your utmost strengths, and this charm'd hour
Fix like the Centre! Make the violent wheels   115
Of Time and Fortune stand, and great Existence
(The Maker's treasury) now not seem to be,
To all but my approaching friends and me!
They come, alas, they come! Fear, fear and hope,
Of one thing, at one instant, fight in me: 120
I love what most I loathe, and cannot live,
Unless I compass that which holds my death:
For life's mere death, loving one that loathes me,
And he I love, will loathe me, when he sees
I fly my sex, my virtue, my renown,   125
To run so madly on a man unknown.   *The vault opens*
See, see, a vault is opening that was never
Known to my lord and husband, nor to any
But him that brings the man I love, and me.
How shall I look on him? How shall I live,   130
And not consume in blushes? I will in,
And cast myself off, as I ne'er had been.

                                                    Exit

              Ascendit Friar *and* D'Ambois

  Friar. Come, worthiest son, I am past measure glad,
That you (whose worth I have approv'd so long)
Should be the object of her fearful love;   135
Since both your wit and spirit can adapt
Their full force to supply her utmost weakness:
You know her worths and virtues, for report
Of all that know is to a man a knowledge:
You know, besides, that our affections' storm,   140
Rais'd in our blood, no reason can reform.
Though she seek then their satisfaction
(Which she must needs, or rest unsatisfied)
Your judgment will esteem her peace thus wrought,
Nothing less dear than if yourself had sought: 145
And (with another colour, which my art
Shall teach you to lay on) yourself must seem
The only agent, and the first orb move
In this our set and cunning world of love.
  Bus. Give me the colour, my most honour'd father,   150
And trust my cunning then to lay it on.
  Friar. 'Tis this, good son; Lord Barrisor (whom you
    slew)

Did love her dearly, and with all fit means
Hath urg'd his acceptation, of all which
She keeps one letter written in his blood :   155
You must say thus, then, that you heard from me
How much herself was touch'd in conscience
With a report (which is, in truth, dispers'd)
That your main quarrel grew about her love,
Lord Barrisor imagining your courtship   160
Of the great Guise's Duchess in the presence,
Was by you made to his elected mistress :
And so made me your mean now to resolve her,
Choosing (by my direction) this night's depth
For the more clear avoiding of all note   165
Of your presumed presence ; and with this
(To clear her hands of such a lover's blood)
She will so kindly thank and entertain you,
(Methinks I see how), ay, and ten to one,
Show you the confirmation in his blood,   170
Lest you should think report and she did feign,
That you shall so have circumstantial means
To come to the direct, which must be used ;
For the direct is crooked ; love comes flying ;
The height of love is still won with denying.   175
   Bus. Thanks, honour'd father.
   Friar.   She must never know
That you know anything of any love
Sustain'd on her part : for, learn this of me,
In anything a woman does alone,
If she dissemble, she thinks 'tis not done ;   180
If not dissemble, nor a little chide,
Give her her wish, she is not satisfied ;
To have a man think that she never seeks,
Does her more good than to have all she likes :
This frailty sticks in them beyond their sex,   185
Which to reform, reason is too perplex :
Urge reason to them, it will do no good ;
Humour (that is the chariot of our food
In everybody) must in them be fed,
To carry their affections by it bred.   190
Stand close !   [*They retire*]

        Enter Tamyra *with a book*

   Tam. Alas, I fear my strangeness will retire him.

If he go back, I die; I must prevent it,
And cheer his onset with my sight at least,
And that's the most; though every step he takes   195
Goes to my heart, I'll rather die than seem
Not to be strange to that I most esteem.
    Friar [*advancing*]. Madam!
    Tam.   Ah!
    Friar.   You will pardon me, I hope,
That so beyond your expectation,
And at a time for visitants so unfit,   200
I (with my noble friend here) visit you:
You know that my access at any time
Hath ever been admitted; and that friend
That my care will presume to bring with me
Shall have all circumstance of worth in him   205
To merit as free welcome as myself.
    Tam. Oh, father, but at this suspicious hour
You know how apt best men are to suspect us,
In any cause, that makes suspicious shadow
No greater than the shadow of a hair: 210
And y'are to blame. What though my lord and husband
Lie forth to-night, and since I cannot sleep
When he is absent I sit up to-night;
Though all the doors are sure, and all our servants
As sure bound with their sleeps; yet there is One   215
That wakes above, whose eye no sleep can bind;
He sees through doors, and darkness, and our thoughts;
And therefore as we should avoid with fear,
To think amiss ourselves before his search;
So should we be as curious to shun   220
All cause that other think not ill of us.
    Bus. [*advancing*] Madam, 'tis far from that; I only heard
By this my honour'd father that your conscience
Made some deep scruple with a false report
That Barrisor's blood should something touch your honour;   225
Since he imagin'd I was courting you,
When I was bold to change words with the Duchess,
And therefore made his quarrel, his long love
And service, as I hear, being deeply vow'd
To your perfections; which my ready presence,   230
Presum'd on with my father at this season
For the more care of your so curious honour,
Can well resolve your conscience is most false.

Tam. And is it therefore that you come, good sir ?
Then crave I now your pardon and my father's,   235
And swear your presence does me so much good,
That all I have it binds to your requital :
Indeed, sir, 'tis most true that a report
Is spread, alleging that his love to me
Was reason of your quarrel ; and because   240
You shall not think I feign it for my glory
That he importun'd me for his court service,
I'll show you his own hand, set down in blood,
To that vain purpose : good sir, then come in.
Father, I thank you now a thousand fold.   245

                    Exit Tamyra *and* D'Ambois
Friar. May it be worth it to you, honour'd daughter.

                    Descendit Friar

FINIS ACTUS SECUNDI

ACTUS TERTII SCENA PRIMA

[*A Room in* Montsurry's *House*]

Enter D'Ambois, Tamyra, *with a Chain of Pearl*

Bus. Sweet mistress, cease, your conscience is too nice,
And bites too hotly of the Puritan spice.
Tam. Oh my dear servant, in thy close embraces
I have set open all the doors of danger
To my encompass'd honour, and my life :   5
Before I was secure against death and hell ;
But now am subject to the heartless fear
Of every shadow, and of every breath,
And would change firmness with an aspen leaf :
So confident a spotless conscience is,   10
So weak a guilty : oh, the dangerous siege
Sin lays about us, and the tyranny
He exercises when he hath expugn'd !
Like to the horror of a winter's thunder,
Mix'd with a gushing storm, that suffer nothing   15
To stir abroad on earth but their own rages,
Is Sin, when it hath gather'd head above us :
No roof, no shelter can secure us so,
But he will drown our cheeks in fear or woe.
Bus. Sin is a coward, madam, and insults   20
But on our weakness, in his truest valour :

And so our ignorance tames us, that we let
His shadows fright us : and like empty clouds,
In which our faulty apprehensions forge
The forms of dragons, lions, elephants,   25
When they hold no proportion, the sly charms
Of the witch Policy makes him like a monster
Kept only to show men for servile money :
That false hag often paints him in her cloth
Ten times more monstrous than he is in troth :   30
In three of us the secret of our meeting
Is only guarded, and three friends as one
Have ever been esteem'd : as our three powers
That in one soul are as one united :
Why should we fear then ? For myself, I swear,   35
Sooner shall torture be the sire to pleasure,
And health be grievous to one long time sick,
Than the dear jewel of your fame in me
Be made an outcast to your infamy ;
Nor shall my value (sacred to your virtues)   40
Only give free course to it, from myself :
But make it fly out of the mouths of kings
In golden vapours and with awful wings.
   Tam. It rests as all kings' seals were set in thee.
Now let us call my father, whom I swear   45
I could extremely chide, but that I fear
To make him so suspicious of my love
Of which, sweet servant, do not let him know
For all the world.
      Bus.   Alas, he will not think it !
   Tam. Come, then.—Ho ! Father, ope, and take your
     friend.   *Ascendit* Friar 50
   Friar. Now, honour'd daughter, is your doubt resolv'd ?
   Tam. Ay, father, but you went away too soon.
   Friar. Too soon ?
   Tam.   Indeed you did, you should have stay'd ;
Had not your worthy friend been of your bringing,
And that contains all laws to temper me,   55
Not all the fearful danger that besieg'd us,
Had aw'd my throat from exclamation.
   Friar. I know your serious disposition well.
Come, son, the morn comes on.
   Bus.   Now, honour'd mistress,
Till farther service call, all bliss supply you !   60

Tam. And you this chain of pearl, and my love only !

Descendit Friar *and* D'Ambois

It is not I, but urgent destiny,
That (as great statesmen for their general end
In politic justice, make poor men offend)
Enforceth my offence to make it just.   65
What shall weak dames do, when th' whole work of nature
Hath a strong finger in each one of us ?
Needs must that sweep away the silly cobweb
Of our still-undone labours, that lays still
Our powers to it : as to the line, the stone,   70
Not to the stone, the line should be oppos'd.
We cannot keep our constant course in virtue :
What is alike at all parts ? Every day
Differs from other : every hour and minute ;
Ay, every thought in our false clock of life,   75
Oft-times inverts the whole circumference :
We must be sometimes one, sometimes another :
Our bodies are but thick clouds to our souls,
Through which they cannot shine when they desire :
When all the stars, and even the sun himself,   80
Must stay the vapours' times that he exhales
Before he can make good his beams to us :
O, how can we, that are but motes to him,
Wandering at random in his order'd rays,
Disperse our passions' fumes, with our weak labours,   85
That are more thick and black than all earth's vapours ?

Enter Montsurry !

Mont. Good day, my love ! What, up and ready too !
Tam. Both, my dear lord ; not all this night made I
Myself unready, or could sleep a wink.
Mont. Alas, what troubled my true love, my peace,   90
From being at peace within her better self ?
Or how could sleep forbear to seize thine eyes,
When he might challenge them as his just prize ?
Tam. I am in no power earthly, but in yours ;
To what end should I go to bed, my lord,   90
That wholly miss'd the comfort of my bed ?
Or how should sleep possess my faculties,
Wanting the proper closer of mine eyes ?
Mont. Then will I never more sleep night from thee :
All mine own business, all the King's affairs,   100

Shall take the day to serve them ; every night
I'll ever dedicate to thy delight.
 Tam. Nay, good my lord, esteem not my desires
Such doters on their humours that my judgment
Cannot subdue them to your worthier pleasure :   105
A wife's pleas'd husband must her object be
In all her acts, not her soothed fantasy.
 Mont. Then come, my love, now pay those rites to sleep
Thy fair eyes owe him ; shall we now to bed ?
 Tam. Oh, no, my lord ; your holy friar says   110
All couplings in the day that touch the bed
Adulterous are, even in the married ;
Whose grave and worthy doctrine, well I know,
Your faith in him will liberally allow.
 Mont. He's a most learned and religious man ; 115
Come to the presence then, and see great D'Ambois
(Fortune's proud mushroom shot up in a night)
Stand like an Atlas under our King's arm ;
Which greatness with him Monsieur now envies
As bitterly and deadly as the Guise.   120
 Tam. What ! He that was but yesterday his maker,
His raiser, and preserver ?
 Mont.   Even the same.
Each natural agent works but to this end,
To render that it works on like itself ;
Which since the Monsieur in his act on D'Ambois 125
Cannot to his ambitious end effect,
But that, quite opposite, the King hath power,
In his love borne to D'Ambois, to convert
The point of Monsieur's aim on his own breast,
He turns his outward love to inward hate :   130
A prince's love is like the lightning's fume,
Which no man can embrace but must consume.

          Exeunt

[SCENA SECUNDA

A Room in the Court]

Henry, D'Ambois, Monsieur, Guise, Duchess, Annable,
Charlotte, Attendants.

 Hen. Speak home, Bussy ! Thy impartial words
Are like brave falcons that dare truss a fowl

Much greater than themselves ; flatterers are kites
That check at sparrows ; thou shalt be my eagle,
And bear my thunder underneath thy wings ;   5
Truth's words, like jewels, hang in th' ears of kings.
   Bus. Would I might live to see no Jews hang there
Instead of jewels—sycophants, I mean,
Who use Truth like the Devil, his true foe,
Cast by the angel to the pit of fears,   10
And bound in chains ; Truth seldom decks kings' ears.
Slave Flattery (like a rippier's legs roll'd up
In boots of hay-ropes) with kings' soothed guts
Swaddled and strappled, now lives only free.
O, 'tis a subtle knave ; how like the plague   .   15
Unfelt he strikes into the brain of man,
And rageth in his entrails when he can,
Worse than the poison of a red-hair'd man.
   Hen. Fly at him and his brood ! I cast thee off,
And once more give thee surname of mine eagle.   20
   Bus. I'll make you sport enough, then : let me have
My lucerns too, or dogs inur'd to hunt
Beasts of most rapine, but to put them up,
And if I truss not, let me not be trusted.
Show me a great man (by the people's voice,   25
Which is the voice of God) that by his greatness
Bombasts his private roofs with public riches ;
That affects royalty, rising from a clapdish ;
That rules so much more by his suffering king,
That he makes kings of his subordinate slaves :   30
Himself and them graduate (like woodmongers,
Piling a stack of billets) from the earth,
Raising each other into steeples' heights ;
Let him convey this on the turning props
Of Protean law, and (his own counsel keeping)   35
Keep all upright—let me but hawk at him,
I'll play the vulture, and so thump his liver,
That, like a huge unlading Argosy,
He shall confess all, and you then may hang him.
Show me a clergyman, that is in voice   40
A lark of heaven, in heart a mole of earth ;
That hath good living, and a wicked life ;
A temperate look, and a luxurious gut,
Turning the rent of his superfluous cures
Into your pheasants and your partridges,   45

Venting their quintessençe as men read Hebrew—
Let me but hawk at him, and, like the other,
He shall confess all, and you then may hang him.
Show me a lawyer that turns sacred law
(The equal rend'rer of each man his own,   50
The scourge of rapine and extortion,
The sanctuary and impregnable defence
Of retir'd learning and besieged virtue)
Into a harpy, that eats all but's own,
Into the damned sins it punisheth ;   55
Into the synagogue of thieves and atheists,
Blood into gold, and justice into lust—
Let me but hawk at him, as at the rest,
He shall confess all, and you then may hang him.

Enter Montsurry, Tamyra, *and* Pero

     Guise.   Where will you find such game as you would hawk
        at ?   60
     Bus.   I'll hawk about your house for one of them.
     Guise.   Come, y'are a glorious ruffian, and run proud
Of the King's headlong graces ; hold your breath,
Or, by that poison'd vapour, not the King
Shall back your murtherous valour against me.   65
     Bus.   I would the King would make his presence free
But for one bout betwixt us : by the reverence
Due to the sacred space 'twixt kings and subjects,
Here would I make thee cast that popular purple,
In which thy proud soul sits and braves thy sovereign.   70
     Mons.   Peace, peace, I pray thee peace.
     Bus.   Let him peace first
That made the first war.
     Mons.   He's the better man.
     Bus.   And, therefore, may do worst ?
     Mons.   He has more titles.
     Bus.   So Hydra had more heads.
     Mons.   He's greater known.
     Bus.   His greatness is the people's ; mine's mine own.   75
     Mons.   He's nobl[ier] born.
     Bus.   He is not ; I am noble.
And noblesse in his blood hath no gradation,
But in his merit.
     Guise.   Th'art not nobly born,
But bastard to the Cardinal of Ambois.

Bus. Thou liest, proud Guisard ; let me fly, my lord.   80
Hen. Not in my face, my eagle ; violence flies
The sanctuaries of a prince's eyes.
   Bus. Still shall we chide and foam upon this bit ?
Is the Guise only great in faction ?
Stands he not by himself ? Proves he th' opinion   85
That men's souls are without them ?   Be a duke,
And lead me to the field.
   Guise.   Come, follow me.
   Hen. Stay them ! Stay, D'Ambois ! Cousin Guise, I
     wonder
Your honour'd disposition brooks so ill
A man so good, that only would uphold   90
Man in his native noblesse, from whose fall
All our dissensions rise ; that in himself
(Without the outward patches of our frailty,
Riches and honour) knows he comprehends
Worth with the greatest : kings had never borne   95
Such boundless empire over other men,
Had all maintain'd the spirit and state of D'Ambois ;
Nor had the full impartial hand of Nature
That all things gave in her original,
Without these definite terms of Mine and Thine,   100
Been turn'd unjustly to the hand of Fortune,
Had all preserv'd her in her prime, like D'Ambois ;
No envy, no disjunction had dissolv'd,
Or pluck'd one stick out of the golden faggot
In which the world of Saturn bound our lives,   105
Had all been held together with the nerves,
The genius, and th' ingenuous soul of D'Ambois.
Let my hand therefore be the Hermean rod
To part and reconcile, and so conserve you,
As my combin'd embracers and supporters.   110
   Bus. 'Tis our King's motion, and we shall not seem
To worst eyes womanish, though we change thus soon
Never so great grudge for his greater pleasure.
   Guise. I seal to that, and so the manly freedom,
That you so much profess, hereafter prove not   115
A bold and glorious licence to deprave,
To me his hand shall hold the Hermean virtue
His grace affects, in which submissive sign
On this his sacred right hand, I lay mine.
   Bus. 'Tis well, my lord, and so your worthy greatness   120

Decline not to the greater insolence,
Nor make you think it a prerogative,
To rack men's freedoms with the ruder wrongs,
My hand (stuck full of laurel, in true sign
'Tis wholly dedicate to righteous peace)   125
In all submission kisseth th' other side.

   Hen.   Thanks to ye both ; and kindly I invite ye
Both to a banquet, where we'll sacrifice
Full cups to confirmation of your loves ;
At which, fair ladies, I entreat your presence ;   130
And hope you, madam [*to the* Duchess], will take one carouse
For reconcilement of your lord and servant.

   Duch.   If I should fail, my lord, some other lady
Would be found there to do that for my servant.

   Mons.   Any of these here ?

   Duch.   Nay, I know not that.   135

   Bus.   [*To* Tamyra]   Think your thoughts like my mistress, honour'd lady ?

   Tam.   I think not on you, sir ; y'are one I know not.

   Bus.   Cry you mercy, madam !

   Mont.   Oh, sir, has she met you ?

        Exeunt Henry, D'Ambois, [*and*] Ladies.

   Mons.   What had my bounty drunk when it rais'd him ?

   Guise.   Y'ave stuck us up a very worthy flag,   140
That takes more wind than we with all our sails.

   Mons.   Oh, so he spreads and flourishes.

   Guise.   He must down,
Upstarts should never perch too near a crown.

   Mons.   'Tis true, my lord ; and as this doting hand,
Even out of earth, like Juno, struck this giant,   145
So Jove's great ordinance shall be here implied
To strike him under th' Etna of his pride :
To which work lend your hands, and let us cast
Where we may set snares for his ranging greatness :
I think it best, amongst our greatest women :   150
For there is no such trap to catch an upstart
As a loose downfall ; for, you know, their falls
Are th' ends of all men's rising : if great men
And wise make scapes to please advantage[s]
'Tis with a woman : women, that worst may,   155
Still hold men's candles : they direct and know
All things amiss in all men, and their women
All things amiss in them ; through whose charm'd mouths,

We may see all the close scapes of the Court.
When the most royal beast of chase, the hart,   160
Being old, and cunning in his lairs and haunts,
Can never be discover'd to the bow,
The piece, or hound, yet where, behind some queach,
He breaks his gall, and rutteth with his hind,
The place is mark'd, and by his venery   165
He still is taken. Shall we then attempt
The chiefest mean to that discovery here,
And court our greatest ladies' chiefest women
With shows of love and liberal promises ?
'Tis but our breath. If something given in hand   170
Sharpen their hopes of more, 'twill be well ventur'd.
   Guise. No doubt of that ; and 'tis the cunning'st point
Of our devis'd investigation.
   Mons. I have broken
The ice to it already with the woman   175
Of your chaste lady, and conceive good hope
I shall wade thorough to some wished shore
At our next meeting.
   Mont.   Nay, there's small hope there.
   Guise. Take say of her, my lord, she comes most fitly.

               Enter Charlotte, Annable, Pero

   Mons. Starting back ?   180
   Guise. Y'are engaged, indeed.
   Anna. Nay, pray, my lord, forbear.
   Mont. What, skittish, servant ?
   Anna. No, my lord, I am not so fit for your service.
   Char. Pray pardon me now, my lord ; my lady expects
me.   185
   Guise. I'll satisfy her expectation, as far as an uncle may.
   Mons. Well said, a spirit of courtship of all hands !
Now, mine own Pero, hast thou remembered me for the dis-
covery I entreated thee to make of thy mistress ? Speak
boldly, and be sure of all things I have sworn to thee.   190
   Pero. Building on that assurance, my lord, I may speak
and much the rather, because my lady hath not trusted me
with that I can tell you ; for now I cannot be said to betray
her.
   Mons. That's all one, so we reach our objects ; forth, I 195
beseech thee.

Pero. To tell you truth, my lord, I have made a strange discovery.

Mons. Excellent ! Pero, thou reviv'st me ; may I sink quick to perdition if my tongue discover it.   200

Pero. 'Tis thus, then : this last night, my lord lay forth, and I, watching my lady's sitting up, stole up at midnight from my pallet, and (having before made a hole both through the wall and arras to her inmost chamber) I saw D'Ambois and herself reading a letter.   205

Mons. D'Ambois ?

Pero. Even he, my lord.

Mons. Dost thou not dream, wench ?

Pero. I swear he is the man.

Mons. [*Aside*] The devil he is, and thy lady his dam ! 210 Why, this was the happiest shot that ever flew ; the just plague of hypocrisy levelled it. Oh, the infinite regions betwixt a woman's tongue and her heart ! Is this our Goddess of chastity ?   I thought I could not be so slighted, if she had not her fraught besides, and therefore plotted this with her 215 woman, never dreaming of D'Ambois.—Dear Pero, I will advance thee for ever ; but tell me now—God's precious, it transforms me with admiration—sweet Pero, whom should she trust with this conveyance ? Or, all the doors being made sure, how should his conveyance be made ?   220

Pero. Nay, my lord, that amazes me ; I cannot by any study so much as guess at it.

Mons. Well, let's favour our apprehensions with forbearing that a little ; for, if my heart were not hooped with adamant, the conceit of this would have burst it.   But hark 225 thee.   *Whispers* [*to* Pero.]

Mont. I pray thee, resolve me : the Duke will never imagine that I am busy about's wife : hath D'Ambois any privy access to her ?

Anna. No, my lord ; D'Ambois neglects her, as she takes 230 it, and is therefore suspicious that either your lady, or the Lady Beaupré, hath closely entertained him.

Mont. By'r lady, a likely suspicion, and very near the life,—especially of my wife.

Mons. [*Aside to* Pero] Come, we'll disguise all with 235 seeming only to have courted.—Away, dry palm ! Sh'as a liver as hard as a biscuit ; a man may go a whole voyage with her, and get nothing but tempests from her wind-pipe.

Guise. Here's one, I think, has swallowed a porcupine, she casts pricks from her tongue so.   240

Mont. And here's a peacock seems to have devoured one
of the Alps, she has so swelling a spirit, and is so cold of her
kindness.

Char. We are no windfalls, my lord; ye must gather
us with the ladder of matrimony, or we'll hang till we be 245
rotten.

Mons. Indeed, that's the way to make ye right open-arses.
But, alas, ye have no portions fit for such husbands as we
wish you.

Pero. Portions, my lord? yes, and such portions as your 250
principality cannot purchase.

Mons. What, woman! what are those portions?

Pero. Riddle my riddle, my lord.

Mons. Ay, marry, wench, I think thy portion is a right
riddle; a man shall never find it out. But let's hear it. 255

Pero. You shall, my lord.

> *What's that, that being most rare's most cheap?*
> *That when you sow, you never reap?*
> *That when it grows most, most you in it;*
> *And still you lose it when you win it?*   260
> *That when 'tis commonest, 'tis dearest,*
> *And when 'tis farthest off, 'tis nearest?*

Mons. Is this your great portion?

Pero. Even this, my lord.

Mons. Believe me, I cannot riddle it.   265

Pero. No, my lord: 'tis my chastity, which you shall
neither riddle nor fiddle.

Mons. Your chastity? Let me begin with the end of it;
how is a woman's chastity nearest a man when 'tis furthest
off?   270

Pero. Why, my lord, when you cannot get it, it goes to th'
heart on you; and that, I think, comes most near you: and
I am sure it shall be far enough off; and so we leave you
to our mercies.   *Exeunt* Women

Mons. Farewell, riddle!   275

Guise. Farewell, medlar!

Mont. Farewell, winter plum!

Mons. Now, my lords, what fruit of our inquisition?
Feel you nothing budding yet? Speak, good my lord
Montsurry.   280

Mont. Nothing but this: D'Ambois is thought negligent in

observing the Duchess, and therefore she is suspicious that
your niece or my wife closely entertains him.

    Mons. Your wife, my lord ? Think you that possible ?

    Mont. Alas, I know she flies him like her last hour.   285

    Mons. Her last hour ? Why, that comes upon her the
more she flies it. Does D'Ambois so, think you ?

    Mont. That's not worth the answering. 'Tis miraculous
to think with what monsters women's imaginations engross
them when they are once enamoured, and what wonders they 290
will work for their satisfaction. They will make a sheep
valiant, a lion fearful.

    Mons. And an ass confident. Well, my lord, more will
come forth shortly ; get you to the banquet.

    Guise. Come, my lord ; I have the blind side of one of 295
them.   *Exit* Guise *cum* Montsurry

    Mons.   O the unsounded sea of women's bloods,
That when 'tis calmest, is most dangerous !
Not any wrinkle creaming in their faces,
When in their hearts are Scylla and Charybdis,   300
Which still are hid in dark and standing fogs,
Where never day shines, nothing ever grows,
But weeds and poisons that no statesman knows :
Not Cerberus ever saw the damned nooks
Hid with the veils of women's virtuous looks.   305
But what a cloud of sulphur have I drawn
Up to my bosom in this dangerous secret !
Which if my haste with any spark should light
Ere D'Ambois were engag'd in some sure plot,
I were blown up ; he would be, sure, my death.   310
Would I had never known it, for before
I shall persuade th' importance to Montsurry,
And make him with some studied stratagem
Train D'Ambois to his wreak, his maid may tell it ;
Or I (out of my fiery thirst to play   315
With the fell tiger, up in darkness tied,
And give it some light) make it quite break loose.
I fear it afore heaven, and will not see
D'Ambois again, till I have told Montsurry,
And set a snare with him to free my fears.   320
Who's there ?

                Enter Maffé

    Maf.   My lord ?

    Mons.   Go call the Count Montsurry,

And make the doors fast; I will speak with none
Till he come to me.

   Maf.   Well, my lord.   *Exiturus*

   Mons.   Or else
Send you some other, and see all the doors
Made safe yourself, I pray; haste, fly about it.   325

   Maf. You'll speak with none but with the Count Mont-
     surry?

   Mons. With none but he, except it be the Guise.

   Maf. See, even by this there's one exception more;
Your Grace must be more firm in the command,
Or else shall I as weakly execute.   330
The Guise shall speak with you?

   Mons.   He shall, I say.

   Maf. And Count Montsurry?

   Mons.   Ay, and Count Montsurry.

   Maf. Your Grace must pardon me, that I am bold
To urge the clear and full sense of your pleasure;
Which whensoever I have known, I hope   335
Your Grace will say I hit it to a hair.

   Mons. You have.

   Maf.   I hope so, or I would be glad—

   Mons. I pray thee get thee gone; thou art so tedious
In the strict form of all thy services
That I had better have one negligent.   340
You hit my pleasure well, when D'Ambois hit you;
Did you not, think you?

   Maf.   D'Ambois? Why, my lord—

   Mons. I pray thee talk no more, but shut the doors:
Do what I charge thee.

   Maf.   I will, my lord, and yet
I would be glad the wrong I had of D'Ambois—   345

   Mons. Precious, then it is a fate that plagues me
In this man's foolery! I may be murther'd
While he stands on protection of his folly.
Avaunt about thy charge!

   Maf.   I go, my lord.
[*Aside.*] I had my head broke in his faithful service;   350
I had no suit the more, nor any thanks,
And yet my teeth must still be hit with D'Ambois—
D'Ambois, my lord, shall know—

   Mons.   The devil and D'Ambois!
                            Exit Maffé

How am I tortur'd with this trusty fool!
Never was any curious in his place   355
To do things justly, but he was an ass ;
We cannot find one trusty that is witty,
And therefore bear their disproportion.
Grant, thou great star and angel of my life,
A sure lease of it but for some few days,   360
That I may clear my bosom of the snake
I cherish'd there, and I will then defy
All check to it but Nature's, and her altars
Shall crack with vessels crown'd with every liquor
Drawn from her highest and most bloody humours.   365
I fear him strangely, his advanced valour
Is like a spirit rais'd without a circle,
Endangering him that ignorantly rais'd him,
And for whose fury he hath learnt no limit.

Enter Maffé hastily

   Maf. I cannot help it : what should I do more ?   370
As I was gathering a fit guard to make
My passage to the doors, and the doors sure,
The man of blood is enter'd.
   Mons.   Rage of death !
If I had told the secret, and he knew it,
Thus had I been endanger'd.   375
Enter D'Ambois.
                         My sweet heart !
How now, what leap'st thou at ?
   Bus.   O royal object !
   Mons. Thou dream'st awake ; object in th' empty air ?
   Bus. Worthy the brows of Titan, worth his chair.
   Mons. Pray thee, what mean'st thou ?
   Bus.   See you not a crown
Impale the forehead of the great King Monsieur ?   380
   Mons. Oh, fie upon thee !
   Bus.   Prince, that is the subject
Of all these your retir'd and sole discourses.
   Mons. Wilt thou not leave that wrongful supposition ?
   Bus. Why wrongful to suppose the doubtless right
To the succession worth the thinking on ?   385
   Mons. Well, leave these jests ! How I am overjoy'd
With thy wish'd presence, and how fit thou com'st,
For, of mine honour, I was sending for thee.

Bus. To what end ?

Mons.   Only for thy company,
Which I have still in thought ; but that's no payment   390
On thy part made with personal appearance.
Thy absence so long suffer'd oftentimes
Put me in some little doubt thou dost not love me.
Wilt thou do one thing therefore now sincerely ?

  Bus. Ay, anything, but killing of the King.   395

  Mons. Still in that discord, and ill-taken note ?
How most unseasonable thou playest the cuckoo,
In this thy fall of friendship !

  Bus.   Then do not doubt.
That there is any act within my nerves,
But killing of the King, that is not yours.   400

  Mons. I will not, then ; to prove which by my love
Shown to thy virtues, and by all fruits else
Already sprung from that still-flourishing tree,
With whatsoever may hereafter spring,
I charge thee utter (even with all the freedom   405
Both of thy noble nature and thy friendship)
The full and plain state of me in thy thoughts.

  Bus. What, utter plainly what I think of you ?

  Mons. Plain as truth !

  Bus. Why, this swims quite against the stream of
    greatness ;   410
Great men would rather hear their flatteries,
And if they be not made fools, are not wise.

  Mons. I am no such great fool, and therefore charge thee
Even from the root of thy free heart display me.

  Bus. Since you affect it in such serious terms,   415
If yourself first will tell me what you think
As freely and as heartily of me,
I'll be as open in my thoughts of you.

  Mons. A bargain, of mine honour ! And make this,
That prove we in our full dissection   420
Never so foul, live still the sounder friends.

  Bus. What else, sir ? Come, pay me home ; I'll bide it
    bravely.

  Mons. I will, I swear. I think thee then a man
That dares as much as a wild horse or tiger,
As headstrong and as bloody ; and to feed   425
The ravenous wolf of thy most cannibal valour,
(Rather than not employ it) thou wouldst turn

Hackster to any whore, slave to a Jew,
Or English usurer, to force possessions
(And cut men's throats) of mortgaged estates ;   430
Or thou wouldst tire thee like a tinker's strumpet,
And murther market-folks ; quarrel with sheep,
And run as mad as Ajax ; serve a butcher ;
Do anything but killing of the King :
That in thy valour th'art like other naturals   435
That have strange gifts in nature, but no soul
Diffus'd quite through, to make them of a piece,
But stop at humours, that are more absurd,
Childish, and villanous than that hackster, whore,
Slave, cut-throat, tinker's bitch, compar'd before ;   440
And in those humours wouldst envy, betray,
Slander, blaspheme, change each hour a religion,
Do anything, but killing of the King :
That in thy valour (which is still the dunghill,
To which hath reference all filth in thy house)   445
Th'art more ridiculous and vain-glorious
Than any mountebank, and impudent
Than any painted bawd ; which not to soothe,
And glorify thee like a Jupiter Hammon,
Thou eat'st thy heart in vinegar, and thy gall   450
Turns all thy blood to poison, which is cause
Of that toad-pool that stands in thy complexion,
And makes thee (with a cold and earthy moisture,
Which is the dam of putrefaction,
As plague to thy damn'd pride) rot as thou liv'st,   455
To study calumnies and treacheries,
To thy friends' slaughters like a screech-owl sing,
And to all mischiefs, but to kill the King.
    Bus.   So ! Have you said ?
    Mons.   How think'st thou ?   Do I flatter ?
Speak I not like a trusty friend to thee ?   460
    Bus.   That ever any man was blest withal ;
So here's for me ! I think you are (at worst)
No devil, since y'are like to be no king ;
Of which, with any friend of yours, I'll lay
This poor stillado here, gainst all the stars,   465
Ay, and gainst all your treacheries, which are more ;
That you did never good, but to do ill.
But ill of all sorts, free and for itself :
That (like a murthering piece, making lanes in armies,

The first man of a rank, the whole rank falling)   470
If you have wrong'd one man, you are so far
From making him amends, that all his race,
Friends, and associates fall into your chase :
That y'are for perjuries the very prince
Of all intelligencers ; and your voice   475
Is like an eastern wind, that, where it flies,
Knits nets of caterpillars, with which you catch
The prime of all the fruits the kingdom yields
That your political head is the curs'd fount
Of all the violence, rapine, cruelty,   480
Tyranny, and atheism flowing through the realm :
That y'ave a tongue so scandalous, 'twill cut
The purest crystal ; and a breath that will
Kill to that wall a spider ; you will jest
With God, and your soul to the Devil tender ;   485
For lust kiss horror, and with death engender :
That your foul body is a Lernean fen
Of all the maladies breeding in all men ;
That you are utterly without a soul ;
And, for your life, the thread of that was spun   490
When Clotho slept, and let her breathing rock
Fall in the dirt ; and Lachesis still draws it,
Dipping her twisting fingers in a bowl
Defil'd, and crown'd with virtue's forced soul :
And lastly (which I must for gratitude   495
Ever remember), that of all my height
And dearest life you are the only spring,
Only in royal hope to kill the King.
    Mons.   Why, now I see thou lovest me ; come to the ban-
    quet.   *Exeunt*

FINIS ACTUS TERTII.

ACTUS QUARTI SCENA PRIMA

[A Room in the Court]

Henry, Monsieur *with a letter*, Guise, Montsurry, Bussy,
    Elenor, Tamyra, Beaupré, Pero, Charlotte, Annable,
    Pyra, *with four* Pages.

    Hen.   Ladies, ye have not done our banquet right,
Nor look'd upon it with those cheerful rays
That lately turn'd your breaths to floods of gold ;
Your looks, methinks, are not drawn out with thoughts

So clear and free as heretofore, but foul,   5
As if the thick complexions of men
Govern'd within them.
    Bus.   'Tis not like, my lord,
That men in women rule, but contrary ;
For as the moon (of all things God created)
Not only is the most appropriate image   10
Or glass to show them how they wax and wane,
But in her height and motion likewise bears
Imperial influences that command
In all their powers, and make them wax and wane ;
So women, that (of all things made of nothing)   15
Are the most perfect idols of the moon,
(Or still-unwean'd sweet moon-calves with white faces)
Not only are patterns of change to men,
But, as the tender moonshine of their beauties
Clears or is cloudy, make men glad or sad :   20
So then they rule in men, not men in them.
    Mons. But here the moons are chang'd, (as the King notes)
And either men rule in them, or some power
Beyond their voluntary faculty,
For nothing can recover their lost faces.   25
    Mont. None can be always one : our griefs and joys
Hold several sceptres in us, and have times
For their divided empires : which grief now in them
Doth prove as proper to his diadem.
    Bus. And grief's a natural sickness of the blood,   30
That time to part asks, as his coming had ;
Only slight fools, griev'd, suddenly are glad ;
A man may say t' a dead man, ' Be reviv'd,'
As well as to one sorrowful, ' Be not griev'd.'
And therefore, princely mistress, [*To the* Duchess] in all wars 35
Against these base foes that insult on weakness,
And still fight hous'd behind the shield of Nature,
Of privilege, law, treachery, or beastly need,
Your servant cannot help ; authority here
Goes with corruption, something like some States   40
That back worst men : valour to them must creep
That, to themselves left, would fear him asleep.
    Duch. Ye all take that for granted that doth rest
Yet to be prov'd ; we all are as we were,
As merry and as free in thought as ever.   45
    Guise. And why then can ye not disclose your thoughts ?

Tam.   Methinks the man hath answer'd for us well.

Mons.   The man ? Why, madam, d'ye not know his name ?

Tam.   Man is a name of honour for a king :

Additions take away from each chief thing.   50

The school of modesty not to learn learns dames :

They sit in high forms there, that know men's names.

Mons. [*To Bussy*] Hark, sweetheart, here's a bar set to
    your valour !

It cannot enter here, no, not to notice

Of what your name is ; your great eagle's beak   55

(Should you fly at her) had as good encounter

An Albion cliff, as her more craggy liver.

Bus.   I'll not attempt her, sir ; her sight and name

(By which I only know her) doth deter me.

Hen.   So they do all men else.

Mons.   You would say so   60

If you knew all.

Tam.   Knew all, my lord ?   What mean you ?

Mons.   All that I know, madam.

Tam.   That you know ! Speak it.

Mons.   No, 'tis enough, I feel it.

Hen.   But, methinks

Her courtship is more pure than heretofore ;

True courtiers should be modest, and not nice,   65

Bold, but not impudent, pleasure love, not vice.

Mons.   Sweetheart, come hither ! What if one should make

Horns at Montsurry ? Would it not strike him jealous

Through all the proofs of his chaste lady's virtues ?

Bus.   If he be wise, not.   70

Mons.   What ? Not if I should name the gardener

That I would have him think hath grafted him ?

Bus.   So the large licence that your greatness uses

To jest at all men, may be taught indeed

To make a difference of the grounds you play on,   75

Both in the men you scandal, and the matter.

Mons.   As how ? As how ?

Bus.   Perhaps led with a train,

Where you may have your nose made less and slit,

Your eyes thrust out.

Mons.   Peace, peace, I pray thee peace.

Who dares do that ? The brother of his King ?   80

Bus.   Were your King brother in you ; all your powers

(Stretch'd in the arms of great men and their bawds),

Set close down by you ; all your stormy laws
Spouted with lawyers' mouths, and gushing blood,
Like to so many torrents ; all your glories   85
(Making you terrible, like enchanted flames)
Fed with bare cockscombs and with crooked hams,
All your prerogatives, your shames and tortures ;
All daring heaven, and opening hell about you—
Were I the man ye wrong'd so and provok'd,   90
Though ne'er so much beneath you, like a box-tree
I would, out of the roughness of my root,
Ram hardness in my lowness and, like Death
Mounted on earthquakes, I would trot through all
Honours and horrors, thorough foul and fair,   95
And from your whole strength toss you into the air.
    Mons. Go, th'art a devil ! Such another spirit
Could not be still'd from all th' Armenian dragons.
O my love's glory, heir to all I have
(That's all I can say, and that all I swear)   100
If thou outlive me, as I know thou must,
Or else hath Nature no proportion'd end
To her great labours ; she hath breathed a mind
Into thy entrails, of desert to swell
Into another great Augustus Cæsar,   105
Organs and faculties fitted to her greatness ;
And should that perish like a common spirit,
Nature's a courtier and regards no merit.
    Hen. Here's nought but whispering with us ; like a calm
Before a tempest, when the silent air   110
Lays her soft ear close to the earth to hearken
For that she fears steals on to ravish her ;
Some fate doth join our ears to hear it coming.
Come, my brave eagle, let's to covert fly ;
I see Almighty Æther in the smoke   115
Of all his clouds descending, and the sky
Hid in the dim ostents of tragedy.
                        Exit Henry *with* D'Ambois *and Ladies*
    Guise [*aside to* Monsieur]. Now stir the humour, and
      begin the brawl.
    Mont. The King and D'Ambois now are grown all one.
    Mons [*making horns at* Montsurry]. Nay, they are two,
      my lord.
    Mont.   How's that ?
    Mons.   No more.   120

Mont.   I must have more, my lord.

Mons.   What, more than two ?

Mont.   How monstrous is this !

Mons.   Why ?

Mont.   You make me horns !

Mons.   Not I, it is a work without my power ;
Married men's ensigns are not made with fingers ;
Of divine fabric they are, not men's hands ;   125
Your wife, you know, is a mere Cynthia.
And she must fashion horns out of her nature.

Mont.   But doth she ? Dare you charge her ? Speak, false
  prince.

Mons.   I must not speak, my lord ; but if you'll use
The learning of a nobleman, and read,   130
Here's something to those points ; soft, you must pawn
Your honour having read it to return it.

Enter Tamyra, Pero.

Mont.   Not I ! I pawn mine honour for a paper ?

Mons.   You must not buy it under.

                     Exeunt Guise *and* Monsieur

Mont.   Keep it then,
And keep fire in your bosom.

Tam.   What says he ?   135

Mont.   You must make good the rest.

Tam.   How fares my lord ?
Takes my love anything to heart he says ?

Mont.   Come y'are a—

Tam.   What, my lord ?

Mont.   The plague of Herod
Feast in his rotten entrails.

Tam.   Will you wreak
Your anger's just cause given by him, on me ?   140

Mont.   By him ?

Tam.   By him, my lord ; I have admir'd
You could all this time be at concord with him,
That still hath play'd such discords on your honour.

Mont.   Perhaps 'tis with some proud string of my wife's.

Tam.   How's that, my lord ?

Mont.   Your tongue will still admire,   145
Till my head be the miracle of the world.

Tam.   O, woe is me !

                     She seems to swound

Pero.   What does your lordship mean ?
Madam, be comforted ; my lord but tries you.
Madam ! Help, good my lord, are you not mov'd ?
Do your set looks print in your words your thoughts ?   150
Sweet lord, clear up those eyes, for shame of noblesse,
Unbend that masking forehead ; whence is it
You rush upon her with these Irish wars,
More full of sound than hurt ? But it is enough,
You have shot home, your words are in her heart ;   155
She has not liv'd to bear a trial now.
   Mont. Look up, my love, and by this kiss receive
My soul amongst thy spirits, for supply
To thine chas'd with my fury.
   Tam.   Oh, my lord,
I have too long liv'd to hear this from you.   160
   Mont. 'Twas from my troubled blood, and not from me.
[*Aside*] I know not how I fare ; a sudden night
Flows through my entrails, and a headlong chaos
Murmurs within me, which I must digest,
And not drown her in my confusions,   165
That was my life's joy, being best inform'd.—
Sweet, you must needs forgive me, that my love
(Like to a fire disdaining his suppression)
Rag'd being discourag'd ; my whole heart is wounded
When any least thought in you is but touch'd,   170
And shall be till I know your former merits,
Your name and memory, altogether crave
In just oblivion their eternal grave ;
And then, you must hear from me, there's no mean
In any passion I shall feel for you ;   175
Love is a razor cleansing, being well us'd,
But fetcheth blood still, being the least abus'd ;
To tell you briefly all—the man that left me
When you appear'd, did turn me worse than woman,
And stabb'd me to the heart thus [*making horns*], with his
      fingers.   180
   Tam. Oh, happy woman ! Comes my stain from him ?
It is my beauty, and that innocence proves
That slew Chymæra, rescued Peleus
From all the savage beasts in Pelion,
And rais'd the chaste Athenian prince from hell :   185
All suffering with me, they for women's lusts,
I for a man's, that the Augean stable

Of his foul sin would empty in my lap ;
How his guilt shunn'd me ! Sacred Innocence,
That where thou fear'st art dreadful, and his face   190
Turn'd in flight from thee, that had thee in chase ;
Come, bring me to him ; I will tell the serpent
Even to his venom'd teeth (from whose curs'd seed
A pitch'd field starts up 'twixt my lord and me)
That his throat lies, and he shall curse his fingers,   195
For being so govern'd by his filthy soul.

    Mont. I know not if himself will vaunt t'have been
The princely author of the slavish sin,
Or any other ; he would have resolv'd me,
Had you not come, not by his word, but writing,   200
Would I have sworn to give it him again,
And pawn'd mine honour to him for a paper.

    Tam. See how he flies me still ! 'Tis a foul heart
That fears his own hand. Good, my lord, make haste
To see the dangerous paper ; papers hold   205
Oft-times the forms and copies of our souls,
And, though the world despise them, are the prizes
Of all our honours ; make your honour then
A hostage for it, and with it confer
My nearest woman here, in all she knows ;   210
Who (if the sun or Cerberus could have seen
Any stain in me) might as well as they ;
And, Pero, here I charge thee by my love,
And all proofs of it (which I might call bounties),
By all that thou hast seen seem good in me,   215
And all the ill which thou shouldst spit from thee,
By pity of the wound this touch hath given me,
Not as thy mistress now, but a poor woman,
To death given over, rid me of my pains ;
Pour on thy powder ; clear thy breast of me :   220
My lord is only here ; here speak thy worst,
Thy best will do me mischief ; if thou spar'st me,
Never shine good thought on thy memory !
Resolve my lord, and leave me desperate.

    Pero. My lord !—My lord hath play'd a prodigal's part, 225
To break his stock for nothing ; and an insolent,
To cut a Gordian when he could not loose it :
What violence is this, to put true fire
To a false train, to blow up long-crown'd peace
With sudden outrage, and believe a man   230

Sworn to the shame of women, gainst a woman
Born to their honours ! But I will to him.
   Tam. No, I will write (for I shall never more
Meet with the fugitive) where I will defy him,
Were he ten times the brother of my king.   235
To him, my lord, and I'll to cursing him.

                                Exeunt

[SCENA SECUNDA

A Room in Montsurry's *House*]

Enter D'Ambois *and* Friar

   Bus. I am suspicious, my most honour'd father,
By some of Monsieur's cunning passages,
That his still ranging and contentious nostrils,
To scent the haunts of Mischief have so us'd
The vicious virtue of his busy sense,   5
That he trails hotly of him, and will rouse him,
Driving him all enrag'd and foaming on us ;
And therefore have entreated your deep skill
In the command of good aërial spirits,
To assume these magic rites, and call up one   10
To know if any have reveal'd unto him
Anything touching my dear love and me.
   Friar. Good son, you have amaz'd me but to make
The least doubt of it, it concerns so nearly
The faith and reverence of my name and order.   15
Yet will I justify, upon my soul,
All I have done ; if any spirit i' th' earth or air
Can give you the resolve, do not despair.

Muzic : and Tamyra *enters with* Pero, *her maid, bearing a letter*

   Tam. Away, deliver it :   *Exit* Pero
               O may my lines,
Fill'd with the poison of a woman's hate,   20
When he shall open them, shrink up his curs'd eyes
With torturous darkness, such as stands in hell,
Stuck full of inward horrors, never lighted,
With which are all things to be fear'd, affrighted ;
   Bus. [advancing] How is it with my honour'd mistress ? 25
   Tam. O servant, help, and save me from the gripes
Of shame and infamy. Our love is known ;

Your Monsieur hath a paper where is writ
Some secret tokens that decipher it.

  Bus. What cold dull Northern brain, what fool but he   30
Durst take into his Epimethean breast
A box of such plagues as the danger yields
Incurr'd in this discovery ? He had better
Ventur'd his breast in the consuming reach
Of the hot surfeits cast out of the clouds,   35
Or stood the bullets that (to wreak the sky)
The Cyclops ram in Jove's artillery.

  Friar. We soon will take the darkness from his face
That did that deed of darkness ; we will know
What now the Monsieur and your husband do,   40
What is contain'd within the secret paper
Offer'd by Monsieur, and your love's events :
To which ends, honour'd daughter, at your motion,
I have put on these exorcising rites,
And, by my power of learned holiness   45
Vouchsaf'd me from above, I will command
Our resolution of a raised spirit.

  Tam. Good father, raise him in some beauteous form,
That with least terror I may brook his sight.

  Friar. Stand sure together, then, whate'er you see,   50
And stir not, as ye tender all our lives.

He puts on his robes

*Occidentalium legionum spiritualium imperator (magnus
ille Behemoth) veni, veni, comitatus cum Astaroth locotenente
invicto. Adjuro te per Stygis inscrutabilia arcana, per ipsos
irremeabiles anfractus Averni : adesto ô Behemoth, tu cui pervia*   55
*sunt Magnatum scrinia ; veni, per Noctis & tenebrarum
abdita profundissima ; per labentia sidera ; per ipsos motus
horarum furtivos, Hecatesque altum silentium ! Appare in
forma spirituali, lucente, splendida & amabili.*

Thunder. Ascendit [Behemoth *with* Cartophylax *and other spirits*]

  Beh. What would the holy Friar ?
  Friar.   I would see   60
What now the Monsieur and Montsurry do,
And see the secret paper that the Monsieur
Offer'd to Count Montsurry, longing much
To know on what events the secret loves
Of these two honour'd persons shall arrive.   65

Beh.   Why call'dst thou me to this accursed light,
To these light purposes ?   I am Emperor
Of that inscrutable darkness where are hid
All deepest truths, and secrets never seen,
All which I know, and command legions   70
Of knowing spirits that can do more than these.
Any of this my guard that circle me
In these blue fires, and out of whose dim fumes
Vast murmurs use to break, and from their sounds
Articulate voices, can do ten parts more   75
Than open such slight truths as you require.
   Friar.   From the last night's black depth I call'd up one
Of the inferior ablest ministers,
And he could not resolve me ; send one then
Out of thine own command, to fetch the paper   80
That Monsieur hath to show to Count Montsurry.
   Beh.   I will.   Cartophylax, thou that properly
Hast in thy power all papers so inscrib'd,
Glide through all bars to it and fetch that paper.
   Car.   I will.   *A torch removes*
   Friar.   Till he returns, great Prince of Darkness, 85
Tell me if Monsieur and the Count Montsurry
Are yet encounter'd ?
   Beh.   Both them and the Guise
Are now together.
   Friar.   Show us all their persons,
And represent the place, with all their actions.
   Beh.   The spirit will straight return, and then I'll show
      thee.   90

                     [*Re-enter* Cartophylax]

See, he is come.   Why brought'st thou not the paper ?
   Car.   He hath prevented me, and got a spirit
Rais'd by another great in our command,
To take the guard of it before I came.
   Beh.   This is your slackness, not t' invoke our powers 95
When first your acts set forth to their effects ;
Yet shall you see it and themselves : behold
They come here, and the Earl now holds the paper.

      Enter [*above*] Monsieur, Guise, Montsurry, *with a paper*

   Bus.   May we not hear them ?
   [*Friar.*]   No, be still and see.
   Bus.   I will go fetch the paper.

Friar.   Do not stir ;   100
There's too much distance and too many locks
'Twixt you and them (how near soe'er they seem),
For any man to interrupt their secrets.
  Tam. O honour'd spirit, fly into the fancy
Of my offended lord, and do not let him   105
Believe what there the wicked man hath written.
  Beh. Persuasion hath already enter'd him
Beyond reflection ; peace till their departure.

  Mons. There is a glass of ink where you may see
How to make ready black-fac'd tragedy :   110
You now discern, I hope, through all her paintings,
Her gasping wrinkles and fame's sepulchres.
  Guise. Think you he feigns, my lord ? What hold you
    now ?
Do we malign your wife, or honour you ?
  Mons. What, stricken dumb ! Nay fie, lord, be not
    daunted ;   115
Your case is common ; were it ne'er so rare,
Bear it as rarely ! Now to laugh were manly ;
A worthy man should imitate the weather
That sings in tempests, and, being clear, is silent.
  Guise. Go home, my lord, and force your wife to write 120
Such loving lines to D'Ambois as she us'd
When she desir'd his presence.
  Mons.   Do, my lord,
And make her name her conceal'd messenger,
That close and most inennerable pander,
That passeth all our studies to exquire ;   125
By whom convey the letter to her love ;
And so you shall be sure to have him come
Within the thirsty reach of your revenge ;
Before which, lodge an ambush in her chamber
Behind the arras, of your stoutest men   130
All close and soundly arm'd ; and let them share
A spirit amongst them that would serve a thousand.

Enter [above] Pero with a letter

  Guise. Yet stay a little ; see, she sends for you.
  Mons. Poor, loving lady ; she'll make all good yet,
Think you not so, my lord ?
                              Montsurry stabs Pero and exit

Guise.   Alas, poor soul !   135
Mons. This was cruelly done, i' faith.
Pero.   'Twas nobly done.
And I forgive his lordship from my soul.
Mons. Then much good do't thee, Pero ! Hast a letter ?
Pero. I hope it rather be a bitter volume
Of worthy curses for your perjury.   140
Guise. To you, my lord.
Mons.   To me ? Now, out upon her.
Guise. Let me see, my lord,
Mons. You shall presently. How fares my Pero ?
Who's there ?
                    Enter Servant.
                              Take in this maid, sh'as caught a clap,
And fetch my surgeon to her ; come, my lord,   145
We'll now peruse our letter.

                    Exeunt Montsurry, Guise

Pero.   Furies rise
Out of the black lines, and torment his soul.
                              [*Servant*] *lead*[*s*] *her out*

Tam. Hath my lord slain my woman ?
Beh.   No, she lives.
Friar. What shall become of us ?
Beh.   All I can say,
Being call'd thus late, is brief, and darkly this :   150
If D'Ambois' mistress dye not her white hand
In his forc'd blood, he shall remain untouch'd ;
So, father, shall yourself, but by yourself :
To make this augury plainer, when the voice
Of D'Ambois shall invoke me, I will rise,   155
Shining in greater light, and show him all
That will betide ye all ; meantime be wise,
And curb his valour with your policies.
                              Descendit cum suis
Bus. Will he appear to me when I invoke him ?
Friar. He will, be sure.
Bus.   It must be shortly then :   160
For his dark words have tied my thoughts on knots
Till he dissolve, and free them.
Tam.   In meantime,
Dear servant, till your powerful voice revoke him,

Be sure to use the policy he advis'd ;
Lest fury in your too quick knowledge taken　　　165
Of our abuse, and your defence of me,
Accuse me more than any enemy ;
And, father, you must on my lord impose
Your holiest charges, and the Church's power
To temper his hot spirit and disperse　　　170
The cruelty and the blood I know his hand
Will shower upon our heads, if you put not
Your finger to the storm, and hold it up,
As my dear servant here must do with Monsieur.

Bus. I'll soothe his plots, and strow my hate with smiles, 175
Till all at once the close mines of my heart
Rise at full date, and rush into his blood :
I'll bind his arm in silk, and rub his flesh,
To make the vein swell, that his soul may gush
Into some kennel where it longs to lie,　　　180
And policy shall be flank'd with policy.
Yet shall the feeling centre where we meet
Groan with the weight of my approaching feet ;
I'll make th' inspired thresholds of his court
Sweat with the weather of my horrid steps,　　　185
Before I enter ; yet will I appear
Like calm security before a ruin ;
A politician must like lightning melt
The very marrow, and not taint the skin :
His ways must not be seen ; the superficies　　　190
Of the green centre must not taste his feet ;
When hell is plow'd up with his wounding tracts ;
And all his harvest reap'd by hellish facts.　　　*Exeunt*

FINIS ACTUS QUARTI

ACTUS QUINTI SCENA PRIMA

[*A Room in* Montsurry's *House*]

Montsurry, *bare, unbraced, pulling* Tamyra *in by the
    hair*, Friar.   *One bearing light, a standish and paper,
    which sets a table.*

　Tam.   O, help me, father !
　Friar.　　　　　　　　Impious earl, forbear.

Take violent hand from her, or, by mine order,
The King shall force thee.
 Mont.   'Tis not violent ;
Come you not willingly ?
 Tam.   Yes, good my lord.
 Friar. My lord, remember that your soul must seek 5
Her peace, as well as your revengeful blood ;
You ever to this hour have prov'd yourself
A noble, zealous, and obedient son,
T'our holy mother ; be not an apostate :
Your wife's offence serves not (were it the worst 10
You can imagine) without greater proofs
To sever your eternal bonds and hearts ;
Much less to touch her with a bloody hand :
Nor is it manly, much less husbandly,
To expiate any frailty in your wife 15
With churlish strokes or beastly odds of strength :
The stony birth of clouds will touch no laurel,
Nor any sleeper ; your wife is your laurel,
And sweetest sleeper ; do not touch her then ;
Be not more rude than the wild seed of vapour 20
To her that is more gentle than that rude ;
In whom kind nature suffer'd one offence
But to set off her other excellence.
 Mont. Good father, leave us ; interrupt no more
The course I must run for mine honour sake. 25
Rely on my love to her, which her fault
Cannot extinguish ; will she but disclose
Who was the secret minister of her love,
And through what maze he serv'd it, we are friends.
 Friar. It is a damn'd work to pursue those secrets, 30
That would ope more sin, and prove springs of slaughter ;
Nor is't a path for Christian feet to tread,
But out of all way to the health of souls,
A sin impossible to be forgiven ;
Which he that dares commit—
 Mont.   Good father, cease your terrors. 35
Tempt not a man distracted ; I am apt
To outrages that I shall ever rue !
I will not pass the verge that bounds a Christian,
Nor break the limits of a man nor husband.
 Friar. Then God inspire you both with thoughts and deeds 40
Worthy his high respect, and your own souls.

Tam.　Father !

Friar.　　　　　　　I warrant thee, my dearest daughter,
He will not touch thee ; think'st thou him a pagan ?
His honour and his soul lies for thy safety.　　　*Exit*

Mont.　Who shall remove the mountain from my breast,　45
Stand the opening furnace of my thoughts,
And set fit outcries for a soul in hell ?

　　　　　　　　　　　　Montsurry *turns a key*

For now it nothing fits my woes to speak
But thunder, or to take into my throat
The trump of Heaven, with whose determinate blasts　　50
The winds shall burst, and the devouring seas
Be drunk up in his sounds ; that my hot woes
(Vented enough) I might convert to vapour,
Ascending from my infamy unseen,
Shorten the world, preventing the last breath　　　55
That kills the living, and regenerates death.

Tam.　My lord, my fault (as you may censure it
With too strong arguments) is past your pardon :
But how the circumstances may excuse me
God knows, and your more temperate mind hereafter　60
May let my penitent miseries make you know.

Mont.　Hereafter ? 'Tis a suppos'd infinite,
That from this point will rise eternally :
Fame grows in going ; in the scapes of virtue
Excuses damn her : they be fires in cities　　　65
Enrag'd with those winds that less lights extinguish.
Come, Siren, sing, and dash against my rocks
Thy ruffian galley, rigg'd with quench for lust !
Sing, and put all the nets into thy voice
With which thou drew'st into thy strumpet's lap　　70
The spawn of Venus, and in which ye danced ;
That, in thy lap's stead, I may dig his tomb,
And quit his manhood with a woman's sleight,
Who never is deceiv'd in her deceit.
Sing (that is, write), and then take from mine eyes　75
The mists that hide the most inscrutable pander
That ever lapp'd up an adulterous vomit ;
That I may see the devil, and survive
To be a devil, and then learn to wive :
That I may hang him, and then cut him down,　　80
Then cut him up, and with my soul's beams search
The cranks and caverns of his brain, and study

The errant wilderness of a woman's face,
Where men cannot get out, for all the comets
That have been lighted at it: though they know   85
That adders lie a-sunning in their smiles,
That basilisks drink their poison from their eyes,
And no way there to coast out to their hearts ;
Yet still they wander there, and are not stay'd
Till they be fetter'd, nor secure before   90
All cares devour them, nor in human consort
Till they embrace within their wife's two breasts
All Pelion and Cythæron with their beasts.
Why write you not ?
   Tam.   O, good my lord, forbear
In wreak of great faults to engender greater,   95
And make my love's corruption generate murther.
   Mont. It follows needfully as child and parent ;
The chain-shot of thy lust is yet aloft,
And it must murther ; 'tis thine own dear twin :
No man can add height to a woman's sin.   100
Vice never doth her just hate so provoke,
As when she rageth under virtue's cloak.
Write ! For it must be ; by this ruthless steel,
By this impartial torture, and the death
Thy tyrannies have invented in my entrails,   105
To quicken life in dying, and hold up
The spirits in fainting, teaching to preserve
Torments in ashes, that will ever last.
Speak ! Will you write ?
   Tam.   Sweet lord, enjoin my sin
Some other penance than what makes it worse :   110
Hide in some gloomy dungeon my loath'd face,
And let condemned murtherers let me down
(Stopping their noses) my abhorred food.
Hang me in chains, and let me eat these arms
That have offended : bind me face to face   115
To some dead woman, taken from the cart
Of execution, till death and time
In grains of dust dissolve me ; I'll endure :
Or any torture that your wrath's invention
Can fright all pity from the world withal :   120
But to betray a friend with show of friendship,
That is too common for the rare revenge
Your rage affecteth ; here then are my breasts,

Last night your pillows; here my wretched arms,
As late the wished confines of your life: 125
Now break them as you please, and all the bounds
Of manhood, noblesse, and religion.
    Mont. Where all these have been broken, they are kept,
In doing their justice there with any show
Of the like cruelty; thine arms have lost   130
Their privilege in lust, and in their torture
Thus they must pay it.   *Stabs her*
    Tam.   O Lord!
    Mont.   Till thou writ'st,
I'll write in wounds (my wrong's fit characters)
Thy right of sufferance. Write!
    Tam.   Oh, kill me, kill me!
Dear husband, be not crueller than death;   135
You have beheld some Gorgon; feel, oh, feel
How you are turn'd to stone; with my heart-blood
Dissolve yourself again, or you will grow
Into the image of all tyranny.
    Mont. As thou art of adultery; I will ever   140
Prove thee my parallel, being most a monster;
Thus I express thee yet.   *Stabs her again*
    Tam.   And yet I live.
    Mont. Ay, for thy monstrous idol is not done yet:
This tool hath wrought enough; [*sheathing his dagger*] now,
    Torture, use
This other engine on th' habituate powers   145
Of her thrice-damn'd and whorish fortitude:

      Enter Servants [*and place* Tamyra *on the rack*]

Use the most madding pains in her that ever
Thy venoms soak'd through, making most of death,
That she may weigh her wrongs with them, and then
Stand, Vengeance, on thy steepest rock, a victor!   150
    Tam. Oh, who is turn'd into my lord and husband?
Husband! My lord! None but my lord and husband!
Heaven, I ask thee remission of my sins,
Not of my pains; husband, oh, help me, husband!

      Ascendit Friar *with a sword drawn*

    Friar. What rape of honour and religion!   155
Oh, wrack of nature!   *Falls and dies*
    Tam.   Poor man! Oh, my father!

Father, look up! Oh, let me down, my lord,
And I will write.
    Mont.   Author of prodigies!
What new flame breaks out of the firmament,
That turns up counsels never known before?   160
Now is it true, earth moves, and heaven stands still;
Even heaven itself must see and suffer ill:
The too huge bias of the world hath sway'd
Her back-part upwards, and with that she braves
This hemisphere, that long her mouth hath mock'd!   165
The gravity of her religious face,
(Now grown too weighty with her sacrilege
And here discern'd sophisticate enough)
Turns to th' Antipodes; and all the forms
That her illusions have impress'd in her,   170
Have eaten through her back; and now all see,
How she is riveted with hypocrisy.
Was this the way? Was he the mean betwixt you?
    Tam.   He was, he was, kind worthy man, he was.
    Mont. Write, write a word or two.   175
    Tam.   I will, I will.
I'll write, but with my blood, that he may see
These lines come from my wounds, and not from me.
                              Writes
    Mont. Well might he die for thought: methinks the frame
And shaken joints of the whole world should crack
To see her parts so disproportionate;   180
And that his general beauty cannot stand
Without these stains in the particular man.
Why wander I so far? Here, here was she
That was a whole world without spot to me,
Though now a world of spots; oh, what a lightning   185
Is man's delight in women! What a bubble,
He builds his state, fame, life on, when he marries!
Since all earth's pleasures are so short and small
The way t'enjoy it, is t'abjure it all.
Enough! I must be messenger myself,   190
Disguis'd like this strange creature: in, I'll after,
To see what guilty light gives this cave eyes,
And to the world sing new impieties.
    Exeunt [Servants]. *He puts the* Friar *in the vault and*
        follows. She wraps herself in the arras.

[SCENA SECUNDA

Another Room in Montsurry's *House*]

Enter Monsieur *and* Guise

Mons. Now shall we see that Nature hath no end
In her great works responsive to their worths ;
That she, that makes so many eyes and souls
To see and foresee, is stark blind herself ;
And as illiterate men say Latin prayers   5
By rote of heart and daily iteration,
Not knowing what they say, so Nature lays
A deal of stuff together, and by use,
Or by the mere necessity of matter,
Ends such a work, fills it, or leaves it empty   10
Of strength or virtue, error or clear truth,
Not knowing what she does ; but usually
Gives that which we call merit to a man,
And believe should arrive him on huge riches,
Honour, and happiness, that effects his ruin ;   15
Right as in ships of war whole lasts of powder
Are laid, men think, to make them last, and guard them,
When a disorder'd spark that powder taking,
Blows up with sudden violence and horror
Ships that (kept empty) had sail'd long with terror.   20
Guise. He that observes but like a worldly man
That which doth oft succeed, and by th' events
Values the worth of things, will think it true
That Nature works at random, just with you :
But with as much proportion she may make   25
A thing that from the feet up to the throat
Hath all the wondrous fabric man should have,
And leave it headless, for a perfect man,
As give a full man valour, virtue, learning,
Without an end more excellent than those   30
On whom she no such worthy part bestows.
Mons. Yet shall you see it here ; here will be one
Young, learned, valiant, virtuous, and full mann'd ;
One on whom Nature spent so rich a hand
That with an ominous eye she wept to see   35
So much consum'd her virtuous treasury.
Yet as the winds sing through a hollow tree
And (since it lets them pass through) let it stand ;

But a tree solid (since it gives no way
To their wild rage) they rend up by the root: 40
So this whole man
(That will not wind with every crooked way,
Trod by the servile world) shall reel and fall
Before the frantic puffs of blind-born chance,
That pipes through empty men, and makes them dance. 45
Not so the sea raves on the Lybian sands,
Tumbling her billows in each others' neck ;
Not so the surges of the Euxine sea
(Near to the frosty pole, where free Boötes
From those dark deep waves turns his radiant team) 50
Swell, being enrag'd, even from their inmost drop,
As Fortune swings about the restless state
Of virtue, now thrown into all men's hate.

Enter Montsurry *disguised* [*as the* Friar] *with the*
Murtherers

Away, my lord ; you are perfectly disguis'd,
Leave us to lodge your ambush. 55
   Mont. Speed me, vengeance ! *Exit*
   Mons. Resolve, my masters, you shall meet with one
Will try what proofs your privy coats are made on :
When he is enter'd, and you hear us stamp,
Approach, and make all sure.
      Murtherers. We will, my lord. *Exeunt*

[SCENA TERTIA

A room in Bussy's *House*]

D'Ambois *with two* Pages *with tapers*

   Bus. Sit up to-night, and watch ; I'll speak with none
But the old Friar, who bring to me.
   Pages. We will, sir. *Exeunt*
   Bus. What violent heat is this ? Methinks the fire
Of twenty lives doth on a sudden flash
Through all my faculties : the air goes high 5
In this close chamber, and the frighted earth   *Thunder*
Trembles, and shrinks beneath me ; the whole house
Nods with his shaken burthen.
      Enter Umbra Friar
                Bless me, heaven !

Umbra.   Note what I want, dear son, and be forewarn'd :
O there are bloody deeds past and to come.   10
I cannot stay ; a fate doth ravish me ;
I'll meet thee in the chamber of thy love.   *Exit*
  Bus.   What dismal change is here ! The good old Friar
Is murther'd, being made known to serve my love ;
And now his restless spirit would forewarn me   15
Of some plot dangerous and imminent.
Note what he wants ? He wants his upper weed,
He wants his life and body : which of these
Should be the want he means, and may supply me
With any fit forewarning ? This strange vision   20
(Together with the dark prediction
Us'd by the Prince of Darkness that was rais'd
By this embodied shadow) stir my thoughts
With reminiscion of the Spirit's promise,
Who told me that by any invocation   25
I should have power to raise him, though it wanted
The powerful words and decent rites of art :
Never had my set brain such need of spirit
T'instruct and cheer it ; now then I will claim
Performance of his free and gentle vow   30
T'appear in greater light, and make more plain
His rugged oracle : I long to know
How my dear mistress fares, and be inform'd
What hand she now holds on the troubled blood
Of her incensed lord : methought the Spirit   35
(When he had utter'd his perplex'd presage)
Threw his chang'd countenance headlong into clouds ;
His forehead bent, as it would hide his face,
He knock'd his chin against his darken'd breast,
And struck a churlish silence through his powers.   40
Terror of darkness ! O, thou King of flames !
That with thy music-footed horse dost strike
The clear light out of crystal on dark earth,
And hurl'st instructive fire about the world,
Wake, wake the drowsy and enchanted night,   45
That sleeps with dead eyes in this heavy riddle !
Or thou great Prince of shades where never sun
Sticks his far-darted beams, whose eyes are made
To shine in darkness, and see ever best
Where men are blindest, open now the heart   50
Of thy abashed oracle, that, for fear,

C.D.W.   F

Of some ill it includes, would fain lie hid,
And rise thou with it in thy greater light.

                      Thunders.   Surgit Spiritus *cum suis*
    Beh.   Thus, to observe my vow of apparition
In greater light, and explicate thy fate,   55
I come ; and tell thee that, if thou obey
The summons that thy mistress next will send thee,
Her hand shall be thy death.
    Bus.   When will she send ?
    Beh.   Soon as I set again, where late I rose.
    Bus.   Is the old Friar slain ?   60
    Beh.   No, and yet lives not.
    Bus.   Died he a natural death ?
    Beh.   He did.
    Bus.   Who then
Will my dear mistress send ?
    Beh.   I must not tell thee.
    Bus.   Who lets thee ?
    Beh.   Fate.
    Bus.   Who are Fate's ministers ?
    Beh.   The Guise and Monsieur.
    Bus.   A fit pair of shears
To cut the threads of kings and kingly spirits,   65
And consorts fit to sound forth harmony
Set to the falls of kingdoms ! Shall the hand
Of my kind mistress kill me ?
    Beh.   If thou yield
To her next summons. Y'are fair-warn'd ; farewell !
                           Thunders.   Exit
    Bus.   I must fare well, however, though I die,   70
My death consenting with his augury :
Should not my powers obey when she commands,
My motion must be rebel to my will,
My will to life. If, when I have obey'd,
Her hand should so reward me, they must arm it,   75
Bind me, or force it ; or, I lay my life,
She rather would convert it many times
On her own bosom, even to many deaths :
But were there danger of such violence,
I know 'tis far from her intent to send :   80
And who she should send is as far from thought,
Since he is dead, whose only mean she us'd.

                            [One] knocks

Who's there ? Look to the door, and let him in,
Though politic Monsieur or the violent Guise.

Enter Montsurry, *like the* Friar, *with a letter written in blood*

 Mont. Hail to my worthy son.　　　　　　　　　　85
 Bus.　　　　　　　　　Oh, lying Spirit,
To say the Friar was dead ! I'll now believe
Nothing of all his forg'd predictions.
My kind and honour'd father, well reviv'd !
I have been frighted with your death and mine,
And told my mistress' hand should be my death,　　90
If I obey'd this summons.
 Mont.　　　　　　I believ'd
Your love had been much clearer than to give
Any such doubt a thought, for she is clear,
And having freed her husband's jealousy
(Of which her much abus'd hand here is witness)　　95
She prays, for urgent cause, your instant presence.
 Bus. Why, then your Prince of Spirits may be call'd
The Prince of liars.
 Mont.　　　　　Holy Writ so calls him.
 Bus. [*Opening the letter*] What ! Writ in blood ?
 Mont.　　　　　　　　　Ay, 'tis the ink of lovers.
 Bus. O, 'tis a sacred witness of her love.　　100
So much elixir of her blood as this,
Dropt in the lightest dame, would make her firm
As heat to fire ; and, like to all the signs,
Commands the life confin'd in all my veins ;
O, how it multiplies my blood with spirit,　　　105
And makes me apt t'encounter Death and Hell.
But come, kind father, you fetch me to heaven,
And to that end your holy weed was given.　　*Exeunt*

[SCENA QUARTA

A Room in Montsurry's *House*]

Thunder. *Intrat* Umbra Friar, *and discovers* Tamyra

Umbra. Up with these stupid thoughts, still loved
 daughter,
And strike away this heartless trance of anguish.

Be like the sun, and labour in eclipses ;
Look to the end of woes : oh, can you sit
Mustering the horrors of your servant's slaughter   5
Before your contemplation, and not study
How to prevent it ? Watch when he shall rise,
And with a sudden outcry of his murther,
Blow his retreat before he be revenged.

    Tam.   O father, have my dumb woes wak'd your death ?   10
When will our human griefs be at their height ?
Man is a tree that hath no top in cares,
No root in comforts ; all his power to live
Is given to no end, but t'have power to grieve.

    Umbra. It is the misery of our creation,   15
Your true friend,
Led by your husband, shadow'd in my weed,
Now enters the dark vault.

    Tam.   But, my dearest father,
Why will not you appear to him yourself,
And see that none of these deceits annoy him ?   20

    Umbra. My power is limited ; alas ! I cannot.
All that I can do—See, the cave opens !

               Exit. D'Ambois [*appears*] *at the Gulf*
    Tam.   Away, my love, away ! Thou wilt be murther'd.

Enter Monsieur *and* Guise *above.*

    Bus.   Murther'd ?   I know not what that Hebrew means :
That word had ne'er been nam'd had all been D'Ambois.   25
Murther'd ? By heaven, he is my murtherer
That shows me not a murtherer ; what such bug
Abhorreth not the very sleep of D'Ambois ?
Murther'd ? Who dares give all the room I see
To D'Ambois' reach, or look with any odds   30
His fight i'th' face, upon whose hand sits death,
Whose sword hath wings, and every feather pierceth ?
If I scape Monsieur's 'pothecary shops,
Foutre for Guise's shambles ! 'Twas ill plotted ;
They should have maul'd me here, when I was rising.   35
I am up and ready.
Let in my politic visitants, let them in,
Though entering like so many moving armours.
Fate is more strong than arms, and sly than treason,
And I at all parts buckled in my fate.   40

Mons. } Why enter not the coward villains ?
Guise. }
Bus.   Dare they not come ?

Enter Murtherers *with* [Umbra] Friar *at the other door*

Tam.   They come.
First Mur.   Come all at once.
Umbra.   Back, coward murtherers, back !
Omnes.   Defend us, heaven !
                    Exeunt all but the first [Murtherer]

First Mur.   Come ye not on ?
Bus.   No, slave, nor goest thou off.
Stand you so firm ?   [*Strikes him with his sword*]   Will it
    not enter here ?   45
You have a face yet.   [*Kills the first* Murtherer]   So ! In thy
    life's flame
I burn the first rites to my mistress' fame.
    Umbra.   Breathe thee, brave son, against the other charge.
    Bus.   Oh, is it true then that my sense first told me ?
Is my kind father dead ?
    Tam.   He is, my love.   50
'Twas the Earl, my husband, in his weed, that brought thee.
    Bus.   That was a speeding sleight, and well resembled.
Where is that angry Earl ?   My lord, come forth
And show your own face in your own affair ;
Take not into your noble veins the blood   55
Of these base villains, nor the light reports
Of blister'd tongues for clear and weighty truth,
But me against the world, in pure defence
Of your rare lady, to whose spotless name
I stand here as a bulwark, and project   60
A life to her renown, that ever yet
Hath been untainted, even in envy's eye,
And, where it would protect, a sanctuary.
Brave Earl, come forth, and keep your scandal in :
'Tis not our fault, if you enforce the spot   65
Nor the wreak yours, if you perform it not.

Enter Montsurry, *with all the* Murtherers

    Mont.   Cowards, a fiend or spirit beat ye off ?
They are your own faint spirits that have forg'd
The fearful shadows that your eyes deluded :
The fiend was in you ; cast him out then, thus.   70

[They fight.] D'Ambois *hath* Montsurry *down*
 Tam. Favour my lord, my love, O, favour him !
 Bus. I will not touch him : take your life, my lord,
And be appeas'd. *Pistols shot within.* [Bussy *is wounded*]
                              O, then the coward Fates
Have maim'd themselves, and ever lost their honour.
 Umbra. What have ye done, slaves ? Irreligious lord !   75
 Bus. Forbear them, father ; 'tis enough for me
That Guise and Monsieur, Death and Destiny,
Come behind D'Ambois. Is my body, then,
But penetrable flesh ? And must my mind
Follow my blood ? Can my divine part add   80
No aid to th' earthly in extremity ?
Then these divines are but for form, not fact :
Man is of two sweet courtly friends compact,
A mistress and a servant : let my death
Define life nothing but a courtier's breath.   85
Nothing is made of nought, of all things made,
Their abstract being a dream but of a shade.
I'll not complain to earth yet, but to heaven,
And, like a man, look upwards even in death.
And if Vespasian thought in majesty   90
An emperor might die standing, why not I ?

                         She offers to help him

Nay, without help, in which I will exceed him ;
For he died splinted with his chamber grooms.
Prop me, true sword, as thou hast ever done !
The equal thought I bear of life and death   95
Shall make me faint on no side ; I am up ;
Here like a Roman statue I will stand
Till death hath made me marble. Oh, my fame,
Live in despite of murther ! Take thy wings
And haste thee where the grey ey'd Morn perfumes   100
Her rosy chariot with Sabæan spices !
Fly, where the Evening from th' Iberian vales
Takes on her swarthy shoulders Hecate,
Crown'd with a grove of oaks : fly where men feel
The burning axletree, and those that suffer   105
Beneath the chariot of the snowy Bear :
And tell them all that D'Ambois now is hasting
To the eternal dwellers ; that a thunder
Of all their sighs together (for their frailties

Beheld in me) may quit my worthless fall   110
With a fit volley for my funeral.
   Umbra.   Forgive thy murtherers.
   Bus.   I forgive them all ;
And you, my lord [*to* Montsurry], their fautor ; for true sign
Of which unfeign'd remission take my sword ;
Take it, and only give it motion,   115
And it shall find the way to victory
By his own brightness, and th' inherent valour
My fight hath still'd into't with charms of spirit.
Now let me pray you that my weighty blood
Laid in one scale of your impartial spleen,   120
May sway the forfeit of my worthy love
Weigh'd in the other ; and be reconcil'd
With all forgiveness to your matchless wife.
   Tam.   Forgive thou me, dear servant, and this hand
That led thy life to this unworthy end ;   125
Forgive it, for the blood with which 'tis stain'd,
In which I writ the summons of thy death—
The forced summons—by this bleeding wound,
By this here in my bosom, and by this
That makes me hold up both my hands imbru'd   130
For thy dear pardon.
   Bus.   O, my heart is broken !
Fate nor these murtherers, Monsieur nor the Guise,
Have any glory in my death, but this,
This killing spectacle, this prodigy :
My sun is turn'd to blood, in whose red beams   135
Pindus and Ossa (hid in drifts of snow,
Laid on my heart and liver) from their veins
Melt like two hungry torrents, eating rocks,
Into the ocean of all human life,
And make it bitter, only with my blood.   140
O frail condition of strength, valour, virtue,
In me (like warning fire upon the top
Of some steep beacon, on a steeper hill)
Made to express it : like a falling star
Silently glanc'd, that like a thunderbolt   145
Look'd to have stuck and shook the firmament.
                                          Moritur

   Umbra.   Farewell, brave relics of a complete man,
Look up and see thy spirit made a star ;
Join flames with Hercules, and when thou sett'st

Thy radiant forehead in the firmament,   150
Make the vast crystal crack with thy receipt ;
Spread to a world of fire, and the aged sky
Cheer with new sparks of old humanity.
[*To* Montsurry]   Son of the earth, whom my unrested soul,
Rues t'have begotten in the faith of heaven,   155
Assay to gratulate and pacify
The soul fled from this worthy by performing
The Christian reconcilement he besought
Betwixt thee and thy lady ; let her wounds
Manlessly digg'd in her, be eas'd and cur'd   160
With balm of thine own tears ; or be assur'd
Never to rest free from my haunt and horror.
  Mont.   See how she merits this ; still kneeling by,
And mourning his fall more than her own fault !
  Umbra.   Remove, dear daughter, and content thy husband ; 165
So piety wills thee, and thy servant's peace.
                          [*Exit* Umbra]
  Tam.   O wretched piety, that art so distract
In thine own constancy, and in thy right
Must be unrighteous : if I right my friend
I wrong my husband ; if his wrong I shun,   170
The duty of my friend I leave undone :
Ill plays on both sides ; here and there, it riseth ;
No place, no good, so good, but ill compriseth ;
O had I never married but for form,
Never vow'd faith but purpos'd to deceive,   175
Never made conscience of any sin,
But cloak'd it privately and made it common ;
Nor never honour'd been in blood or mind ;
Happy had I been then, as others are
Of the like licence ; I had then been honour'd ;   180
Liv'd without envy ; custom had benumb'd
All sense of scruple and all note of frailty ;
My fame had been untouch'd, my heart unbroken :
But (shunning all) I strike on all offence,
O husband ! Dear friend ! O my conscience !   185
  Mons.   Come, let's away ; my senses are not proof
Against those plaints.
           Exeunt Guise *and* Monsieur. D'Ambois *is borne off*
  Mont.   I must not yield to pity, nor to love
So servile and so traitorous : cease, my blood,
To wrestle with my honour, fame, and judgment :   190

Away, forsake my house, forbear complaints
Where thou hast bred them : here [are] all things
Of their own shame and sorrow ; leave my house.

   Tam.   Sweet lord, forgive me, and I will be gone,
And till these wounds (that never balm shall close   195
Till death hath enter'd at them, so I love them,
Being open'd by your hands) by death be cur'd,
I never more will grieve you with my sight,
Never endure that any roof shall part
Mine eyes and heaven ; but to the open deserts   200
(Like to a hunted tigress) I will fly,
Eating my heart, shunning the steps of men,
And look on no side till I be arriv'd.

   Mont.   I do forgive thee, and upon my knees,
With hands held up to heaven, wish that mine honour   205
Would suffer reconcilement to my love ;
But since it will not, honour never serve
My love with flourishing object, till it sterve !
And as this taper, though it upwards look,
Downwards must needs consume, so let our love !   210
As, having lost his honey, the sweet taste
Runs into savour, and will needs retain
A spice of his first parents, till, like life,
It sees and dies ; so let our love ! And lastly,
As when the flame is suffer'd to look up,   215
It keeps his lustre, but, being thus turn'd down,
(His natural course of useful light inverted),
His own stuff puts it out, so let our love !
Now turn from me, as here I turn from thee,
And may both points of heaven's straight axle-tree   220
Conjoin in one, before thyself and me.

                                                 Exeunt severally

FINIS ACTUS QUINTI ET ULTIMI

EPILOGUE

With many hands you have seen D'Ambois slain,
Yet by your grace he may revive again,
And every day grow stronger in his skill
To please, as we presume he is in will.
The best deserving actors of the time   5
Had their ascents ; and by degrees did climb
To their full height, a place to study due.
To make him tread in their path lies in you ;
He'll not forget his makers, but still prove
His thankfulness, as you increase your love.   10

FINIS

THE REVENGE OF BUSSY D'AMBOIS

A TRAGEDY

The Revenge of Bussy d'Ambois

A TRAGEDY

TO

THE RIGHT VIRTUOUS AND TRULY NOBLE KNIGHT

SIR THOMAS HOWARD, Etc.

Sir—

Since works of this kind have been lately esteemed worthy the patronage of some of our worthiest nobles, I have made no doubt to prefer this of mine to your undoubted virtue and exceeding true noblesse, as containing matter no less deserving your reading, and excitation to heroical life, than any such late dedication. Nor have the greatest Princes of Italy and other countries conceived it any least diminution to their greatness to have their names winged with these tragic plumes, and dispersed by way of patronage through the most noble notices of Europe.

Howsoever therefore in the scenical presentation it might meet with some maligners, yet considering even therein it passed with approbation of more worthy judgments, the balance of their side (especially being held by your impartial hand) I hope will to no grain abide the out-weighing. And for the autentical truth of either person or action, who (worth the respecting) will expect it in a poem, whose subject is not truth, but things like truth ? Poor envious souls they are that cavil at truth's want in these natural fictions ; material instruction, elegant and sententious excitation to virtue, and deflection from her contrary, being the soul, limbs, and limits of an autentical tragedy. But whatsoever merit of your full countenance and favour suffers defect in this, I shall soon supply with some other of more general account : wherein your right virtuous name made famous and preserved to posterity, your future comfort and honour in your present acceptation, and love of all virtuous and divine expression, may be so much past others of your rank increased, as they are short of your judicial ingenuity in their due estimation.

For, howsoever those ignoble and sour-browed worldlings are careless of whatsoever future or present opinion spreads of them, yet (with the most divine philosopher, if Scripture did not confirm it) I make it matter of my faith, that we truly retain an intellectual feeling of good or bad after this life, proportionably answerable to the love or neglect we bear here to all virtue, and truly humane instruction : in whose favour and honour I wish you most eminent ; and rest ever,

Your true virtue's
Most true observer,
GEO. CHAPMAN

THE ACTORS' NAMES

Henry, *the King*

Monsieur, *his brother*

Guise, *a Duke*

Renel, *a Marquess*

Montsurry, *an Earl*

Baligny, *Lord-Lieutenant* [*of Cambrai*]

Clermont d'Ambois

Maillard,
Chalon, } *captains*
Aumale,

Epernon,
Soissons, }

Perricot, *an Usher* [*to Guise*]

[An Usher to the Countess]

The Guard

Soldiers

Servants

The ghost[*s*] *of* {
Bussy
Monsieur
Guise
Cardinal Guise
Chatillon
}

The Countess of Cambrai

Tamyra, *wife to Montsurry.*

Charlotte, *wife to Baligny*

Riova, *a servant*

ACTUS PRIMI SCENA PRIMA

[A Room in the Court]

Enter Baligny *and* Renel

Bal. To what will this declining kingdom turn,
Swinging in every licence, as in this
Stupid permission of brave D'Ambois' murther?
Murther made parallel with law! Murther us'd
To serve the kingdom, given by suit to men   5
For their advancement, suffer'd scarecrow-like
To fright adultery! What will policy
At length bring under his capacity?
Ren. All things: for as when the high births of kings,
Deliverances, and coronations,   10
We celebrate with all the cities' bells
Jangling together in untun'd confusion,
All order'd clocks are tied up; so when glory,
Flattery, and smooth applauses of things ill,
Uphold th' inordinate swinge of downright power,   15
Justice and truth, that tell the bounded use,
Virtuous and well-distinguish'd forms of time
Are gagg'd and tongue-tied. But we have observ'd
Rule in more regular motion: things most lawful
Were once most royal; kings sought common good,   20
Men's manly liberties, though ne'er so mean,
And had their own swinge so more free, and more.
But when pride enter'd them, and rule by power,
All brows that smil'd beneath them, frown'd; hearts griev'd
By imitation; virtue quite was vanish'd,   25
And all men studied self-love, fraud, and vice;
Then no man could be good but he was punish'd:
Tyrants being still more fearful of the good
Than of the bad; their subjects' virtues ever
Manag'd with curbs and dangers, and esteem'd   30
As shadows and detractions to their own.

Bal. Now all is peace, no danger : now what follows ?
Idleness rusts us, since no virtuous labour
Ends ought rewarded : ease, security,
Now all the palm wears : we made war before   35
So to prevent war ; men with giving gifts,
More than receiving, made our country strong ;
Our matchless race of soldiers then would spend
In public wars, not private brawls, their spirits,
In daring enemies, arm'd with meanest arms,   40
Not courting strumpets, and consuming birthrights
In apishness and envy of attire.
No labour then was harsh, no way so deep,
No rock so steep, but if a bird could scale it,
Up would our youth fly too. A foe in arms   45
Stirr'd up a much more lust of his encounter,
Than of a mistress never so be-painted :
Ambition then, was only scaling walls,
And over-topping turrets ; fame was wealth ;
Best parts, best deeds, were best nobility ;   50
Honour with worth, and wealth well got or none :
Countries we won with as few men as countries ;
Virtue subdu'd all.
     Ren.   Just : and then our nobles
Lov'd virtue so, they prais'd and us'd it too :
Had rather do than say, their own deeds hearing   55
By others glorified, than be so barren
That their parts only stood in praising others.
     Bal. Who could not do, yet prais'd, and envied not ;
Civil behaviour flourish'd ; bounty flow'd ;
Avarice to upland boors, slaves, hangmen, banish'd. 60
     Ren. 'Tis now quite otherwise : but to note the cause
Of all these foul digressions and revolts
From our first natures, this 'tis in a word :
Since good arts fail, crafts and deceits are us'd ;
Men ignorant are idle ; idle men   65
Most practise what they most may do with ease,
Fashion, and favour ; all their studies aiming
At getting money, which no wise man ever
Fed his desires with.
     Bal.   Yet now none are wise
That think not heaven's tru[th] foolish, weigh'd with that. 70
Well, thou most worthy to be greatest Guise,
Make with thy greatness a new world arise.

Such depress'd nobles, followers of his,
As you, [yourself], my lord, will find a time
When to revenge your wrongs.
   Ren.   I make no doubt :   75
In mean time, I could wish the wrong were righted
Of your slain brother-in-law, brave Bussy d'Ambois.
   Bal. That one accident was made my charge.
My brother Bussy's sister, now my wife,
By no suit would consent to satisfy   80
My love of her with marriage, till I vow'd,
To use my utmost to revenge my brother :
But Clermont d'Ambois, Bussy's second brother,
Had, since, his apparition and excitement
To suffer none but his hand in his wreak,   85
Which he hath vow'd, and so will needs acquit
Me of my vow, made to my wife, his sister,
And undertake himself Bussy's revenge ;
Yet loathing any way to give it act,
But in the noblest and most manly course,   90
If th' Earl dares take it, he resolves to send
A challenge to him, and myself must bear it ;
To which delivery I can use no means,
He is so barricado'd in his house,
And arm'd with guard still.   95
   Ren.   That means lay on me,
Which I can strangely make. My last lands' sale,
By his great suit, stands now on price with him,
And he, as you know, passing covetous,
With that blind greediness that follows gain,
Will cast no danger where her sweet feet tread.   100
Besides, you know, his lady by his suit,
(Wooing as freshly, as when first Love shot
His faultless arrows from her rosy eyes)
Now lives with him again, and she, I know,
Will join with all helps in her friend's revenge.   105
   Bal. No doubt, my lord, and therefore let me pray you
To use all speed ; for so on needles' points
My wife's heart stands with haste of the revenge,
Being, as you know, full of her brother's fire,
That she imagines I neglect my vow ;   110
Keeps off her kind embraces, and still asks,
' When, when, will this revenge come ? When perform'd
Will this dull vow be ? ' and, I vow to heaven,

So sternly, and so past her sex she urges
My vow's performance, that I almost fear   115
To see her, when I have awhile been absent,
Not showing her, before I speak, the blood
She so much thirsts for, freckling hands and face.
   Ren. Get you the challenge writ, and look from me
To hear your passage clear'd no long time after.   120

                                  Exit Renel
   Bal. All restitution to your worthiest lordship
Whose errand I must carry to the King,
As having sworn my service in the search
Of all such malcontents and their designs,
By seeming one affected with their faction   125
And discontented humours gainst the state :
Nor doth my brother Clermont scape my counsel
Given to the King about his Guisean greatness,
Which, as I spice it, hath possess'd the King
(Knowing his daring spirit) of much danger   130
Charg'd in it to his person ; though my conscience
Dare swear him clear of any power to be
Infected with the least dishonesty :
Yet that sincerity, we politicians
Must say, grows out of envy, since it cannot   135
Aspire to policy's greatness ; and the more
We work on all respects of kind and virtue,
The more our service to the King seems great,
In sparing no good that seems bad to him :
And the more bad we make the most of good,   140
The more our policy searcheth, and our service
Is wonder'd at for wisdom and sincereness.
'Tis easy to make good suspected still,
Where good and God are made but cloaks for ill.

Enter Henry, Monsieur, Guise, Clermont, Epernon, Soissons.
   Monsieur *taking leave of the* King, [*who then goes out*]

See Monsieur taking now his leave for Brabant,   145
The Guise, and his dear minion, Clermont d'Ambois,
Whispering together, not of state affairs
I durst lay wagers (though the Guise be now
In chief heat of his faction), but of something
Savouring of that which all men else despise,
How to be truly noble, truly wise.

Mon.   See how he hangs upon the ear of Guise,
Like to his jewel.
    Ep.   He's now whispering in
Some doctrine of stability and freedom,
Contempt of outward greatness, and the guises   155
That vulgar great ones make their pride and zeal,
Being only servile trains, and sumptuous houses,
High places, offices.
    Mon.   Contempt of these
Does he read to the Guise ? 'Tis passing needful ;
And he, I think, makes show t'affect his doctrine.   160
    Ep.   Commends, admires it—
    Mon.   And pursues another.
'Tis fine hypocrisy, and cheap, and vulgar,
Known for a covert practice, yet believ'd,
By those abus'd souls that they teach and govern
No more than wives' adulteries by their husbands,   165
They bearing it with so unmov'd aspects,
Hot coming from it, as 'twere not [at] all,
Or made by custom nothing. This same D'Ambois
Hath gotten such opinion of his virtues,
Holding all learning but an art to live well,   170
And showing he hath learn'd it in his life,
Being thereby strong in his persuading others,
That this ambitious Guise, embracing him,
Is thought t'embrace his virtues.
    Ep.   Yet in some
His virtues are held false for th' other's vices :   175
For 'tis more cunning held, and much more common,
To suspect truth than falsehood : and of both
Truth still fares worse, as hardly being believ'd,
As 'tis unusual and rarely known.
    Mon.   I'll part engendering virtue. Men affirm   180
Though this same Clermont hath a D'Ambois' spirit,
And breathes his brother's valour, yet his temper
Is so much past his, that you cannot move him :
I'll try that temper in him. [*To* Guise *and* Clermont] Come,
    you two
Devour each other with your virtue's zeal,   185
And leave for other friends no fragment of ye :
I wonder, Guise, you will thus ravish him
Out of my bosom that first gave the life
His manhood breathes, spirit, and means, and lustre.

What do men think of me, I pray thee, Clermont ?   190
Once give me leave (for trial of that love
That from thy brother Bussy thou inherit'st)
T'unclasp thy bosom.
    Cler.   As how, sir ?
    Mon. Be a true glass to me, in which I may
Behold what thoughts the many-headed beast,   195
And thou thyself, breathes out concerning me,
My ends, and new-upstarted state in Brabant,
For which I now am bound, my higher aims
Imagin'd here in France : speak, man, and let
Thy words be born as naked as thy thoughts :   200
Oh, were brave Bussy living !
    Cler.   ' Living,' my lord ?
    Mon. 'Tis true thou art his brother, but durst thou
Have brav'd the Guise ; maugre his presence courted
His wedded lady ; emptied even the dregs
Of his worst thoughts of me even to my teeth ;   205
Discern'd not me, his rising sovereign,
From any common groom, but let me hear
My grossest faults as gross-full as they were ?
Durst thou do this ?
    Cler.   I cannot tell : a man
Does never know the goodness of his stomach   210
Till he sees meat before him. Were I dar'd,
Perhaps, as he was, I durst do like him.
    Mon. Dare then to pour out here thy freest soul
Of what I am.
    Cler.   'Tis stale ; he told you it.
    Mon. He only jested, spake of spleen and envy ;   215
Thy soul, more learn'd, is more ingenious,
Searching, judicial ; let me then from thee
Hear what I am.
    Cler.   What but the sole support,
And most expectant hope of all our France,
The toward victor of the whole Low Countries ?   220
    Mon. Tush, thou wilt sing encomions of my praise !
Is this like D'Ambois ? I must vex the Guise,
Or never look to hear free truth ; tell me,
For Bussy lives not ; he durst anger me,
Yet, for my love, would not have fear'd to anger   225
The King himself. Thou understand'st me, dost not ?
    Cler. I shall, my lord, with study.

Mon.   Dost understand thyself ?   I pray thee tell me,
Dost never search thy thoughts what my design
Might be to entertain thee and thy brother,   230
What turn I meant to serve with you ?
  Cler.   Even what you please to think.
  Mon.   But what think'st thou ?
Had I no end in't, think'st ?
  Cler.   I think you had.
  Mon.   When I took in such two as you two were,
A ragged couple of decay'd commanders,   235
When a French crown would plentifully serve
To buy you both to anything i' th' earth.
  Cler.   So it would you.
  Mon.   Nay, bought you both outright,
You, and your trunks—I fear me, I offend thee.
  Cler.   No, not a jot.
  Mon.   The most renowned soldier,   240
Epaminondas (as good authors say),
Had no more suits than backs, but you two shar'd
But one suit 'twixt you both, when both your studies
Were not what meat to dine with, if your partridge,
Your snipe, your wood-cock, lark, or your red herring,   245
But where to beg it ; whether at my house
Or at the Guise's (for you know you were
Ambitious beggars), or at some cook's-shop,
T'eternize the cook's trust, and score it up.
Does't not offend thee ?
  Cler.   No, sir.   Pray proceed.   250
  Mon.   As for thy gentry, I dare boldly take
Thy honourable oath : and yet some say
Thou and thy most renowned noble brother,
Came to the Court first in a keel of sea-coal ;
Does't not offend thee ?
  Cler.   Never doubt it, sir.   255
  Mon.   Why do I love thee, then ? Why have I rak'd thee
Out of the dung-hill, cast my cast wardrobe on thee ?
Brought thee to Court too, as I did thy brother ?
Made ye my saucy boon companions ?
Taught ye to call our greatest noblemen   260
By the corruption of their names, Jack, Tom ?
Have I blown both for nothing to this bubble ?
Though thou art learn'd, th'ast no enchanting wit ;
Or were thy wit good, am I therefore bound

To keep thee for my table ?

Cler.   Well, sir, 'twere   265
A good knight's place. Many a proud dubb'd gallant
Seeks out a poor knight's living from such emrods.

[*Mons.*] Or what use else should I design thee to ?
Perhaps you'll answer me, to be my pander.

Cler. Perhaps I shall.

Mon.   Or did the sly Guise put thee   270
Into my bosom t'undermine my projects ?
I fear thee not ; for though I be not sure
I have thy heart, I know thy brain-pan yet
To be as empty a dull piece of wainscot
As ever arm'd the scalp of any courtier ;   275
A fellow only that consists of sinews,
Mere Swisser, apt for any execution.

Cler. But killing of the King !

Mon.   Right ; now I see
Thou understand'st thyself.

Cler.   Ay, and you better :
You are a king's son born.

Mon.   Right !

Cler.   And a king's brother. 280

Mon. True !

Cler. And might not any fool have been so too,
As well as you ?

Mon. A pox upon you !

Cler.   You did no princely deeds
Ere you're born, I take it, to deserve it ;   285
Nor did you any since that I have heard ;
Nor will do ever any, as all think.

Mon. The devil take him ! I'll no more of him.

Guise. Nay : stay, my lord, and hear him answer you.

Mon. No more, I swear. Farewell !

                         Exeunt Monsieur, Epernon, Soissons

Guise.   No more ? Ill fortune ! 290
I would have given a million to have heard
His scoffs retorted, and the insolence
Of his high birth and greatness (which were never
Effects of his deserts, but of his fortune)
Made show to his dull eyes beneath the worth   295
That men aspire to by their knowing virtues,
Without which greatness is a shade, a bubble.

Cler. But what one great man dreams of that but you ?

All take their births and birth-rights left to them
(Acquir'd by others) for their own worth's purchase,   300
When many a fool in both is great as they :
And who would think they could win with their worths
Wealthy possessions, when, won to their hands,
They neither can judge justly of their value,
Nor know their use ? And therefore they are puff'd   305
With such proud tumours as this Monsieur is,
Enabled only by the goods they have
To scorn all goodness : none great fill their fortunes ;
But as those men that make their houses greater,
Their households being less, so Fortune raises   310
Huge heaps of outside in these mighty men,
And gives them nothing in them.
   Guise.   True as truth :
And therefore they had rather drown their substance
In superfluities of bricks and stones
(Like Sisyphus, advancing of them ever,   315
And ever pulling down), than lay the cost
Of any sluttish corner on a man,
Built with God's finger, and enstyl'd his temple.
   Bal. 'Tis nobly said, my lord.
   Guise.   I would have **these things**
Brought upon stages, to let mighty misers   320
See all their grave and serious miseries play'd,
As once they were in Athens and old Rome.
   Cler. Nay, we must now have nothing brought on stages
But puppetry, and pied ridiculous antics :
Men thither come to laugh, and feed fool-fat,   325
Check at all goodness there, as being profan'd :
When, wheresoever goodness comes, she makes
The place still sacred, though with other feet
Never so much 'tis scandal'd and polluted.
Let me learn anything that fits a man,   330
In any stables shown, as well as stages.
   Bal. Why, is not all the world esteem'd a stage ?
   Cler. Yes, and right worthily ; and stages too
Have a respect due to them, if but only,
For what the good Greek moralist says of them :   335
' Is a man proud of greatness, or of riches ?
Give me an expert actor, I'll show all
That can within his greatest glory fall
Is a man fray'd with poverty and lowness ?

Give me an actor, I'll show every eye   340
What he laments so, and so much doth fly,
The best and worst of both.' If but for this then,
To make the proudest outside, that most swells
With things without him and above his worth,
See how small cause he has to be so blown up,   345
And the most poor man to be griev'd with poorness,
Both being so easily borne by expert actors,
The stage and actors are not so contemptful
As every innovating Puritan,
And ignorant sweater-out of zealous envy,   350
Would have the world imagine. And besides
That all things have been liken'd to the mirth
Us'd upon stages, and for stages fitted,
The splenative philosopher that ever
Laugh'd at them all, were worthy the enstaging :   355
All objects, were they ne'er so full of tears,
He so conceited that he could distil thence
Matter that still fed his ridiculous humour.
Heard he a lawyer, never so vehement pleading
He stood and laugh'd. Heard he a tradesman swearing   360
Never so thriftily selling of his wares,
He stood and laugh'd. Heard he an holy brother,
For hollow ostentation, at his prayers
Ne'er so impetuously, he stood and laugh'd.
Saw he a great man never so insulting,   365
Severely inflicting, gravely giving laws,
Not for their good, but his, he stood and laugh'd.
Saw he a youthful widow
Never so weeping, wringing of her hands,
For her lost lord, still the philosopher laugh'd.   370
Now whether he suppos'd all these presentments
Were only maskeries, and wore false faces,
Or else were simply vain, I take no care ;
But still he laugh'd, how grave soe'er they were.

    Guise.   And might right well, my Clermont ; and for this   375
Virtuous digression, we will thank the scoffs
Of vicious Monsieur. But now for the main point
Of your late resolution for revenge
Of your slain [brother.]

    Cler.   I have here my challenge,
Which I will pray my brother Baligny   380
To bear the murtherous Earl.

Bal.   I have prepar'd
Means for access to him through all his guard.
    Guise.   About it then, my worthy Baligny,
And bring us the success.
    Bal.   I will, my Lord.   *Exeunt*

[SCENA SECUNDA

A Room in Montsurry's *House*]

Tamyra *sola*

    Tam.   Revenge, that ever red sitt'st in the eyes
Of injur'd ladies, till we crown thy brows
With bloody laurel, and receive from thee
Justice for all our [honour's] injury ;
Whose wings none fly, that wrath or tyranny   5
Have ruthless made and bloody, enter here,
Enter, O enter ! And, though length of time
Never lets any scape thy constant justice,
Yet now prevent that length. Fly, fly, and here
Fix thy steel footsteps : here, O here, where still   10
Earth, mov'd with pity, yielded and embrac'd
My love's fair figure, drawn in his dear blood,
And mark'd the place, to show thee where was done
The cruell'st murther that e'er fled the sun.
O Earth, why keep'st thou not as well his spirit   15
To give his form life ? No, that was not earthly ;
That (rarefying the thin and yielding air)
Flew sparkling up into the sphere of fire,
Whence endless flames it sheds in my desire :
Here be my daily pallet ; here all nights   20
That can be wrested from thy rival's arms,
O my dear Bussy, I will lie and kiss
Spirit into thy blood, or breathe out mine
In sighs, and kisses, and sad tunes to thine.   *She sings*

Enter Montsurry

    Mont.   Still on this haunt ? Still shall adulterous blood   25
Affect thy spirits ? Think, for shame, but this,
This blood that cockatrice-like thus thou brood'st
Too dry is to breed any quench to thine.
And therefore now (if only for thy lust

A little cover'd with a veil of shame)   30
Look out for fresh life, rather than witchlike
Learn to kiss horror, and with death engender.
Strange cross in nature, purest virgin shame
Lies in the blood, as lust lies ; and together
Many times mix too ; and in none more shameful   35
Than in the shamefac'd. Who can then distinguish
'Twixt their affections ; or tell when he meets
With one not common ? Yet, as worthiest poets
Shun common and plebeian forms of speech,
Every illiberal and affected phrase,   40
To clothe their matter ; and together tie
Matter and form with art and decency ;
So worthiest women should shun vulgar guises,
And though they cannot but fly out for change,
Yet modesty, the matter of their lives,   45
Be it adulterate, should be painted true
With modest out-parts ; what they should do still
Grac'd with good show, though deeds be ne'er so ill.
    Tam. That is so far from all ye seek of us,
That (though yourselves be common as the air)   50
We must not take the air, we must not fit
Our actions to our own affections :
But as geometricians, you still say,
Teach that no lines nor superficies
Do move themselves, but still accompany   55
The motions of their bodies ; so poor wives
Must not pursue, nor have their own affections ;
But to their husbands' earnests, and their jests,
To their austerities of looks, and laughters
(Though ne'er so foolish and injurious),   60
Like parasites and slaves, fit their disposures,
    Mont. I us'd thee as my soul, to move and rule me.
    Tam. So said you, when you woo'd. So soldiers tortur'd
With tedious sieges of some well-wall'd town
Propound conditions of most large contents,   65
Freedom of laws, all former government ;
But having once set foot within the walls,
And got the reins of power into their hands,
Then do they tyrannize at their own rude swinges,
Seize all their goods, their liberties, and lives, 70
And make advantage and their lusts their laws.
    Mont. But love me, and perform a wife's part yet,

With all my love before I swear forgiveness.

Tam.   Forgiveness ! That grace you should seek of me :
These tortur'd fingers and these stabb'd-through arms   75
Keep that law in their wounds yet, unobserv'd,
And ever shall.

Mont.   Remember their deserts.

Tam.   Those with fair warnings might have been reform'd,
Not these unmanly rages. You have heard
The fiction of the north wind and the sun,   80
Both working on a traveller, and contending
Which had most power to take his cloak from him :
Which when the wind attempted, he roar'd out
Outrageous blasts at him to force it off,
That wrapt it closer on : when the calm sun   85
(The wind once leaving) charg'd him with still beams,
Quiet and fervent, and therein was constant,
Which made him cast off both his cloak and coat ;
Like whom should men do. If ye wish your wives
Should leave dislik'd things, seek it not with rage,   90
For that enrages ; what ye give, ye have :
But use calm warnings and kind manly means,
And that in wives most prostitute will win
Not only sure amends, but make us wives
Better than those that ne'er led faulty lives.   95

Enter a Soldier

Sold.   My lord !

Mont.   How now ? Would any speak with me ?

Sold.   Ay, sir.

Mont.   Perverse and traitorous miscreant,
Where are your other fellows of my guard ?
Have I not told you I will speak with none
But Lord Renel ?

Sold.   And 'tis he that stays you.   100

Mont.   O, is it he ? 'Tis well ; attend him in :
I must be vigilant ; the Furies haunt me.
Do you hear, dame ?

Enter Renel *with the* Soldier

Ren.   [*Aside to the* Soldier] Be true now for your lady's
     injur'd sake,
Whose bounty you have so much cause to honour :   105
For her respect is chief in this design,

And therefore serve it; call out of the way
All your confederate fellows of his guard,
Till Monsieur Baligny be enter'd here.

Sold. Upon your honour, my lord shall be free   110
From any hurt, you say?

Ren. Free as myself. Watch then, and clear his entry.

Sold. I will not fail, my lord.

Exit Soldier

Ren.   God save your lordship!

Mont. My noblest Lord Renel, past all men welcome!
Wife, welcome his lordship.

Osculatur

Ren.   I much joy   115
In your return here.

Tam.   You do more than I.

Mont. She's passionate still, to think we ever parted,
By my too stern injurious jealousy.

Ren. 'Tis well your lordship will confess your error
In so good time yet.

Enter Baligny *with a challenge*

Mont.   Death! Who have we here?   120
Ho! Guard! Villains!

Bal.   Why exclaim you so?

Mont. Negligent traitors! Murther, murther, murther!

Bal. Y'are mad. Had mine intent been so, like yours,
It had been done ere this.

Ren.   Sir, your intent,
And action, too, was rude to enter thus.   125

Bal. Y'are a decay'd lord to tell me of rudeness,
As much decay'd in manners as in means.

Ren. You talk of manners, that thus rudely thrust
Upon a man that's busy with his wife.

Bal. And kept your lordship then the door?

Ren.   The door? 130

Mont. [*To* Renel] Sweet lord, forbear.—Show, show
    your purpose, sir,
To move such bold feet into others' roofs.

Bal. This is my purpose, sir; from Clermont d'Ambois
I bring this challenge.

Mont.   Challenge! I'll touch none.

Bal. I'll leave it here then.

Ren.   Thou shalt leave thy life first. 135

Mont. Murther, murther!

Ren.   Retire, my lord; get off.

[*To* Baligny] Hold, or thy death shall hold thee.—Hence,
    my lord!

Bal. There lie the challenge.

> *They all fight, and* Baligny *drives in* Montsurry.
> *Exit* Montsurry

Ren.   Was not this well handled?

Bal. Nobly, my lord. All thanks!

>   *Exit* Baligny

Tam.   I'll make him read it

>   *Exit* Tamyra

Ren. This was a sleight well mask'd. O, what is man,   140
Unless he be a politician!   *Exit*

FINIS ACTUS PRIMI

ACTUS SECUNDI SCENA PRIMA

[*A Room in the Court*]

Henry, Baligny

Hen. Come, Baligny, we now are private; say,
What service bring'st thou? Make it short; the Guise
(Whose friend thou seem'st) is now in Court, and near,
And may observe us.

Bal.   This, sir, then, in short.
The faction of the Guise (with which my policy,   5
For service to your Highness seems to join)
Grows ripe, and must be gather'd into hold;
Of which my brother Clermont being a part
Exceeding capital, deserves to have
A capital eye on him. And, as you may   10
With best advantage and your speediest charge,
Command his apprehension: which (because
The Court, you know, is strong in his defence)
We must ask country swinge and open fields.
And, therefore, I have wrought him to go down   15
To Cambrai with me (of which government
Your Highness' bounty made me your Lieutenant)
Where when I have him, I will leave my house,
And feign some service out about the confines;
When in the meantime, if you please to give   20

Command to my lieutenant, by your letters,
To train him to some muster, where he may,
(Much to his honour) see for him your forces
Put into battle, when he comes, he may
With some close stratagem be apprehended :   25
For otherwise your whole powers there will fail
To work his apprehension : and with that
My hand needs never be discern'd therein.
   Hen. Thanks, honest Baligny.
   Bal.   Your Highness knows
I will be honest, and betray for you   30
Brother and father : for, I know, my lord,
Treachery for kings is truest loyalty ;
Nor is to bear the name of treachery,
But grave, deep policy. All acts that seem
Ill in particular respects are good   35
As they respect your universal rule.
As in the main sway of the universe
The supreme Rector's general decrees,
To guard the migl ty globes of earth and heaven,
Since they make good that guard to preservation   40
Of both those in their order and first end,
No man's particular (as he thinks) wrong
Must hold him wrong'd ; no, not though all men's reasons,
All law, all conscience, concludes it wrong.
Nor is comparison a flatterer   45
To liken you here to the King of kings ;
Nor any man's particular offence
Against the world's sway, to offence at yours
In any subject ; who as little may
Grudge at their particular wrong, if so it seem,   50
For th' universal right of your estate :
As, being a subject of the world's whole sway
As well as yours, and being a righteous man
To whom Heaven promises defence, and blessing,
Brought to decay, disgrace, and quite defenceless,   55
He may complain of Heaven for wrong to him.
   Hen. 'Tis true : the simile at all parts holds,
As all good subjects hold that love our favour.
   Bal. Which is our heaven here ; and a misery
Incomparable, and most truly hellish,   60
To live depriv'd of our King's grace and countenance,
Without which best conditions are most cursed :

Life of that nature, howsoever short,
Is a most lingering and tedious life ;
Or rather no life, but a languishing,   65
And an abuse of life.
    Hen.   'Tis well conceited.
    Bal.   I thought it not amiss to yield your Highness
A reason of my speeches ; lest perhaps
You might conceive I flatter'd, which, I know,
Of all ills under heaven you most abhor.   70
    Hen.   Still thou art right, my virtuous Baligny ;
For which I thank and love thee. Thy advice
I'll not forget ; haste to thy government,
And carry D'Ambois with thee. So farewell !   *Exit*
    Bal.   Your Majesty fare ever like itself.   75

Enter Guise

    Guise.   My sure friend Baligny !
    Bal.   Noblest of princes !
    Guise.   How stands the state of Cambrai ?
    Bal.   Strong, my lord,
And fit for service : for whose readiness
Your creature, Clermont d'Ambois, and myself
Ride shortly down.
    Guise.   That Clermont is my love ;   80
France never bred a nobler gentleman
For all parts ; he exceeds his brother Bussy.
    Bal.   Ay, my lord ?
    Guise.   Far ; because, besides his valour,
He hath the crown of man, and all his parts,
Which learning is ; and that so true and virtuous   85
That it gives power to do as well as say
Whatever fits a most accomplish'd man ;
Which Bussy, for his valour's season, lack'd ;
And so was rapt with outrage oftentimes
Beyond decorum ; where this absolute Clermont,   90
Though (only for his natural zeal to right)
He will be fiery, when he sees it cross'd,
And in defence of it, yet when he lists
He can contain that fire, as hid in embers.
    Bal.   No question, he's a true, learn'd gentleman.   95
    Guise.   He is as true as tides, or any star
Is in his motion ; and for his rare learning,
He is not (as all else are that seek knowledge)

C.D.W.   H

Of taste so much deprav'd, that they had rather
Delight, and satisfy themselves to drink   100
Of the stream troubled, wand'ring ne'er so far
From the clear fount, than of the fount itself.
In all, Rome's Brutus is reviv'd in him,
Whom he of industry doth imitate.
Or rather, as great Troy's Euphorbus was   105
After Pythagoras ; so is Brutus, Clermont.
And, were not Brutus a conspirator—
    Bal. ' Conspirator,' my lord ?   Doth that impair him ?
Cæsar began to tyrannize ; and when virtue
Nor the religion of the gods could serve   110
To curb the insolence of his proud laws,
Brutus would be the gods' just instrument.
What said the Princess, sweet Antigone,
In the grave Greek tragedian, when the question
'Twixt her and Creon is for laws of kings ?   115
Which, when he urges, she replies on him ;
Though his laws were a king's, they were not God's ;
Nor would she value Creon's written laws
With God's unwrit edicts ; since they last not
This day, and the next, but every day and ever ;   120
Where kings' laws alter every day and hour,
And in that change imply a bounded power.
    Guise.   Well, let us leave these vain disputings what
Is to be done, and fall to doing something.
When are you for your government in Cambrai ?   125
    Bal.   When you command, my lord.
    Guise.   Nay, that's not fit.
Continue your designments with the King,
With all your service ; only, if I send,
Respect me as your friend, and love my Clermont.
    Bal.   Your Highness knows my vows.
    Guise.   Ay, 'tis enough. 130
                Exit Guise.   *Manet* Baligny
    Bal.   Thus must we play on both sides, and thus hearten
In any ill those men whose good we hate.
Kings may do what they list, and for kings, subjects,
Either exempt from censure or exception ;
For, as no man's worth can be justly judg'd   135
But when he shines in some authority,⟩   'Αμήχανον δὲ παντὸς,
So no authority should suffer censure   &c. *Impossible*
But by a man of more authority.   *est viri cognoscere*

Great vessels into less are emptied never,   *mentem ac vol-*
There's a redundance past their continent ever.   *untatem, prius-* 140
                                                  quam in Magis.
These *virtuosi* are the poorest creatures ;   *tratibus apparet.*
For look how spinners weave out of themselves Sopho. Antig.
Webs, whose strange matter none before can see ;
So these, out of an unseen good in virtue,
Make arguments of right and comfort in her,   145
That clothe them like the poor web of a spinner.

Enter Clermont

  Cler. Now, to my challenge. What's the place, the
    weapon ?
  Bal. Soft, sir ! Let first your challenge be received :
He would not touch, nor see it.
  Cler.   Possible !
How did you then ?
  Bal.   Left it in his despite.   150
But when he saw me enter so expectless,
To hear his base exclaims of ' murther, murther,'
Made me think noblesse lost, in him quick buried.
  Cler. They are the breathing sepulchres of noblesse :
No trulier noble men, than lions' pictures   155
Hung up for signs, are lions. Who knows not   *Quo mollius*
That lions the more soft kept, are more servile ? *degunt, eo*
And look how lions close kept, fed by hand,   *servilius.*
Lose quite th' innative fire of spirit and greatness *Epict.*
That lions free breathe, foraging for prey,   160
And grow so gross that mastiffs, curs, and mongrels
Have spirit to cow them : so our soft French nobles,
Chain'd up in ease and numb'd security
(Their spirits shrunk up like their covetous fists,
And never open'd but Domitian-like,   165
And all his base obsequious minions
When they were catching, though it were but flies),
Besotted with their peasants' love of gain,
Rusting at home, and on each other preying,
Are for their greatness but the greater slaves,   170
And none is noble but who scrapes and saves.
  Bal. 'Tis base, tis base ! and yet they think them high.
  Cler. So children mounted on their hobby-horse
Think they are riding, when with wanton toil
They bear what should bear them. A man may well   175
Compare them to those foolish great-spleen'd camels,

That to their high heads, begg'd of Jove horns higher ;
Whose most uncomely and ridiculous pride
When he had satisfied, they could not use,
But where they went upright before, they stoop'd,   180
And bore their heads much lower for their horns.   *Simile.*
As these high men do, low in all true grace,
Their height being privilege to all things base.
And as the foolish poet that still writ
All his most self-lov'd verse in paper royal,   185
Or parchment rul'd with lead, smooth'd with the pumice,
Bound richly up, and strung with crimson strings ;
Never so blest as when he writ and read
The ape-lov'd issue of his brain, and never
But joying in himself, admiring ever :   190
Yet in his works behold him, and he show'd
Like to a ditcher. So these painted men,
All set on out-side, look upon within,
And not a peasant's entrails you shall find
More foul and measled, nor more starv'd of mind.   195
   Bal.   That makes their bodies fat. I fain would know
How many millions of our other nobles
Would make one Guise. There is a true tenth Worthy,
Who, did not one act only blemish him—
   Cler.   One act ? What one ?
   Bal.   One, that, though years past done, 200
Sticks by him still, and will distain him ever.
   Cler.   Good heaven, wherein ? What one act can you
       name
Suppos'd his stain, that I'll not prove his lustre ?
   Bal.   To satisfy you, 'twas the Massacre.
   Cler.   The Massacre ? I thought 'twas some such blemish. 205
   Bal.   Oh, it was heinous
   Cler.   To a brutish sense,
But not a manly reason. We so tender
The vile part in us, that the part divine
We see in hell, and shrink not. Who was first
Head of that massacre ?
   Bal.   The Guise.
   Cler.   'Tis nothing so.   210
Who was in fault for all the slaughters made
In Ilion, and about it ? Were the Greeks ?
Was it not Paris ravishing the Queen
Of Lacedæmon ; breach of shame and faith

And all the laws of hospitality ?   215
This is the beastly slaughter made of men,
When truth is overthrown, his laws corrupted ;
When souls are smother'd in the flatter'd flesh,
Slain bodies are no more than oxen slain.
   Bal. Differ not men from oxen ?
   Cler.   Who says so ?   220
But see wherein ; in the understanding rules
Of their opinions, lives, and actions ;
In their communities of faith and reason.
Was not the wolf that nourish'd Romulus
More human than the men that did expose him ?   225
   Bal. That makes against you.
   Cler.   Not, sir, if you note
That by that deed, the actions difference make
'Twixt men and beasts, and not their names nor forms.
Had faith, nor shame, all hospitable rights
Been broke by Troy, Greece had not made that slaughter.   230
Had that been sav'd (says a philosopher)
The Iliads and Odysseys had been lost ;
Had faith and true religion been preferr'd,
Religious Guise had never massacred.
   Bal. Well, sir, I cannot when I meet with you   235
But thus digress a little, for my learning,
From any other business I intend.
But now the voyage we resolv'd for Cambrai,
I told the Guise begins, and we must haste.
And till the Lord Renel hath found some mean,   240
Conspiring with the Countess, to make sure
Your sworn wreak on her husband, though this fail'd,
In my so brave command we'll spend the time,
Sometimes in training out in skirmishes
And battles all our troops and companies ;   245
And sometimes breathe your brave Scotch running horse,
That great Guise gave you, that all th' horse in France
Far overruns at every race and hunting
Both of the hare and deer. You shall be honour'd
Like the great Guise himself, above the King.   250
And (can you but appease your great-spleen'd sister
For our delay'd wreak of your brother's slaughter)
At all parts you'll be welcom'd to your wonder.
   Cler. I'll see my lord the Guise again before
We take our journey.

Bal.   O, sir, by all means ;   255
You cannot be too careful of his love,
That ever takes occasion to be raising
Your virtues past the reaches of this age,
And ranks you with the best of th' ancient Romans.
    Cler. That praise at no part moves me, but the worth 260
Of all he can give others spher'd in him.
    Bal. He ýet is thought to entertain strange aims.
    Cler. He may be well, yet not as you think strange.
His strange aims are to cross the common custom
Of servile nobles, in which he's so ravish'd,   265
That quite the earth he leaves, and up he leaps
On Atlas' shoulders, and from thence looks down,
Viewing how far off other high ones creep ;
Rich, poor of reason, wander ; all pale looking,
And trembling but to think of their sure deaths,   270
Their lives so base are, and so rank their breaths.
Which I teach Guise to heighten, and make sweet
With life's dear odours, a good mind and name ;
For which he only loves me, and deserves
My love and life, which through all deaths I vow :   275
Resolving this, whatever change can be,
Thou hast created, thou hast ruin'd me.

                                    Exeunt

FINIS   CTUS SECUNDI

ACTUS TERTII SCENA PRIMA

[*A Field near Cambrai*]

A march of Captains *over the stage.* Maillard, Chalon, Aumale
following with Soldiers

    Mail. These troops and companies come in with wings :
So many men, so arm'd, so gallant horse,
I think no other government in France
So soon could bring together. With such men
Methinks a man might pass th' insulting pillars   5
Of Bacchus and Alcides.
    Chal.   I much wonder
Our Lord-Lieutenant brought his brother down
To feast and honour him, and yet now leaves him
At such an instance.

Mail.   'Twas the King's command :
For whom he must leave brother, wife, friend, all things.   10
    Aum. The confines of his government, whose view
Is the pretext of his command, hath need
Of no such sudden expedition.
    Mail. We must not argue that.   The King's command
Is need and right enough : and that he serves   15
(As all true subjects should) without disputing.
    Chal. But knows not he of your command to take
His brother Clermont ?
    Mail.   No : the King's will is
Expressly to conceal his apprehension
From my Lord Governor. Observ'd ye not ?   20
Again peruse the letters. Both you are
Made my assistants, and have right and trust
In all the weighty secrets like myself.
    Aum. 'Tis strange a man that had, through his life past,
So sure a foot in virtue and true knowledge   25
As Clermont d'Ambois, should be now found tripping,
And taken up thus, so to make his fall
More steep and headlong.
    Mail.   It is Virtue's fortune,
To keep her low, and in her proper place ;
Height hath no room for her. But as a man   30
That hath a fruitful wife, and every year
A child by her, hath every year a month
To breathe himself, where he that gets no child
Hath not a night's rest (if he will do well) ;
So, let one marry this same barren Virtue,   35
She never lets him rest, where fruitful Vice
Spares her rich drudge, gives him in labour breath,
Feeds him with bane, and makes him fat with death.
    Chal. I see that good lives never can secure
Men from bad livers. Worst men will have best   40
As ill as they, or heaven to hell they'll wrest.
    Aum. There was a merit for this, in the fault
That Bussy made, for which he (doing penance)
Proves that these foul adulterous guilts will run
Through the whole blood, which not the clear can shun. 45
    Mail. I'll therefore take heed of the bastarding
Whole innocent races ; 'tis a fearful thing.
And as I am true bachelor, I swear
To touch no woman (to the coupling ends)

Unless it be mine own wife, or my friend's.   50
I may make bold with him.
   Aum.   'Tis safe and common.
The more your friend dares trust, the more deceive him.
And as through dewy vapours the sun's form
Makes the gay rainbow girdle to a storm,
So in hearts hollow, friendship (even the sun   55
To all good growing in society)
Makes his so glorious and divine name hold
Colours for all the ill that can be told. *Trumpets within.*
   Mail. Hark, our last troops are come.   *Drums beat*
   Chal.   Hark, our last foot.
   Mail. Come, let us put all quickly into battle,   60
And send for Clermont, in whose honour all
This martial preparation we pretend.
   Chal. We must bethink us, ere we apprehend him,
(Besides our main strength) of some stratagem
To make good our severe command on him,   65
As well to save blood as to make him sure :
For if he come on his Scotch horse, all France
Put at the heels of him will fail to take him.
   Mail. What think you if we should disguise a brace
Of our best soldiers in fair lackeys' coats,   70
And send them for him, running by his side,
Till they have brought him in some ambuscado
We close may lodge for him, and suddenly
Lay sure hand on him, plucking him from horse.
   Aum. It must be sure and strong hand ; for if once   75
He feels the touch of such a stratagem,
'Tis not the choicest brace of all our bands
Can manacle or quench his fiery hands.
   Mail. When they have seiz'd him, the ambush shall make in.
   Aum. Do as you please ; his blameless spirit deserves   80
(I dare engage my life) of all this nothing.
   Chal. Why should all this stir be, then ?
   Aum.   Who knows not
The bombast Polity thrusts into his giant,
To make his wisdom seem of size as huge,
And all for slight encounter of a shade,   85
So he be touch'd, he would have heinous made ?
   Mail. It may be once so, but so ever, never :
Ambition is abroad, on foot, on horse ;
Faction chokes every corner, street, the Court ;

Whose faction 'tis you know, and who is held   90
The fautor's right hand ; how high his aims reach
Nought but a crown can measure. This must fall
Past shadows' weights, and is most capital.
   Chal. No question ; for since he is come to Cambrai,
The malcontent, decay'd Marquess Renel   95
Is come, and new arriv'd, and made partaker
Of all the entertaining shows and feasts
That welcom'd Clermont to the brave virago,
His manly sister. Such we are esteem'd
As are our consorts. Marquess Malcontent   100
Comes where he knows his vein hath safest vent.
   Mail. Let him come at his will, and go as free ;
Let us ply Clermont, our whole charge is he.
                              Exeunt

[SCENA SECUNDA

A Room in the Castle]

Enter a Gentleman Usher *before* Clermont, Renel, Charlotte
   with two women attendants, *with others : shows having
   passed within.*

   Char. This for your lordship's welcome into Cambrai.
   Ren. Noblest of ladies, 'tis beyond all power
(Were my estate at first full) in my means
To quit or merit.
   Cler.   You come something later
From Court, my lord, than I : and since news there   5
Is every day increasing with th' affairs,
Must I not ask now what the news is there ?
Where the Court lies ? What stir, change, what advice
From England, Italy ?
   Ren.   You must do so,
If you'll be call'd a gentleman well qualified,   10
And wear your time and wits in those discourses.
   Cler. The Locrian Princes therefore were brave rulers ;
For whosoever there came new from country
And in the city ask'd 'What news ? ' was punish'd ;
Since commonly such brains are most delighted   15
With innovations, gossips' tales, and mischiefs :
But as of lions it is said, and eagles,
That, when they go, they draw their seres and talons
Close up, to shun rebating of their sharpness :

So our wit's sharpness, which we should employ   20
In noblest knowledge, we should never waste
In vile and vulgar admirations.
   Ren.   'Tis right ; but who, save only you, performs it,
And your great brother ?   Madam, where is he ?
   Char.   Gone, a day since, into the country's confines,   25
To see their strength and readiness for service.
   Ren.   'Tis well ; his favour with the King hath made him
Most worthily great, and live right royally.
   Cler.   Ay : would he would not do so ! Honour never
Should be esteem'd with wise men, as the price   30
And value of their virtuous services,
But as their sign or badge ; for that bewrays
More glory in the outward grace of goodness,
Than in the good itself ; and then 'tis said,
Who more joy takes that men his good advance   35
Than in the good itself, does it by chance.
   Char.   My brother speaks all principle.   What man
Is mov'd with your soul, or hath such a thought
In any rate of goodness ?
   Cler.   'Tis their fault.
We have examples of it, clear and many.   40
Demetrius Phalereus, an orator,
And (which not oft meet) a philosopher,
So great in Athens grew that he erected
Three hundred statues of him ; of all which,
No rust nor length of time corrupted one ;   45
But in his life time all were overthrown.
And Demades (that pass'd Demosthenes
For all extemporal orations)
Erected many statues, which (he living)
Were broke, and melted into chamber-pots.   50
Many such ends have fallen on such proud honours,
No more because the men on whom they fell
Grew insolent and left their virtues' state,
Than for their hugeness, that procur'd their hate :
And therefore little pomp in men most great   55
Makes mightily and strongly to the guard
Of what they win by chance or just reward.
Great and immodest braveries again,
Like statues much too high made for their bases,
Are overturn'd as soon as given their places.   60

Enter a Messenger *with a Letter*

Mes. Here is a letter, sir, deliver'd me,
Now at the fore-gate by a gentleman.
　Cler. What gentleman ?
　Mes.　　　　　　　　　He would not tell his name ;
He said, he had not time enough to tell it,
And say the little rest he had to say.　　　　　　65
　Cler. That was a merry saying ; he took measure
Of his dear time like a most thrifty husband. [*Reads*]
　Char. What news ?
　Cler.　　　　　　Strange ones, and fit for a novation ;
Weighty, unheard of, mischievous enough.
　Ren. Heaven shield ! What are they ?
　Cler.　　　　　　　　Read them, good my lord.　70
　Ren. [*reads*] ' You are betray'd into this country.'
　　Monstrous !
　Char. How's that ?
　Cler. Read on.
　Ren. ' Maillard, your brother's Lieutenant, that yester-
day invited you to see his musters, hath letters and strict　75
charge from the King to apprehend you.'
　Char. To apprehend him ?
　Ren. ' Your brother absents himself of purpose.'
　Cler. That's a sound one !
　Char. That's a lie !　　　　　　　　　80
　Ren. ' Get on your Scotch horse, and retire to your
strength ; you know where it is, and there it expects you.
Believe this as your best friend had sworn it. Fare well, if
you will. ANONYMOS.' What's that ?
　Cler. Without a name.　　　　　　　85
　Char. And all his notice, too, without all truth.
　Cler. So I conceive it, sister : I'll not wrong
My well-known brother for Anonymos.
　Char. Some fool hath put this trick on you, yet more
T'uncover your defect of spirit and valour,　　　90
First shown in ling'ring my dear brother's wreak.
See what it is to give the envious world
Advantage to diminish eminent virtue.
Send him a challenge ? Take a noble course
To wreak a murther done so like a villain ?　　95
　Cler. Shall we revenge a villany with villany ?
　Char. Is it not equal ?

Cler.   Shall we equal be
With villains ? Is that your reason ?
    Char.   Cowardice evermore
Flies to the shield of reason.
    Cler.   Nought that is
Approv'd by reason can be cowardice.   100
    Char. Dispute, when you should fight ! Wrong, wreakless
        sleeping,
Makes men die honourless ; one borne, another
Leaps on our shoulders.
    Cler.   We must wreak our wrongs
So as we take not more.
    Char.   One wreak'd in time
Prevents all other. Then shines virtue most   105
When time is found for facts ; and found, not lost.
    Cler. No time occurs to kings, much less to virtue ;
Nor can we call it virtue that proceeds
From vicious fury. I repent that ever
(By any instigation in th' appearance   110
My brother's spirit made, as I imagin'd)
That e'er I yielded to revenge his murther.
All worthy men should ever bring their blood
To bear all ill, not to be wreak'd with good :
Do ill for no ill ; never private cause   115
Should take on it the part of public laws.
    Char. A D'Ambois bear in wrong so tame a spirit !
    Ren. Madam, be sure there will be time enough
For all the vengeance your great spirit can wish.
The course yet taken is allow'd by all,   120
Which being noble, and refus'd by th' Earl,
Now makes him worthy of your worst advantage ;
And I have cast a project with the Countess
To watch a time when all his wariest guards
Shall not exempt him. Therefore give him breath ;   125
Sure death delay'd is a redoubled death.
    Cler. Good sister, trouble not yourself with this ;
Take other ladies' care ; practise your face.
There's the chaste matron, Madam Perigot,
Dwells not far hence ; I'll ride and send her to you.   130
She did live by retailing maiden-heads
In her minority ; but now she deals
In wholesale altogether for the Court.
I tell you, she's the only fashion-monger

For your complexion, powdering of your hair,   135
Shadows, rebatoes, wires, tires, and such tricks,
That Cambrai, or I think, the Court affords :
She shall attend you, sister, and with these
Womanly practices employ your spirit ;
This other suits you not, nor fits the fashion.   140
Though she be dear, lay't on, spare for no cost,
Ladies in these have all their bounties lost.
   Ren.   Madam, you see his spirit will not check
At any single danger, when it stands
Thus merrily firm against an host of men,   145
Threaten'd to be [in] arms for his surprise.
   Char.   That's a mere bugbear, an impossible mock.
If he, and him I bound by nuptial faith,
Had not been dull and drossy in performing
Wreak of the dear blood of my matchless brother,   150
What prince, what king, which of the desperat'st ruffians,
Outlaws in Arden, durst have tempted thus
One of our blood and name, be't true or false ?
   Cler.   This is not caus'd by that ; 'twill be as sure
As yet it is not, though this should be true.   155
   Char.   True ? 'Tis past thought false.
   Cler.   I suppose the worst,
Which far I am from thinking ; and despise
The army now in battle that should act it.
   Char.   I would not let my blood up to that thought,
But it should cost the dearest blood in France.   160
   Cler.   Sweet sister, far be both off as the fact
Of my feign'd apprehension.   *Osculatur*
   Char.   I would once
Strip off my shame with my attire, and try
If a poor woman, votist of revenge,
Would not perform it with a precedent   165
To all you bungling, foggy-spirited men ;
But for our birthright's honour, do not mention
One syllable of any word may go
To the begetting of an act so tender
And full of sulphur as this letter's truth ;   170
It comprehends so black a circumstance
Not to be nam'd, that but to form one thought,
It is, or can be so, would make me mad ;
Come, my lord, you and I will fight this dream
Out at the chess.

Ren.   Most gladly, worthiest lady.   175
                      Exeunt Charlotte and Renel

                      Enter a Messenger

Mes. Sir, my Lord Governor's Lieutenant prays
Access to you.
    Cler.   Himself alone ?
    Mes.   Alone, sir.
    Cler. Attend him in. *Exit* Messenger
                      Now comes this plot to trial.
I shall discern (if it be true as rare)
Some sparks will fly from his dissembling eyes.   180
I'll sound his depth.

                  Enter Maillard *with the* Messenger

Mail.   Honour, and all things noble !
    Cler. As much to you, good Captain. What's th' affair ?
    Mail. Sir, the poor honour we can add to all
Your studied welcome to this martial place,
In presentation of what strength consists   185
My lord your brother's government, is ready.
I have made all his troops and companies
Advance and put themselves rang'd in battalia,
That you may see both how well-arm'd they are,
How strong is every troop and company,   190
How ready, and how well prepar'd for service.
    Cler. And must they take me ?
    Mail.   Take you, sir ? O, heaven ! [*turning away*]
    Mes. [*Aside to Clermont*] Believe it, sir ; his count'nance
      chang'd in turning.
    Mail. What do you mean, sir ?
    Cler.   If you have charg'd them,
You being charg'd yourself, to apprehend me,   195
Turn not your face ; throw not your looks about so.
    Mail. Pardon me, sir. You amaze me to conceive
From whence our wills to honour you should turn
To such dishonour of my lord your brother.
Dare I, without him, undertake your taking ?   200
    Cler. Why not, by your direct charge from the King ?
    Mail. By my charge from the King ? Would he so much
Disgrace my lord, his own Lieutenant here,
To give me his command without his forfeit ?

Cler.   Acts that are done by kings are not ask'd why.   205
I'll not dispute the case, but I will search you.
   Mail. Search me ? For what ?
   Cler.   For letters.
   Mail.   I beseech you,
Do not admit one thought of such a shame
To a commander.
   Cler.   Go to ! I must do't.
Stand and be search'd ; you know me.
   Mail.   You forget   210
What 'tis to be a captain, and yourself.
   Cler.   Stand, or I vow to heaven, I'll make you lie,
Never to rise more.
   Mail.   If a man be mad
Reason must bear him.
   Cler.   So coy to be search'd ?
   Mail. 'Sdeath, sir ! Use a captain like a carrier ?   215
   Cler.   Come, be not furious ; when I have done
You shall make such a carrier of me,
If't be your pleasure ; you're my friend, I know,
And so am bold with you.
   Mail.   You'll nothing find
Where nothing is.
   Cler.   Swear you have nothing.   220
   Mail.   Nothing you seek, I swear : I beseech you
Know I desir'd this out of great affection,
To th' end my lord may know out of your witness
His forces are not in so bad estate
As he esteem'd them lately in your hearing :   225
For which he would not trust me with the confines,
But went himself to witness their estate.
   Cler.   I heard him make that reason, and am sorry
I had no thought of it before I made
Thus bold with you, since 'tis such rhubarb to you.   230
I'll therefore search no more. If you are charg'd
(By letters from the King, or otherwise)
To apprehend me, never spice it more
With forc'd terms of your love, but say ; I yield ;
Hold, take my sword, here ; I forgive thee freely ;   235
Take, do thine office.
   Mail.   'Sfoot, you make m' a hangman ;
By all my faith to you, there's no such thing.
   Cler.   Your faith to me ?

Mail.   My faith to God ; all's one,
Who hath no faith to men, to God hath none.
    Cler.   In that sense I accept your oath, and thank you :   240
I gave my word to go, and I will go.   *Exit* Clermont
    Mail.   I'll watch you whither.   *Exit* Maillard
    Mes.   If he goes, he proves
How vain are men's foreknowledges of things,
When Heaven strikes blind their powers of note and use ;
And makes their way to ruin seem more right   245
Than that which safety opens to their sight.
Cassandra's prophecy had no more profit
With Troy's blind citizens, when she foretold
Troy's ruin ; which, succeeding, made her use
This sacred inclamation : ' God ' (said she)   250
' Would have me utter things uncredited :
For which now they approve what I presag'd ;
They count me wise that said before I rag'd.'   [*Exit*]

[SCENA TERTIA

In the Camp]

Enter Chalon *with two* Soldiers

    Chal.   Come, soldiers, you are downwards fit for lackeys ;
Give me your pieces, and take you these coats,
To make you complete footmen, in whose forms
You must be complete soldiers ; you two only
Stand for our army.
    1st Sold.   That were much.
    Chal.   Tis true ;   5
You two must do, or enter, what our army
Is now in field for.
    2nd Sold.   I see then our guerdon
Must be the deed itself, 'twill be such honour.
    Chal.   What fight soldiers most for ?
    1st Sold.   Honour only.
    Chal.   Yet here are crowns beside.
    Ambo.   We thank you, captain.   10
    2nd Sold.   Now, sir, how show we ?
    Chal.   As you should at all parts.
Go now to Clermont d'Ambois, and inform him
Two battles are set ready in his honour,

And stay his presence only for their signal,
When they shall join : and that t'attend him hither,   15
Like one we so much honour, we have sent him—
  1st Sold.   Us two in person.
  Chal.   Well, sir, say it so ;
And having brought him to the field, when I
Fall in with him, saluting, get you both
Of one side of his horse, and pluck him down,   20
And I with the ambush laid will second you.
  1st Sold,   Nay, we shall lay on hands of too much strength
To need your secondings.
  2nd Sold.   I hope we shall.
Two are enough to encounter Hercules.
  Chal.   'Tis well said, worthy soldiers ; haste, and haste him.   25
                               [Exeunt]

[SCENA QUARTA

A Room in the Castle]

Enter Clermont, Maillard *close following him*

  Cler. [*To himself*].   My Scotch horse to their army—
  Mail.   Please you, sir ?
  Cler. 'Sdeath, you're passing diligent !
  Mail.   Of my soul
'Tis only in my love to honour you
With what would grace the King ; but since I see
You still sustain a jealous eye on me,   5
I'll go before.
  Cler.   'Tis well ; I'll come ; my hand.
  Mail.   Your hand, sir !   Come, your word ; your choice
  be used.   *Exit*

Clermont *solus*

  Cler. I had an aversation to this voyage,
When first my brother mov'd it ; and have found
That native power in me was never vain ;   10
Yet now neglected it.   I wonder much
At my inconstancy in these decrees,
I every hour set down to guide my life.
When Homer made Achilles passionate,
Wrathful, revengeful, and insatiate   15
  C.D.W.   I

In his affections, what man will deny
He did compose it all of industry,
To let men see that men of most renown,
Strong'st, noblest, fairest, if they set not down
Decrees within them, for disposing these,   20
Of judgment, resolution, uprightness,
And certain knowledge of their use and ends,
Mishap and misery no less extends
To their destruction, with all that they priz'd,
Than to the poorest, and the most despis'd.   25

Enter Renel

  Ren.   Why, how now, friend, retir'd ?   Take heed you
    prove not
Dismay'd with this strange fortune : all observe you.
Your government's as much mark'd as the King's.
What said a friend to Pompey ?
  Cler.   What ?
  Ren.   The people
Will never know, unless in death thou try,   30
That thou know'st how to bear adversity.
  Cler. I shall approve how vile I value fear
Of death at all times ; but to be too rash,
Without both will and care to shun the worst
(It being in power to do, well and with cheer)   35
Is stupid negligence, and worse than fear.
  Ren. Suppose this true now.
  Cler.   No, I cannot do't.
My sister truly said, there hung a tail
Of circumstance so black on that supposure,
That to sustain it thus abhorr'd our metal.   40
And I can shun it too, in spite of all,
Not going to field ; and there too, being so mounted
As I will, since I go.
  Ren.   You will then go ?
  Cler. I am engag'd, both in my word and hand ;
But this is it that makes me thus retir'd   45
To call myself t'account how this affair
Is to be manag'd if the worst should chance ;
With which I note how dangerous it is
For any man to press beyond the place
To which his birth, or means, or knowledge ties him ;   50

For my part, though of noble birth, my birthright
Had little left it, and I know 'tis better
To live with little, and to keep within
A man's own strength still, and in man's true end,
Than run a mix'd course. Good and bad hold never   55
Anything common ; you can never find
Things' outward care, but you neglect your mind.
God hath the whole world perfect made and free,
His parts to th' use of th' All ; men then that [be]
Parts of that All, must, as the general sway   60
Of that importeth, willingly obey
In everything without their power to change.
He that, unpleas'd to hold his place, will range,
Can in no other be contain'd that's fit,
And so resisting th' All, is crush'd with it.   65
But he, that knowing how divine a frame
The whole world is ; and of it all, can name
(Without self-flattery) no part so divine
As he himself, and therefore will confine
Freely his whole powers in his proper part,   70
Goes on most God-like. He that strives t'invert
The Universal's course with his poor way,
Not only dust-like shivers with the sway,
But, crossing God in his great work, all earth
Bears not so cursed and so damn'd a birth.   75
    Ren. Go on ; I'll take no care what comes of you ;
Heaven will not see it ill, howe'er it show :
But the pretext to see these battles rang'd
Is much your honour.
    Cler.   As the world esteems it.
But to decide that, you make me remember   80
An accident of high and noble note,
And fits the subject of my late discourse
Of holding on our free and proper way.
I overtook, coming from Italy,
In Germany, a great and famous earl   85
Of England, the most goodly-fashion'd man
I ever saw ; from head to foot in form
Rare and most absolute ; he had a face
Like one of the most ancient honour'd Romans,
From whence his noblest family was deriv'd ;   90
He was beside of spirit passing great,
Valiant, and learn'd, and liberal as the sun,

Spoke and writ sweetly, or of learned subjects,
Or of the discipline of public weals ;
And 'twas the Earl of Oxford ; and being offer'd   95
At that time, by Duke Casimir, the view
Of his right royal army then in field,
Refus'd it, and no foot was mov'd to stir
Out of his own free fore-determin'd course :
I, wondering at it, ask'd for it his reason,   100
It being an offer so much for his honour.
He, all acknowledging, said 'twas not fit
To take those honours that one cannot quit.
   Ren.   'Twas answer'd like the man you have describ'd.
   Cler.   And yet he cast it only in the way,   105
To stay and serve the world. Nor did it fit
His own true estimate how much it weigh'd,
For he despis'd it ; and esteem'd it freer
To keep his own way straight, and swore that he
Had rather make away his whole estate   110
In things that cross'd the vulgar, than he would
Be frozen up stiff (like a Sir John Smith,
His countryman) in common nobles' fashions,
Affecting, as the end of noblesse were,
Those servile observations.
   Ren.   It was strange.   115
   Cler.   O, 'tis a vexing sight to see a man,
Out of his way, stalk proud as he were in ;
Out of his way to be officious,
Observant, wary, serious, and grave,
Fearful, and passionate, insulting, raging,   120
Labour with iron flails to thresh down feathers
Flitting in air.
   Ren.   What one considers this,
Of all that are thus out, or once endeavours,
Erring, to enter on man's right-hand path ?
   Cler.   These are too grave for brave wits ; give them toys ; 125
Labour bestow'd on these is harsh and thriftless.
If you would Consul be (says one) of Rome,
You must be watching, starting out of sleeps ;
Every way whisking ; glorifying Plebeians ;
Kissing Patricians' hands, rot at their doors ;   130
Speak and do basely ; every day bestow
Gifts and observance upon one or other :
And what's th' event of all ? Twelve rods before thee ;

Three or four times sit for the whole tribunal ;
Exhibit Circene games ; make public feasts ;   135
And for these idle outward things (says he)
Would'st thou lay on such cost, toil, spend thy spirits ?
And to be void of perturbation,
For constancy, sleep when thou would'st have sleep,
Wake when thou would'st wake, fear nought, vex for nought, 140
No pains wilt thou bestow, no cost, no thought ?
  Ren.   What should I say ?   As good consort with you
As with an angel ; I could hear you ever.
  Cler.   Well, in, my lord, and spend time with my sister,
And keep her from the field with all endeavour ;   145
The soldiers love her so, and she so madly
Would take my apprehension, if it chance,
That blood would flow in rivers.
  Ren.   Heaven forbid !
And all with honour your arrival speed !   *Exit*

Enter Messenger *with two* Soldiers *like lackeys*

  Mes.   Here are two lackeys, sir, have message to you.   150
  Cler.   What is your   message,   and from whom,   my
    friends ?
  1st Sold.   From the Lieutenant, Colonel, and the Captains ;
Who sent us to inform you that the battles
Stand ready rang'd, expecting but your presence
To be their honour'd signal when to join,   155
And we are charg'd to run by, and attend you.
  Cler.   I come.   I pray you see my running horse
Brought to the back-gate to me.
  Mes.   Instantly.
Exit Messenger.
  Cler.   Chance what can chance me, well or ill is equal
In my acceptance, since I joy in neither,   160
But go with sway of all the world together.
In all successes Fortune and the day
To me alike are ; I am fix'd, be she
Never so fickle ; and will there repose,
Far past the reach of any die she throws.   165
Exit cum Pedisequis

FINIS ACTUS TERTII

ACTUS QUARTI SCENA PRIMA

[A Field near Cambrai]

Alarum within : excursions over the Stage

The [Soldiers *disguised like*] Lackeys *running*, Maillard *following them*

Mail.   Villains, not hold him when ye had him down !
1st Lackey.   Who can hold lightning ?   'Sdeath, a man as
    well
Might catch a cannon-bullet in his mouth,
And spit it in your hands, as take and hold him.
Mail.   Pursue, enclose him ! Stand or fall on him,   5
And ye may take him.   'Sdeath, they make him guards !
                        Exit [*with the Lackeys*]

Alarum still, and enter Chalon [*with two* Soldiers]

Chal.   Stand, cowards,   stand,   strike,   send your
    bullets at him !
1st Sold.   We came to entertain him, sir, for honour.
2nd Sold.   Did ye not say so ?
Chal.   Slaves, he is a traitor !
Command the horse troops to over-run the traitor.   10
                              Exeunt

*Shouts within.   Alarum still, and chambers shot off.   Then
enter* Aumale

Aum.   What spirit breathes thus in this more than man,
Turns flesh to air possess'd, and in a storm
Tears men about the field like autumn leaves ?
He turn'd wild lightning in the lackeys' hands,
Who, though their sudden violent twitch unhors'd him,   15
Yet when he bore himself, their saucy fingers
Flew as too hot off, as he had been fire.
The ambush then made in, through all whose force,
He drave as if a fierce and fire-given cannon
Had spit his iron vomit out amongst them.   20
The battles then in two half-moons enclos'd him,
In which he show'd as if he were the light,
And they but earth, who wond'ring what he was,
Shrunk their steel horns, and gave him glorious pass :

And as a great shot from a town besieg'd   25
At foes before it flies forth black and roaring,
But they too far, and that with weight oppress'd,
(As if disdaining earth) doth only graze,
Strike earth, and up again into the air;
Again sinks to it, and again doth rise,   30
And keeps such strength that when it softliest moves,
It piecemeal shivers any let it proves:
So flew brave Clermont forth, till breath forsook him,
Then fell to earth; and yet (sweet man) even then
His spirit's convulsions made him bound again   35
Past all their reaches; till, all motion spent,
His fix'd eyes cast a blaze of such disdain,
All stood and star'd, and untouch'd let him lie,
As something sacred fallen out of the sky.

                                        A cry within
O now some rude hand hath laid hold on him!   40

Enter Maillard, Chalon *leading* Clermont, Captains *and*
                    Soldiers *following*

See prisoner led, with his bands honour'd more
Than all the freedom he enjoy'd before.
    Mail.   At length we have you, sir.
    Cler.   You have much joy too;
I made you sport yet; but I pray you tell me,
Are not you perjur'd?
    Mail.   No; I swore for the King.   45
    Cler.   Yet perjury, I hope, is perjury.
    Mail.   But thus forswearing is not perjury.
You are no politician: not a fault,
How foul soever, done for private ends,
Is fault in us sworn to the public good: 50
We never can be of the damned crew,
We may impolitic ourselves (as 'twere)
Into the kingdom's body politic,
Whereof indeed we're members; you miss terms.
    Cler.   The things are yet the same.   55
    Mail.   'Tis nothing so; the property is alter'd;
Y'are no lawyer. Or say that oath and oath
Are still the same in number, yet their species
Differ extremely, as, for flat example,
When politic widows try men for their turn,   60

Before they wed them, they are harlots then,
But when they wed them, they are honest women ;
So private men, when they forswear, betray,
Are perjur'd treachers, but being public once,
That is, sworn, married, to the public good—   65
   Cler. Are married women public ?
   Mail.   Public good ;
For marriage makes them, being the public good,
And could not be without them. So I say
Men public, that is, being sworn or married
To the good public, being one body made   70
With the realm's body politic, are no more
Private, nor can be perjur'd, though forsworn,
More than a widow, married for the act
Of generation, is for that an harlot,
Because for that she was so, being unmarried :   75
An argument *a paribus*.
   Chal.   'Tis a shrewd one.
   Cler. ' Who hath no faith to men, to God hath none ' :
Retain you that, sir ? Who said so ?
   Mail.   'Twas I.
   Cler. Thy own tongue damn thy infidelity !
But, captains all, you know me nobly born,   80
Use ye t'assault such men as I with lackeys ?
   Chal. They are no lackeys, sir, but soldiers
Disguis'd in lackeys' coats.
   1st Sold.   Sir, we have seen the enemy.
   Cler. Avaunt, ye rascals ! Hence !
   Mail.   Now leave your coats.
   Cler. Let me not see them more.   85
   Aum. I grieve that virtue lives so undistinguish'd
From vice in any ill, and though the crown
Of sovereign law, she should be yet her footstool,
Subject to censure, all the shame and pain
Of all her rigour.
   Cler.   Yet false policy   90
Would cover all, being like offenders hid,
That (after notice taken where they hide)
The more they crouch and stir, the more are spied.
   Aum. I wonder how this chanc'd you.
   Cler.   Some informer
Bloodhound to mischief, usher to the hangman,   95
Thirsty of honour for some huge state act,

Perceiving me great with the worthy Guise,
And he (I know not why) held dangerous,
Made me the desperate organ of his danger,
Only with that poor colour: 'tis the common   100
And more than whore-like trick of treachery
And vermin bred to rapine and to ruin:
For which this fault is still to be accus'd,
Since good acts fail, crafts and deceits are us'd.
If it be other, never pity me.   105
   Aum. Sir, we are glad, believe it, and have hope,
The King will so conceit it.
   Cler.   At his pleasure.
In meantime, what's your will, Lord Lieutenant?
   Mail. To leave your own horse, and to mount the trum-
     pet's.
   Cler. It shall be done.   This heavily prevents   110
My purpos'd recreation in these parts;
Which now I think on, let me beg you, sir,
To lend me some one captain of your troops
To bear the message of my hapless service
And misery to my most noble mistress,   115
Countess of Cambrai; to whose house this night
I promis'd my repair, and know most truly,
With all the ceremonies of her favour,
She sure expects me.
   Mail.   Think you now on that?
   Cler. On that, sir? Ay, and that so worthily,   120
That if the King, in spite of your great service,
Would send me instant promise of enlargement,
Condition I would set this message by,
I would not take it, but had rather die.
   Aum. Your message shall be done, sir; I myself   125
Will be for you a messenger of ill.
   Cler. I thank you, sir, and doubt not yet to live
To quite your kindness.
   Aum.   Mean space use your spirit
And knowledge for the cheerful patience
Of this so strange and sudden consequence.   130
   Cler. Good sir, believe that no particular torture
Can force me from my glad obedience
To anything the high and general Cause
To match with his whole fabric hath ordain'd:
And know ye all (though far from all your aims   135

Yet worth them all, and all men's endless studies)
That in this one thing, all the discipline
Of manners and of manhood is contain'd :
A man to join himself with th' Universe
In his main sway, and make (in all things fit)   140
One with that All, and go on round as it ;
Not plucking from the whole his wretched part,
And into straits, or into nought revert,
Wishing the complete Universe might be
Subject to such a rag of it as he ;   145
But to consider great Necessity
All things as well refract as voluntary
Reduceth to the prime celestial cause ;
Which he that yields to with a man's applause,
And cheek by cheek goes, crossing it no breath,   150
But, like God's image, follows to the death,
That man is truly wise, and everything
(Each cause, and every part distinguishing)
In nature with enough art understands,
And that full glory merits at all hands,   155
That doth the whole world at all parts adorn,
And appertains to one celestial born.   *Exeunt omnes*

[SCENA SECUNDA

A Room in the Court]

Enter Baligny, Renel

Bal. So foul a scandal never man sustain'd,
Which, caus'd by th' King, is rude and tyrannous :
Give me a place, and my Lieutenant make
The filler of it !
Ren.   I should never look
For better of him ; never trust a man   5
For any justice, that is rapt with pleasure ;
To order arms well, that makes smocks his ensigns
And his whole government's sails : you heard of late,
He had the four and twenty ways of venery
Done all before him.
Bal.   'Twas abhorr'd and beastly.   10
Ren. 'Tis more than Nature's mighty hand can do
To make one human and a lecher too.

Look how a wolf doth like a dog appear,
So like a friend is an adulterer :
Voluptuaries, and these belly-gods,   15
No more true men are than so many toads.
A good man happy, is a common good ;
Vile men advanc'd live of the common blood.
    Bal.   Give and then take, like children !
    Ren.   Bounties are
As soon repented as they happen rare.   20
    Bal.   What should kings do, and men of eminent places,
But, as they gather, sow gifts to the Graces ?
And where they have given, rather give again,
(Being given for virtue) than like babes and fools,
Take and repent gifts ? Why are wealth and power ?   25
    Ren.   Power and wealth move to tyranny, not bounty ;
The merchant for his wealth is swoln in mind,
When yet the chief lord of it is the wind.
    Bal.   That may so chance to our state-merchants too ;
Something perform'd, that hath not far to go.   30
    Ren.   That's the main point, my lord ; insist on that.
    Bal.   But doth this fire rage further ? Hath it taken
The tender tinder of my wife's sere blood ?
Is she so passionate ?
    Ren.   So wild, so mad,
She cannot live, and this unwreak'd sustain.   35
The woes are bloody that in women reign.
The Sicile gulf keeps fear in less degree ;
There is no tiger not more tame than she.
    Bal.   There is no looking home, then ?
    Ren.   Home ! Medea
With all her herbs, charms, thunders, lightnings,   40
Made not her presence and black haunts more dreadful.
    Bal.   Come to the King ; if he reform not all,
Mark the event, none stand where that must fall. *Exeunt*

[SCENA TERTIA

A Room in the House of the Countess of Cambrai].

Enter Countess, Riova, *and an* Usher

    Ush.   Madam, a captain come from Clermont d'Ambois
Desires access to you.

Count. And not himself ?
Ush. No, madam.
Count. That's not well. Attend him in.
The last hour of his promise now run out, *Exit* Usher
And he break ? Some brack's in the frame of nature 5
That forceth his breach.

Enter Usher *and* Aumale

Aum. Save your ladyship!
Count. All welcome ! Come you from my worthy servant ?
Aum. Ay, madam ; and confer such news from him—
Count. Such news ? What news ?
Aum. News that I wish some other had the charge of. 10
Count. Oh, what charge ? What news ?
Aum. Your ladyship must use some patience
Or else I cannot do him that desire
He urg'd with such affection to your graces.
Count. Do it, for heaven's love do it ! If you serve 15
His kind desires, I will have patience.
Is he in health ?
Aum. He is.
Count. Why, that's the ground
Of all the good estate we hold in earth ;
All our ill built upon that is no more
Than we may bear, and should ; express it all. 20
Aum. Madam, 'tis only this ; his liberty—
Count. His liberty ! Without that, health is nothing.
Why live I, but to ask, in doubt of that,
Is that bereft him ?
Aum. You'll again prevent me.
Count. No more, I swear ; I must hear, and together 25
Come all my misery ! I'll hold though I burst.
Aum. Then, madam, thus it fares. He was invited,
By way of honour to him, to take view
Of all the powers his brother Baligny
Hath in his government ; which rang'd in battles, 30
Maillard, Lieutenant to the Governor,
Having receiv'd strict letters from the King
To train him to the musters, and betray him
To their surprise, which, with Chalon in chief,
And other captains (all the field put hard 35
By his incredible valour for his scape)

They haplessly and guiltlessly perform'd,
And to Bastile he's now led prisoner.
   Count.   What change is here ! How are my hopes prevented !
O my most faithful servant, thou betray'd !   40
Will kings make treason lawful ?   Is society
(To keep which only kings were first ordain'd)
Less broke in breaking faith 'twixt friend and friend,
Than 'twixt the king and subject ?   Let them fear.
Kings' precedents in licence lack no danger.   45
Kings are compar'd to gods, and should be like them,
Full in all right, in nought superfluous,
Nor nothing straining past right for their right :
Reign justly and reign safely.   Policy
Is but a guard corrupted, and a way   50
Ventur'd in deserts, without guide or path.
Kings punish subjects' errors with their own.
Kings are like archers, and their subjects, shafts :
For as when archers let their arrows fly,
They call to them, and bid them fly or fall,   55
As if 'twere in the free power of the shaft
To fly or fall, when only 'tis the strength,
Straight shooting, compass, given it by the archer,
That makes it hit or miss ; and doing either,
He's to be prais'd or blam'd, and not the shaft :   60
So kings to subjects crying, ' Do, do not this ',
Must to them by their own examples' strength,
The straightness of their acts, and equal compass,
Give subjects power t' obey them in the like ;
Not shoot them forth with faulty aim and strength,   65
And lay the fault in them for flying amiss.
   Aum.   But, for your servant, I dare swear him guiltless.
   Count.   He would not for his kingdom traitor be ;
His laws are not so true to him as he.
O knew I how to free him, by way forc'd   70
Through all their army, I would fly, and do it :
And had I of my courage and resolve
But ten such more, they should not all retain him ;
But I will never die before I give
Maillard an hundred slashes with a sword,   75
Chalon an hundred breaches with a pistol.
They could not all have taken Clermont d'Ambois
Without their treachery ; he had bought his bands out
With their slave bloods ; but he was credulous ;

He would believe, since he would be believ'd ;   80
Your noblest natures are most credulous.
Who gives no trust, all trust is apt to break ;
Hate like hell-mouth who think not what they speak.
    Aum. Well, madam, I must tender my attendance
On him again. Will't please you to return   85
No service to him by me ?
    Count.   Fetch me straight
My little cabinet. (*Exit* Ancilla) 'Tis little, tell him,
And much too little for his matchless love :
But as in him the worths of many men
Are close contracted (*Intrat* Ancilla), so in this are jewels   90
Worth many cabinets. Here, with this (good sir),
Commend my kindest service to my servant,
Thank him, with all my comforts, and, in them
With all my life for them : all sent from him
In his remembrance of me, and true love ;   95
And look you tell him, tell him how I lie
                              She kneels down at his feet
Prostrate at feet of his accurs'd misfortune,
Pouring my tears out, which shall ever fall
Till I have pour'd for him out eyes and all.
    Aum. O, madam, this will kill him : comfort you   100
With full assurance of his quick acquittal :
Be not so passionate : rise, cease your tears.
    Count. Then must my life cease. Tears are all the vent
My life hath to scape death. Tears please me better
Than all life's comforts, being the natural seed   105
Of hearty sorrow. As a tree fruit bears,
So doth an undissembled sorrow tears.
                    He raises her, and leads her out. Exeunt
    Ush.   This might have been before, and sav'd much charge.
                                                        Exit

[SCENA QUARTA

A Room in the Court]

Enter Henry, Guise, Baligny, Epernon, Soissons, Perricot *with
                    pen, ink, and paper*

    Guise. Now, sir, I hope your much abus'd eyes see,
In my word for my Clermont, what a villain

He was that whisper'd in your jealous ear
His own black treason in suggesting Clermont's,
Colour'd with nothing but being great with me.   5
Sign then this writ for his delivery;
Your hand was never urg'd with worthier boldness:
Come, pray, sir, sign it: why should kings be pray'd
To acts of justice? 'Tis a reverence
Makes them despis'd, and shows they stick and tire   10
In what their free powers should be hot as fire.
   Hen. Well, take your will, sir;—I'll have mine ere
     long.—   *Aversus*
But wherein is this Clermont such a rare one?
   Guise. In his most gentle and unwearied mind
Rightly to virtue fram'd, in very nature,   15
In his most firm inexorable spirit
To be remov'd from anything he chooseth
For worthiness, or bear the least persuasion
To what is base, or fitteth not his object,
In his contempt of riches and of greatness,   20
In estimation of th'idolatrous vulgar,
His scorn of all things servile and ignoble,
Though they could gain him never such advancement,
His liberal kind of speaking what is truth
In spite of temporizing, the great rising   25
And learning of his soul, so much the more
Against ill Fortune, as she set herself
Sharp against him, or would present most hard
To shun the malice of her deadliest charge;
His detestation of his special friends,   30
When he perceiv'd their tyrannous will to do,
Or their abjection basely to sustain
Any injustice that they could revenge;
The flexibility of his most anger,
Even in the main career and fury of it,   35
When any object of desertful pity
Offers itself to him; his sweet disposure,
As much abhorring to behold as do
Any unnatural and bloody action;
His just contempt of jesters, parasites,   40
Servile observers, and polluted tongues:
In short, this Senecal man is found in him,
He may with heaven's immortal powers compare,
To whom the day and fortune equal are;

Come fair or foul, whatever chance can fall,   45
Fix'd in himself, he still is one to all.
    Hen. Shows he to others thus ?
    Omnes.   To all that know him.
    Hen. And apprehend I this man for a traitor ?
    Guise. These are your Machiavellian villains,
Your bastard Teucers, that, their mischiefs done,   50
Run to your shield for shelter, Cacusses
That cut their too large murtherous thieveries
To their dens' length still : woe be to that state
Where treachery guards, and ruin makes men great !
    Hen. Go, take my letters for him, and release him.   55
    Omnes. Thanks to your Highness ! Ever live your High-
      ness !   *Exeunt [all but* Baligny]
    Bal. Better a man were buried quick, than live
A property for state, and spoil to thrive   *Exit*

[SCENA QUINTA

On the Road to Paris]

Enter Clermont, Maillard, Chalon, *with* Soldiers

    Mail. We joy you take a chance so ill, so well.
    Cler. Who ever saw me differ in acceptance
Of either fortune ?
    Chal.   What, love bad like good !
How should one learn that ?
    Cler.   To love nothing outward,
Or not within our own powers to command ;   5
And so being sure of everything we love,
Who cares to lose the rest ? If any man
Would neither live nor die in his free choice,
But as he sees necessity will have it
(Which if he would resist, he strives in vain)   10
What can come near him, that he doth not [will,]
And if in worst events his will be done,
How can the best be better ? All is one.
    Mail. Methinks 'tis pretty.
    Cler.   Put no difference
If you have this, or not this ; but as children   15
Playing at quoits, ever regard their game,
And care not for their quoits, so let a man

The things themselves that touch him not esteem,
But his free power in well disposing them.
   Chal.   Pretty, from toys !
   Cler.   Methinks this double distich   20
Seems prettily too to stay superfluous longings :
' Not to have want, what riches doth exceed ?
Not to be subject, what superior thing ?
He that to nought aspires, doth nothing need ;
Who breaks no law is subject to no king '.   25
   Mail.   This goes to mine ear well, I promise you.
   Chal.   O, but 'tis passing hard to stay one thus.
   Cler.   'Tis so ; rank custom raps men so beyond it ;
And as 'tis hard so well men's doors to bar
To keep the cat out, and th' adulterer ;   30
So 'tis as hard to curb affections so
We let in nought to make them overflow.
And as of Homer's verses many critics
On those stand, of which Time's old moth hath eaten
The first or last feet, and the perfect parts   35
Of his unmatched poem sink beneath,
With upright gasping and sloth dull as death :
So the unprofitable things of life,
And those we cannot compass, we affect ;
All that doth profit, and we have, neglect ;   40
Like covetous and basely getting men,
That, gathering much, use never what they keep ;
But for the least they lose, extremely weep.
   Mail.   This pretty talking, and our horses walking
Down this steep hill, spends time with equal profit.   45
   Cler.   'Tis well bestow'd on ye ; meat and men sick
Agree like this and you : and yet even this
Is th' end of all skill, power, wealth, all that is.
   Chal.   I long to hear, sir, how your mistress takes this.

Enter Aumale *with a cabinet*

   Mail.   We soon shall know it ; see Aumale return'd   50
   Aum.   Ease to your bands, sir !
   Cler.   Welcome, worthy friend !
   Chal.   How took his noblest mistress your sad message ?
   Aum.   As great rich men take sudden poverty.
I never witness'd a more noble love,
Nor a more ruthful sorrow : I well wish'd   55
Some other had been master of my message.

Mail.   Y' are happy, sir, in all things, but this one
Of your unhappy apprehension.
Cler.   This is to me, compar'd with her much moan,
As one tear is to her whole passion.   60
Aum.   Sir, she commends her kindest service to you,
And this rich cabinet.
Chal.   O happy man !
This may enough hold to redeem your bands.
Cler.   These clouds, I doubt not, will be soon blown over.

Enter Baligny *with his discharge*, Renel, *and others*

Aum.   Your hope is just and happy ; see, sir, both,   65
In both the looks of these.
Bal.   Here's a discharge
For this your prisoner, my good Lord Lieutenant.
Mail.   Alas, sir ! I usurp that style, enforc'd,
And hope you know it was not my aspiring.
Bal.   Well, sir, my wrong aspir'd past all men's hopes.   70
Mail.   I sorrow for it, sir.
Ren.   You see, sir, there
Your prisoner's discharge autentical.
Mail.   It is, sir, and I yield it him with gladness.
Bal.   Brother, I brought you down to much good purpose.
Cler.   Repeat not that, sir ; the amends makes all.   75
Ren.   I joy in it, my best and worthiest friend ;
O y'have a princely fautor of the Guise.
Bal.   I think I did my part too.
Ren   Well, sir, all
Is in the issue well : and, worthiest friend,
Here's from your friend, the Guise ; here from the Countess,
Your brother's mistress, [*giving letters*], the contents whereof 80
I know, and must prepare you now to please
Th' unrested spirit of your slaughter'd brother,
If it be true, as you imagin'd once
His apparition show'd it ; the complot   85
Is now laid sure betwixt us ; therefore haste
Both to your great friend (who hath some use weighty
For your repair to him) and to the Countess,
Whose satisfaction is no less important.
Cler.   I see all, and will haste as it importeth ;   90
And, good friend, since I must delay a little
My wish'd attendance on my noblest mistress,
Excuse me to her, with return of this,

And endless protestation of my service ;
And now become as glad a messenger   95
As you were late a woful.

   Aum.   Happy change !
I ever will salute thee with my service.   *Exit*

   Bal.   Yet more news, brother ; the late jesting Monsieur
Makes now your brother's dying prophecy equal
At all parts, being dead as he presag'd.   100

   Ren.   Heaven shield the Guise from seconding that truth,
With what he likewise prophesied on him.

   Cler.   It hath enough, 'twas grac'd with truth in one ;
To th' other falsehood and confusion !
Lead to th' Court, sir.

   Bal.   You I'll lead no more,   105
It was too ominous and foul before.   *Exeunt*

FINIS ACTUS QUARTI

ACTUS QUINTI SCENA PRIMA

[A Room in the House of Guise]

Ascendit Umbra Bussy

   Umb.   Up from the chaos of eternal night
(To which the whole digestion of the world
Is now returning) once more I ascend,
And bide the cold damp of this piercing air,
To urge the justice whose almighty word   5
Measures the bloody acts of impious men
With equal penance, who in th' act itself
Includes th' infliction, which like chained shot
Batter together still ; though as the thunder
Seems, by men's duller hearing than their sight,   10
To break a great time after lightning forth,
Yet both at one time tear the labouring cloud,
So men think penance of their ills is slow,
Though th' ill and penance still together go.
Reform, ye ignorant men, your manless lives,   15
Whose laws ye think are nothing but your lusts,
When leaving but for supposition' sake
The body of felicity, religion
(Set in the midst of Christendom, and her head
Cleft to her bosom, one half one way swaying,   20
Another th' other), all the Christian world

And all her laws, whose observation
Stands upon faith, above the power of reason—
Leaving (I say) all these, this might suffice
To fray ye from your vicious swinge in ill,   25
And set you more on fire to do more good,
That since the world (as which of you denies ?)
Stands by proportion, all may thence conclude
That all the joints and nerves sustaining nature
As well may break, and yet the world abide,   30
As any one good unrewarded die,
Or any one ill scape his penalty.   *The* Ghost *stands close*

Enter Guise, Clermont

Guise.   Thus (friend) thou seest how all good men would thrive,
Did not the good thou prompt'st me with prevent
The jealous ill pursuing them in others.   35
But now thy dangers are dispatch'd, note mine :
Hast thou not heard of that admired voice
That at the barricadoes spake to me
(No person seen), ' Let's lead my lord to Rheims ' ?
   Cler.   Nor could you learn the person ?
   Guise.   By no means.   40
   Cler.   'Twas but your fancy, then, a waking dream :
For as in sleep, which binds both th' outward senses,
And the sense common too, th' imagining power
(Stirr'd up by forms hid in the memory's store,
Or by the vapours of o'erflowing humours   45
In bodies full and foul, and mix'd with spirits)
Feigns many strange, miraculous images,
In which act it so painfully applies
Itself to those forms that the common sense
It actuates with his motion, and thereby   50
Those fictions true seem, and have real act :
So, in the strength of our conceits awake,
The cause alike doth [oft] like fictions make.
   Guise.   Be what it will, 'twas a presage of something
Weighty and secret, which th' advertisements   55
I have receiv'd from all parts, both without
And in this kingdom, as from Rome and Spain,
[Lorraine] and Savoy, gives me cause to think,
All writing that our plot's catastrophe,
For propagation of the Catholic cause,   60

Will bloody prove, dissolving all our counsels.
  Cler. Retire, then, from them all.
  Guise.   I must not do so.
The Archbishop of Lyons tells me plain
I shall be said then to abandon France
In so important an occasion ;   65
And that mine enemies (their profit making
Of my faint absence) soon would let that fall,
That all my pains did to this height exhale.
  Cler. Let all fall that would rise unlawfully :
Make not your forward spirit in virtue's right   70
A property for vice, by thrusting on
Further than all your powers can fetch you off.
It is enough, your will is infinite
To all things virtuous and religious,
Which, within limits kept, may without danger   75
Let virtue some good from your graces gather.
Avarice of all is ever nothing's father.
  Umb. [*advancing*] Danger (the spur of all great minds)
    is ever
The curb to your tame spirits ; you respect not
(With all your holiness of life and learning)   80
More than the present, like illiterate vulgars ;
Your mind (you say) kept in your flesh's bounds,
Shows that man's will must rul'd be by his power :
When (by true doctrine) you are taught to live
Rather without the body than within,   85
And rather to your God still than yourself ;
To live to Him, is to do all things fitting
His image, in which, like Himself, we live ;
To be His image is to do those things
That make us deathless, which by death is only   90
Doing those deeds that fit eternity ;
And those deeds are the perfecting that justice
That makes the world last, which proportion is
Of punishment and wreak for every wrong,
As well as for right a reward as strong.   95
Away, then ! Use the means thou hast to right
The wrong I suffer'd. What corrupted law
Leaves unperform'd in kings, do thou supply,
And be above them all in dignity.   *Exit*
  Guise. Why stand'st thou still thus, and apply'st thine ears 100
And eyes to nothing ?

Cler.   Saw you nothing here ?
Guise.   Thou dream'st awake now ; what was here to see ?
Cler.   My brother's spirit, urging his revenge.
Guise.   Thy brother's spirit !   Pray thee mock me not.
Cler.   No, by my love and service !
Guise.   Would he rise,   105
And not be thund'ring threats against the Guise ?
    Cler.   You make amends for enmity to him
With ten parts more love and desert of me ;
And as you make your hate to him no let
Of any love to me, no more bears he   110
(Since you to me supply it) hate to you.
Which reason and which justice is perform'd
In spirits ten parts more than fleshy men ;
To whose fore-sights our acts and thoughts lie open :
And therefore, since he saw the treachery   115
Late practis'd by my brother Baligny,
He would not honour his hand with the justice
(As he esteems it) of his blood's revenge,
To which my sister needs would have him sworn,
Before she would consent to marry him.   120
    Guise.   O Baligny !—Who would believe there were
A man, that (only since his looks are rais'd
Upwards, and have but sacred heaven in sight)
Could bear a mind so more than devilish
As, for the painted glory of the countenance,   125
Flitting in kings, doth good for nought esteem,
And the more ill he does, the better seem ?
    Cler.   We easily may believe it, since we see
In this world's practice few men better be.
Justice to live doth nought but justice need,   130
But policy must still on mischief feed.
Untruth, for all his ends, truth's name doth sue in ;
None safely live but those that study ruin.
A good man happy is a common good ;
Ill men advanc'd live of the common blood.   135
    Guise.   But this thy brother's spirit startles me,
These spirits seld or never haunting men
But some mishap ensues.
    Cler.   Ensue what can ;
Tyrants may kill, but never hurt a man ;
All to his good makes, spite of death and hell.   140

Enter Aumale

Aum.   All the desert of good renown, your Highness !.
Guise.   Welcome, Aumale !
Cler.   My good friend, friendly welcome !
How took my noblest mistress the chang'd news ?
  Aum.   It came too late, sir ; for those loveliest eyes
(Through which a soul look'd so divinely loving)   145
Tears nothing uttering her distress enough,
She wept quite out, and like two falling stars
Their dearest sights quite vanish'd with her tears.
  Cler.   All good forbid it !
  Guise.   What events are these ?
  Cler.   All must be borne, my lord ; and yet this chance   150
Would willingly enforce a man to cast off
All power to bear with comfort, since he sees
In this our comforts made our miseries.
  Guise.   How strangely thou art lov'd of both the sexes ;
Yet thou lov'st neither, but the good of both.   155
  Cler.   In love of women, my affection first
Takes fire out of the frail parts of my blood ;
Which, till I have enjoy'd, is passionate
Like other lovers ; but, fruition past,
I then love out of judgment, the desert   160
Of her I love still sticking in my heart,
Though the desire and the delight be gone,
Which must chance still, since the comparison
Made upon trial 'twixt what reason loves,
And what affection, makes in me the best   165
Ever preferr'd, what most love, valuing lest.
  Guise.   Thy love being judgment then, and of the mind,
Marry thy worthiest mistress now being blind.
  Cler.   If there were love in marriage, so I would :
But I deny that any man doth love,   170
Affecting wives, maid, widows, any women :
For neither flies love milk, although they drown
In greedy search thereof ; nor doth the bee
Love honey, though the labour of her life
Is spent in gathering it ; nor those that fat   175
O[n] beasts or fowls, do anything therein
For any love : for as when only Nature
Moves men to meat, as far as her power rules,
She doth it with a temperate appetite,

The too much men devour abhorring Nature ;   180
And in our most health is our most disease ;
So, when humanity rules men and women,
'Tis for society confin'd in reason.
But what excites the bed's desire in blood,
By no means justly can be constru'd love ;   185
For when love kindles any knowing spirit,
It ends in virtue and effects divine,
And is in friendship chaste and masculine.
 Guise. Thou shalt my mistress be ; methinks my blood
Is taken up to all love with thy virtues.   190
And howsoever other men despise
These paradoxes strange and too precise,
Since they hold on the right way of our reason,
I could attend them ever. Come, away !
Perform thy brother's thus importun'd wreak ;   195
And I will see what great affairs the King
Hath to employ my counsel, which he seems
Much to desire, and more and more esteems. *Exeunt*

[SCENA SECUNDA

A Room in the Court]

Enter Henry, Baligny *with six of the* Guard

 Hen. Saw you his saucy forcing of my hand
To D'Ambois' freedom ?
 Bal.   Saw, and through mine eyes
Let fire into my heart, that burn'd to bear
An insolence so giantly austere.
 Hen. The more kings bear at subjects' hands, the more   5
Their ling'ring justice gathers, that resembles
The weighty and the goodly-bodied eagle,
Who (being on earth) before her shady wings
Can raise her into air, a mighty way
Close by the ground she runs ; but being aloft,   10
All she commands, she flies at ; and the more
Death in her seres bears, the more time she stays
Her thund'ry stoop from that on which she preys.
 Bal. You must be then more secret in the weight
Of these your shady counsels, who will else   15
Bear (where such sparks fly as the Guise and D'Ambois)

Powder about them. Counsels (as your entrails)
Should be unpierc'd and sound kept; for not those,
Whom you discover, you neglect; but ope
A ruinous passage to your own best hope.   20
  Hen. We have spies set on us, as we on others;
And therefore they that serve us must excuse us,
If what we most hold in our hearts take wind;
Deceit hath eyes that see into the mind.
But this plot shall be quicker than their twinkling,   25
On whose lids Fate with her dead weight shall lie,
And Confidence that lightens ere she die.
Friends of my guard, as ye gave oath to be
True to your Sovereign, keep it manfully;
Your eyes have witness'd oft th' ambition   30
That never made access to me in Guise
But treason ever sparkled in his eyes;
Which if you free us of, our safety shall
You not our subjects but our patrons call.
  Omnes. Our duties bind us; he is now but dead.   35
  Hen. We trust in it, and thank ye. Baligny,
Go lodge their ambush, and thou God, that art
Fautor of princes, thunder from the skies
Beneath his hill of pride this giant Guise.   *Exeunt*

[SCENA TERTIA

A Room in Montsurry's *House*]

Enter Tamyra *with a letter*, Charlotte *in man's attire*

  Tam. I see y'are servant, sir, to my dear sister,
The lady of her loved Baligny.
  Char. Madam, I am bound to her virtuous bounties
For that life which I offer in her service
To the revenge of her renowned brother.   5
  Tam. She writes to me as much, and much desires
That you may be the man, whose spirit she knows
Will cut short off these long and dull delays
Hitherto bribing the eternal Justice!
Which I believe, since her unmatched spirit   10
Can judge of spirits that have her sulphur in them;
But I must tell you that I make no doubt
Her living brother will revenge her dead,

On whom the dead impos'd the task, and he,
I know, will come t'effect it instantly.   15
   Char.   They are but words in him ; believe them not.
   Tam.   See ; this is the vault where he must enter ;
Where now I think he is.

     Enter Renel *at the vault, with the* Countess *being blind*
   Ren.   God save you, lady !
What gentleman is this, with whom you trust
The deadly weighty secret of this hour ?   20
   Tam.   One that yourself will say I well may trust.
   Ren.   Then come up, madam.

                 He helps the Countess *up*
              See here, honour'd lady,
A Countess, that in love's mishap doth equal
At all parts your wrong'd self, and is the mistress
Of your slain servant's brother ; in whose love,   25
For his late treacherous apprehension,
She wept her fair eyes from her ivory brows,
And would have wept her soul out, had not I
Promis'd to bring her to this mortal quarry,
That by her lost eyes for her servant's love,   30
She might conjure him from this stern attempt,
In which (by a most ominous dream she had)
She knows his death fix'd, and that never more
Out of this place the sun shall see him live.
   Char.   I am provided, then, to take his place   35
And undertaking on me.
   Ren.   You, sir ! Why ?
   Char.   Since I am charg'd so by my mistress
His mournful sister.
   Tam.   See her letter, sir.   *He reads*
Good madam, I rue your fate more than mine,
And know not how to order these affairs,   40
They stand on such occurrents.
   Ren.   This, indeed,
I know to be your lady mistress' hand,
And know, besides, his brother will and must
Endure no hand in this revenge but his.

        Enter Umbra Bussy
   Umb.   Away, dispute no more ; get up and see !   45
Clermont must author this just tragedy.

Count.   Who's that ?
Ren.   The spirit of Bussy.
Tam.   O, my servant !
Let us embrace.
Umb.   Forbear ! The air, in which
My figure's likeness is impress'd, will blast ;
Let my revenge for all loves satisfy,   50
In which, dame, fear not, Clermont shall not die :
No word dispute more ; up, and see th' event.
                                        Exeunt Ladies
Make the guard sure, Renel ; and then the doors
Command to make fast when the Earl is in.   *Exit* Renel
The black soft-footed hour is now on wing,   55
Which, for my just wreak, ghosts shall celebrate
With dances dire and of infernal state.   *Exit*

[SCENA QUARTA

An Ante-room in the Palace]

Enter Guise

Guise.   Who says that death is natural, when nature
Is with the only thought of it dismay'd ?
I have had lotteries set up for my death,
And I have drawn beneath my trencher one,
Knit in my handkerchief another lot,   5
The word being, ' Y'are a dead man if you enter ' ;
And these words this imperfect blood and flesh
Shrink at in spite of me, their solid'st part
Melting like snow within me with cold fire :
I hate myself, that, seeking to rule kings,   10
I cannot curb my slave.   Would any spirit,
Free, manly, princely, wish to live to be
Commanded by this mass of slavery,
Since reason, judgment, resolution,
And scorn of what we fear, will yield to fear ?   15
While this same sink of sensuality swells,
Who would live sinking in it, and not spring
Up to the stars, and leave this carrion here
For wolves and vultures, and for dogs to tear ?
O Clermont d'Ambois, wert thou here to chide   20
This softness from my flesh, far as my reason,

Far as my resolution not to stir
One foot out of the way, for death and hell !
Let my false man by falsehood perish here ;
There's no way else to set my true man clear.   25

Enter Messenger

   Mes. The King desires your Grace to come to Council.
   Guise. I come. It cannot be : he will not dare
To touch me with a treachery so profane.
Would Clermont now were here, to try how he
Would lay about him, if this plot should be :   30
Here would be tossing souls into the sky.
Who ever knew blood sav'd by treachery ?
Well, I must on, and will ; what should I fear ?
Not against two Alcides ? Against two,
And Hercules to friend, the Guise will go.   35

He takes up the arras, and the Guard *enters upon him : he draws*
Hold, murtherers ! So then, this is confidence
                    They strike him down
In greatness, not in goodness : where is the King ?

The King *comes in sight with* Epernon, Soissons, *and others*
Let him appear to justify his deed
In spite of my betray'd wounds, ere my soul
Take her flight through them, and my tongue hath strength   40
To urge his tyranny.
   Hen.   See, sir, I am come
To justify it before men, and God,
Who knows with what wounds in my heart for woe
Of your so wounded faith I made these wounds,
Forc'd to it by an insolence of force   45
To stir a stone ; nor is a rock, oppos'd
To all the billows of the churlish sea,
More beat and eaten with them than was I
With your ambitious mad idolatry ;
And this blood I shed is to save the blood   50
Of many thousands.
   Guise.   That's your white pretext,
But you will find one drop of blood shed lawless
Will be the fountain to a purple sea :
The present lust and shift made for kings' lives
Against the pure form and just power of law,   55

Will thrive like shifters' purchases ; there hangs
A black star in the skies, to which the sun
Gives yet no light, will rain a poison'd shower
Into your entrails, that will make you feel
How little safety lies in treacherous steel.   60
   Hen. Well, sir, I'll bear it ; y' have a brother too,
Bursts with like threats, the scarlet Cardinal :
Seek, and lay hands on him ; and take this hence.
Their bloods, for all you, on my conscience.   *Exit*
   Guise. So, sir, your full swinge take ; mine, death hath
     curb'd.   65
Clermont, farewell, O didst thou see but this !
But it is better ; see by this the ice
Broke to thine own blood, which thou wilt despise,
When thou hear'st mine shed. Is there no friend here
Will bear my love to him ?
   Aum.   I will, my lord.   70
   Guise. Thanks with my last breath : recommend me, then,
To the most worthy of the race of men.
               Dies. Exeunt [*the* guard *with the body*]

[SCENA QUINTA

A Room in Montsurry's *House*]

Enter Montsurry *and* Tamyra

   Mont. Who have you let into my house ?
   Tam.   I ? None.
   Mont. 'Tis false ; I savour the rank blood of foes
In every corner.
   Tam.   That you may do well,
It is the blood you lately shed you smell.
   Mont. 'Sdeath, the vault opes.   *The gulf opens*
   Tam.   What vault ? Hold your sword.   5
           Clermont *ascends*
   Cler. No, let him use it.
   Mont.   Treason, murther, murther !
   Cler. Exclaim not ; 'tis in vain, and base in you,
Being one to only one.
   Mont.   O bloody strumpet !
   Cler. With what blood charge you her ? It may be mine
As well as yours ; there shall not any else   10

Enter or touch you ; I confer no guards,
Nor imitate the murtherous course you took ;
But single here will have my former challenge
Now answer'd single ; not a minute more
My brother's blood shall stay for his revenge,   15
If I can act it ; if not, mine shall add
A double conquest to you, that alone
Put it to fortune now, and use no odds.
Storm not, nor beat yourself thus 'gainst the doors,
Like to a savage vermin in a trap ;   20
All doors are sure made, and you cannot scape
But by your valour.

    Mont.   No, no ; come and kill me.

                            [Throws himself down]

    Cler. If you will die so like a beast, you shall ;
But when the spirit of a man may save you,
Do not so shame man, and a nobleman.   25

    Mont. I do not show this baseness that I fear thee,
But to prevent and shame thy victory,
Which of one base is base, and so I'll die.

    Cler. Here, then.   *[Offers to kill* Montsurry]

    Mont.   Stay, hold ! One thought hath harden'd me ;

                              He starts up

And since I must afford thee victory,   30
It shall be great and brave, if one request
Thou wilt admit me.

    Cler.   What's that ?

    Mont.   Give me leave
To fetch and use the sword thy brother gave me
When he was bravely giving up his life.

    Cler. No, I'll not fight against my brother's sword ;   35
Not that I fear it, but since 'tis a trick
For you to show your back.

    Mont.   By all truth, no :
Take but my honourable oath, I will not.

    Cler. Your honourable oath ! Plain truth no place has
Where oaths are honourable.

    Tam.   Trust not his oath.   40
He will lie like a lapwing ; when she flies
Far from her sought nest, still ' Here 'tis ', she cries.

    Mont. Out on thee, dam of devils ! I will quite
Disgrace thy brave[r']s conquest, die, not fight. *Lies down*

    Tam. Out on my fortune, to wed such an abject !   45

Now is the people's voice the voice of God ;
He that to wound a woman vaunts so much
(As he did me), a man dares never touch.

    Cler. Revenge your wounds now, madam ; I resign him
Up to your full will, since he will not fight.   50
First you shall torture him (as he did you,
And Justice wills), and then pay I my vow.
Here, take this poniard.

    Mont.   Sink earth, open heaven,
And let fall vengeance !

    Tam.   Come, sir ; good sir, hold him.

    Mont. O, shame of women, whither art thou fled !   55

    Cler. Why (good my lord), is it a greater shame
For her than you ? Come, I will be the bands
You us'd to her, profaning her fair hands.

    Mont. No, sir ; I'll fight now, and the terror be
Of all you champions to such as she.   60
I did but thus far dally : now observe.
O all you aching foreheads that have robb'd
Your hands of weapons and your hearts of valour,
Join in me all your rages and rebutters,
And into dust ram this same race of furies ;   65
In this one relic of the [D']Ambois gall,
In his one purple soul shed, drown it all.   *Fight*
Now give me breath a while.

    Cler.   Receive it freely.

    Mont. What think y'o' this now ?

    Cler.   It is very noble,
Had it been free, at least, and of yourself ;   70
And thus we see (where valour most doth vaunt)
What 'tis to make a coward valiant.

    Mont. Now I shall grace your conquest.

    Cler.   That you shall.

    Mont. If you obtain it.

    Cler.   True, sir, 'tis in fortune.

    Mont. If you were not a D'Ambois, I would scarce   75
Change lives with you, I feel so great a change
In my tall spirits ; breath'd, I think, with the breath
A D'Ambois breathes here ; and Necessity
(With whose point now prick'd on, and so, whose help
My hands may challenge), that doth all men conquer,   80
If she except not you of all men only,
May change the case here.

Cler.   True, as you are chang'd ;
Her power, in me urg'd, makes y'another man
Than yet you ever were.
    Mont.   Well, I must on.
    Cler. Your lordship must by all means.
    Mont.   Then at all.   85
            Fights, and D'Ambois *hurts him*

        [*Enter* Renel, *the* Countess *and*] Charlotte *above*

    Char. Death of my father, what a shame is this !
Stick in his hands thus ?
    Ren. [*trying to stop her*].   Gentle sir, forbear.
    Count. Is he not slain yet ?   [Charlotte] *gets down*
    Ren.   No, madam, but hurt
In divers parts of him.
    Mont.   Y'have given it me,
And yet I feel life for another veney.   90

                Enter Charlotte [*below*]

    Cler. [*To* Charlotte] What would you, sir ?
    Char.   I would perform this combat.
    Cler. Against which of us ?
    Char.   I care not much if 'twere
Against thyself : thy sister would have sham'd
To have thy brother's wreak with any man
In single combat stick so in her fingers.   95
    Cler. My sister ? Know you her ?
    Tam.   Ay, sir, she sent him
With this kind letter to perform the wreak
Of my dear servant.
    Cler.   Now, alas, good sir !
Think you you could do more ?
    Char.   Alas ; I do !
And wer't not I, fresh, sound, should charge a man   100
Weary and wounded, I would long ere this
Have prov'd what I presume on.
    Cler.   Y'have a mind
Like to my sister, but have patience now ;
If next charge speed not, I'll resign to you.
    Mont. [*To* Clermont] Pray thee, let him decide it.
    Cler.   No, my lord,   105
I am the man in fate, and since so bravely

Your lordship stands me, scape but one more charge,
And, on my life, I'll set your life at large.
   Mont.   Said like a D'Ambois, and if now I die,
Sit joy and all good on thy victory !   *Fights and falls down* 110
Farewell, I heartily forgive thee ;   wife,
And thee ;   let penitence spend thy rest of life.
             He gives his hand to Clermont *and his wife*
   Cler.   Noble and Christian !
   Tam.   O, it breaks my heart !
   Cler.   And should ;   for all faults found in him before,
These words, this end, makes full amends and more.   115
Rest, worthy soul ;   and with it the dear spirit
Of my lov'd brother rest in endless peace !
Soft lie thy bones, Heaven be your soul's abode,
And to your ashes be the earth no load !

Music, and the Ghost of Bussy *enters, leading the Ghosts of the*
     Guise, Monsieur, Cardinal Guise, *and* Chatillon ;   *they*
     dance about the dead body, and exeunt.

   Cler.   How strange is this ! The Guise amongst these spirits, 120
And his great brother Cardinal, both yet living !
And that the rest with them with joy thus celebrate
This our revenge !   This certainly presages
Some instant death both to the Guise and Cardinal.
That the Chatillon's ghost too should thus join   125
In celebration of this just revenge,
With Guise, that bore a chief stroke in his death,
It seems that now he doth approve the act,
And these true shadows of the Guise and Cardinal,
Fore-running thus their bodies, may approve   130
That all things to be done, as here we live,
Are done before all times in th' other life.
That spirits should rise in these times yet are fables ;
Though learned'st men hold that our sensive spirits
A little time abide about the graves   135
Of their deceased bodies, and can take
In cold condens'd air the same forms they had
When they were shut up in this body's shade.

               Enter Aumale

   Aum.   O sir, the Guise is slain !
   Cler.   Avert it, heaven !

Aum.   Sent for to Council, by the King, an ambush   140
(Lodg'd for the purpose) rush'd on him, and took
His princely life ; who sent (in dying then)
His love to you, as to the best of men.
   Cler.   The worst, and most accursed of things creeping
On earth's sad bosom.   Let me pray ye all   145
A little to forbear, and let me use
Freely mine own mind in lamenting him.
I'll call ye straight again.
   Aum.   We will forbear,
And leave you free, sir.   *Exeunt*
   Cler.   Shall I live, and he
Dead, that alone gave means of life to me ?   150
There's no disputing with the acts of kings,
Revenge is impious on their sacred persons :
And could I play the worldling (no man loving
Longer than gain is reap'd, or grace from him)
I should survive, and shall be wonder'd at   155
Though (in mine own hands being) I end with him :
But friendship is the cement of two minds,
As of one man the soul and body is,
Of which one cannot sever, but the other
Suffers a needful separation.   160
   Ren.   I fear your servant, madam, let's descend.
                     Descend Renel *and* Countess
   Cler.   Since I could skill of man, I never liv'd
To please men worldly, and shall I in death,
Respect their pleasures, making such a jar
Betwixt my death and life, when death should make   165
The consort sweetest, th' end being proof and crown
To all the skill and worth we truly own ?
Guise, O my lord, how shall I cast from me
The bands and coverts hind'ring me from thee ?
The garment or the cover of the mind,   170
The human soul is ; of the soul, the spirit
The proper robe is ; of the spirit, the blood ;
And of the blood, the body is the shroud.
With that must I begin then to unclothe,
And come at th' other.   Now, then, as a ship,   175
Touching at strange and far-removed shores,
Her men ashore go, for their several ends,
Fresh water, victuals, precious stones, and pearl,
All yet intentive (when the master calls,

The ship to put off ready) to leave all   180
Their greediest labours, lest they there be left
To thieves or beasts, or be the country's slaves :
So, now my master calls, my ship, my venture,
All in one bottom put, all quite put off,
Gone under sail, and I left negligent,   185
To all the horrors of the vicious time,
The far-remov'd shores to all virtuous aims,
None favouring goodness, none but he respecting
Piety or manhood—shall I here survive,
Not cast me after him into the sea,   190
Rather than here live, ready every hour
To feed thieves, beasts, and be the slave of power ?
I come, my lord ! Clermont, thy creature, comes.

                                        He kills himself

Enter Aumale, Tamyra, Charlotte

   Aum.   What, lie and languish, Clermont ? Cursed man,
To leave him here thus ! He hath slain himself.   195
   Tam.   Misery on misery ! O me, wretched dame
Of all that breathe ! All heaven turn all his eyes
In hearty envy thus on one poor dame !
   Char.   Well done, my brother ! I did love thee ever,
But now adore thee : loss of such a friend   200
None should survive, of such a brother [none] ;
With my false husband live, and both these slain !
Ere I return to him, I'll turn to earth.

Enter Renel, *leading the* Countess

   Ren.   Horror of human eyes ! O Clermont d'Ambois !
Madam, we stay'd too long ; your servant's slain.   205
   Count.   It must be so ; he liv'd but in the Guise,
As I in him. O follow, life, mine eyes !
   Tam.   Hide, hide thy snaky head ! To cloisters fly,
In penance pine ! Too easy 'tis to die.
   Char.   It is. In cloisters, then, let's all survive.   210
Madam, since wrath nor grief can help these fortunes,
Let us forsake the world in which they reign,
And for their wish'd amends to God complain.
   Count.   'Tis fit and only needful : lead me on,
In heaven's course comfort seek, in earth is none.   215

                                        Exeunt

Enter Henry, Epernon, Soissons, *and others*

Hen.   We came indeed too late, which much I rue,
And would have kept this Clermont as my crown.
Take in the dead, and make this fatal room
(The house shut up) the famous D'Ambois tomb.

Exeunt [*with the bodies*]

FINIS

THE CONSPIRACY AND TRAGEDY
OF
CHARLES DUKE OF BYRON

The Conspiracy and Tragedy

of

Charles Duke of Byron

TO

MY HONOURABLE AND CONSTANT FRIEND,

SIR THO: WALSINGHAM, KNIGHT;

AND TO

MY MUCH LOVED FROM HIS BIRTH, THE RIGHT

TOWARD AND WORTHY GENTLEMAN HIS SON,

THOMAS WALSINGHAM, ESQUIRE

Sir, Though I know you ever stood little affected to these unprofitable rites of Dedication (which disposition in you hath made me hitherto dispense with your right in my other impressions), yet, lest the world may repute it a neglect in me of so ancient and worthy a friend, having heard your approbation of these in their presentment, I could not but prescribe them with your name; and that my affection may extend to your posterity, I have entitled to it, herein, your hope and comfort in your generous son; whom I doubt not that most reverenced Mother of manly sciences, to whose instruction your virtuous care commits him, will so profitably initiate in her learned labours, that they will make him flourish in his riper life over the idle lives of our ignorant gentlemen, and enable him to supply the honourable places of your name; extending your years and his right noble mother's, in the true comforts of his virtues, to the sight of much and most happy progeny ; which most affectionately wishing, and dividing these poor dismembered poems betwixt you, I desire to live still in your graceful loves, and ever

The most assured at your commandments,

GEORGE CHAPMAN

PROLOGUS

WHEN the uncivil civil wars of France
Had pour'd upon the country's beaten breast
Her batter'd cities, press'd her under hills
Of slaughter'd carcasses, set her in the mouths
Of murtherous breaches, and made pale Despair,   5
Leave her to Ruin, through them all, Byron
Stepp'd to her rescue, took her by the hand;
Pluck'd her from under her unnatural press,
And set her shining in the height of peace.
And now new cleans'd from dust, from sweat, and blood,   10
And dignified with title of a Duke,
As when in wealthy Autumn his bright star
Wash'd in the lofty ocean, thence ariseth,
Illustrates heaven, and all his other fires
Out-shines and darkens, so admir'd Byron   15
All France exempted from comparison.
He touch'd heaven with his lance, nor yet was touch'd
With hellish treachery; his country's love
He yet thirsts, not the fair shades of himself;
Of which empoison'd spring when Policy drinks,   20
He bursts in growing great, and, rising, sinks:
Which now behold in our conspirator,
And see in his revolt how honour's flood
Ebbs into air, when men are great, not good.

DRAMATIS PERSONAE

Henry IV, *King of France.*
Albert, *Archduke* of *Austria.*
The Duke of Savoy
The Duke of Byron
D'Auvergne, *a friend of Byron*
Nemours,
Soissons,
D'Aumont, }*French Noblemen*
Crequi,
Epernon,
Bellièvre, }*French Commis-*
Brulart, }*sioners at Brussels*
D'Aumale, *a French exile at Brussels*
Picoté, *a Frenchman in the Spanish service at Brussels*

Orange, }*Noblemen in the*
Mansfield, }*Archduke's Court*
Roiseau, *a French gentleman attending the Embassy*
La Fin, *a ruined French noble*
Roncas, *the Ambassador of Savoy at Paris*
Rochette, }*Lords attending the*
Breton, }*Duke of Savoy*
Vitry, *Captain of the Guard*
Janin, *a French minister*
La Brosse, *an astrologer*

Three Ladies *at the French Court*

ACTUS I SCENA I

[Paris.   A Room in the Court]

Enter Savoy, Roncas, Rochette, Breton

Sav. I would not for half Savoy but have bound
France to some favour by my personal presence
More than your self, my Lord Ambassador,
Could have obtain'd ; for all ambassadors,
You know, have chiefly these instructions :   5
To note the state and chief sway of the Court
To which they are employ'd ; to penetrate
The heart and marrow of the King's designs,
And to observe the countenances and spirits
Of such as are impatient of rest,   10
And wring beneath some private discontent :
But, past all these, there are a number more
Of these state criticisms that our personal view
May profitably make, which cannot fall
Within the powers of our instruction   15
To make you comprehend ; I will do more
With my mere shadow than you with your persons.
All you can say against my coming here
Is that, which I confess, may for the time
Breed strange affections in my brother Spain ;   20
But when I shall have time to make my cannons
The long-tongued heralds of my hidden drifts,
Our reconcilement will be made with triumphs.
   Ron. If not, your Highness hath small cause to care,
Having such worthy reason to complain   25
Of Spain's cold friendship and his ling'ring succours,
Who only entertains your griefs with hope
To make your med'cine desperate.
   Roch.   My lord knows
The Spanish gloss too well ; his form, stuff, lasting,

And the most dangerous conditions   30
He lays on them with whom he is in league.
Th' injustice in the most unequal dower
Given with th' Infanta, whom my lord espous'd,
Compar'd with that her elder sister had,
May tell him how much Spain's love weighs to him,   35
When of so many globes and sceptres held
By the great King, he only would bestow
A portion but of six-score thousand crowns
In yearly pension with his Highness' wife,
When the Infanta, wedded by the Archduke,   40
Had the Franche-Comté, and Low Provinces.
    Bret. We should not set these passages of spleen
'Twixt Spain and Savoy : to the weaker part
More good by suff'rance grows than deeds of heart ;
The nearer princes are, the further off   45
In rites of friendship ; my advice had never
Consented to this voyage of my lord,
In which he doth endanger Spain's whole loss,
For hope of some poor fragment here in France.
    Sav. My hope in France you know not, though my
        counsel ;   50
And for my loss of Spain, it is agreed
That I should slight it ; oft-times princes' rules
Are like the chymical philosophers' ;
Leave me then to mine own projection
In this our thrifty alchemy of state ;   55
Yet help me thus far, you that have been here
Our Lord Ambassador, and in short inform me
What spirits here are fit for our designs.
    Ron. The new-created Duke Byron is fit,
Were there no other reason for your presence,   60
To make it worthy ; for he is a man
Of matchless valour, and was ever happy
In all encounters, which were still made good
With an unwearied sense of any toil,
Having continued fourteen days together   65
Upon his horse ; his blood is not voluptuous,
Nor much inclined to women ; his desires
Are higher than his state, and his deserts
Not much short of the most he can desire
If they be weigh'd with what France feels by them :
He is past measure glorious ; and that humour   70

Is fit to feed his spirits, whom it possesseth,
With faith in any error, chiefly where
Men blow it up with praise of his perfections ;
The taste whereof in him so soothes his palate,   75
And takes up all his appetite, that oft-times
He will refuse his meat and company
To feast alone with their most strong conceit ;
Ambition also cheek by cheek doth march
With that excess of glory, both sustain'd   80
With an unlimited fancy that the King,
Nor France itself, without him can subsist.
    Sav. He is the man, my lord, I come to win ;
And that supreme intention of my presence
Saw never light till now, which, yet I fear,   85
The politic King suspecting, is the cause,
That he hath sent him so far from my reach,
And made him chief in the commission
Of his ambassage to my brother Archduke,
With whom he is now ; and, as I am told,   90
So entertain'd and fitted in his humour,
That ere I part, I hope he will return
Prepar'd and made the more fit for the physic
That I intend to minister.
    Ron.   My lord,
There is another discontented spirit   95
Now here in Court, that for his brain and aptness
To any course that may recover him
In his declined and litigious state
Will serve Byron, as he were made for him,
In giving vent to his ambitious vein,   100
And that is, de La Fin.
    Sav.   You tell me true,
And him I think you have prepar'd for me.
    Ron. I have, my lord, and doubt not he will prove
Of the yet taintless fortress of Byron
A quick expugner, and a strong abider.   105
    Sav. Perhaps the batt'ry will be brought before him
In this ambassage, for I am assur'd
They set high price of him, and are inform'd
Of all the passages, and means for mines
That may be thought on to his taking in.   110

Enter Henry *and* La Fin

The King comes, and La Fin; the King's aspect
Folded in clouds.

Hen.   I will not have my train
Made a retreat for bankrouts, nor my Court
A hive for drones: proud beggars and true thieves,
That with a forced truth they swear to me   115
Rob my poor subjects, shall give up their arts,
And henceforth learn to live by their deserts;
Though I am grown, by right of birth and arms,
Into a greater kingdom, I will spread
With no more shade than may admit that kingdom   120
Her proper, natural, and wonted fruits;
Navarre shall be Navarre, and France still France:
If one may be the better for the other
By mutual rites, so; neither shall be worse.
Thou art in law, in quarrels, and in debt,   125
Which thou would'st quit with count'nance; borrowing
With thee is purchase, and thou seek'st by me,
In my supportance, now our old wars cease,
To wage worse battles with the arms of peace.

La F.   Peace must not make men cowards, nor keep calm 130
Her pursy regiment with men's smother'd breaths;
I must confess my fortunes are declin'd,
But neither my deservings nor my mind:
I seek but to sustain the right I found
When I was rich, in keeping what is left,   135
And making good my honour as at best,
Though it be hard; man's right to everything
Wanes with his wealth, wealth is his surest king;
Yet Justice should be still indifferent.
The overplus of kings, in all their might,   140
Is but to piece out the defects of right:
And this I sue for, nor shall frowns and taunts
(The common scare-crows of all poor men's suits)
Nor misconstruction that doth colour still
Licentiate justice, punishing good for ill,   145
Keep my free throat from knocking at the sky,
If thunder chid me, for my equity.

Hen.   Thy equity is to be ever banish'd
From Court and all society of noblesse,
Amongst whom thou throw'st balls of all dissension; 150

Thou art at peace with nothing but with war,
Hast no heart but to hurt, and eat'st thy heart,
If it but think of doing any good :
Thou witchest with thy smiles, suck'st blood with praises,
Mock'st all humanity ; society poison'st,   155
Cozen'st with virtue ; with religion
Betray'st and massacrest ; so vile thyself,
That thou suspect'st perfection in others :
A man must think of all the villanies
He knows in all men to decipher thee,   160
That art the centre to impiety :
Away, and tempt me not.
   La F.   But you tempt me,
To what, thou, Sun, be judge, and make him see.   *Exit*
   Sav.   Now by my dearest Marquisate of Saluces,
Your Majesty hath with the greatest life   165
Describ'd a wicked man, or rather thrust
Your arm down through him to his very feet
And pluck'd his inside out, that ever yet
My ears did witness, or turn'd ears to eyes ;
And those strange characters, writ in his face,   170
Which at first sight were hard for me to read,
The doctrine of your speech hath made so plain
That I run through them like my natural language :
Nor do I like that man's aspect, methinks,
Of all looks where the beams of stars have carv'd   175
Their powerful influences ; and (O rare)
What an heroic, more than royal spirit
Bewray'd you in your first speech, that defies
Protection of vile drones that eat the honey
Sweat from laborious virtue, and denies   180
To give those of Navarre, though bred with you,
The benefits and dignities of France.
When little rivers by their greedy currents
(Far far extended from their mother springs)
Drink up the foreign brooks still as they run,   185
And force their greatness, when they come to sea,
And justle with the Ocean for a room,
O how he roars, and takes them in his mouth,
Digesting them so to his proper streams
That they are no more seen, he nothing rais'd   190
Above his usual bounds, yet they devour'd
That of themselves were pleasant, goodly floods.

Hen. I would do best for both, yet shall not be secure,
Till in some absolute heirs my crown be settled ;
There is so little now betwixt aspirers   195
And their great object in my only self,
That all the strength they gather under me
Tempts combat with mine own : I therefore make
Means for some issue by my marriage,
Which with the Great Duke's niece is now concluded,   200
And she is coming ; I have trust in heaven
I am not yet so old, but I may spring,
And then I hope all trait'rous hopes will fade.
  Sav. Else may their whole estates fly, rooted up,
To ignominy and oblivion :   205
And (being your neighbour, servant, and poor kinsman)
I wish your mighty race might multiply,
Even to the period of all empery.
  Hen. Thanks to my princely cousin : this your love
And honour shown me in your personal presence   210
I wish to welcome to your full content ;
The peace now made with your brother Archduke
By Duke Byron, our Lord Ambassador,
I wish may happily extend to you,
And that at his return we may conclude it.   215
  Sav. It shall be to my heart the happiest day
Of all my life, and that life all employ'd
To celebrate the honour of that day.   *Exeunt*

[SCENA II

Brussels.   *A Room in the* Archduke's *Court*]

Enter Roiseau

Rois. The wondrous honour done our Duke Byron
In his ambassage here, in th' Archduke's court,
I fear will taint his loyalty to our King ;
I will observe how they observe his humour
And glorify his valour, and how he   5
Accepts and stands attractive to their ends,
That so I may not seem an idle spot
In train of this ambassage, but return
Able to give our King some note of all,
Worth my attendance ; and see, here's the man,   10

Who (though a Frenchman and in Orleans born,
Serving the Archduke) I do most suspect,
Is set to be the tempter of our Duke;
I'll go where I may see, although not hear.   [*Retires*]

Enter Picoté, *with two others, spreading a carpet*

Pic.   Spread here this history of Catiline,   15
That earth may seem to bring forth Roman spirits
Even to his genial feet, and her dark breast
Be made the clear glass of his shining graces;
We'll make his feet so tender they shall gàll
In all paths but to empire; and therein   20
I'll make the sweet steps of his state begin.

Exit [Picoté *with* Servants]

Loud music, and enter Byron

Byr.   What place is this, what air, what region,
In which a man may hear the harmony
Of all things moving? Hymen marries here
Their ends and uses, and makes me his temple.   25
Hath any man been blessed, and yet liv'd?
The blood turns in my veins; I stand on change,
And shall dissolve in changing; 'tis so full
Of pleasure not to be contain'd in flesh:
To fear a violent good abuseth goodness,   30
'Tis immortality to die aspiring,
As if a man were taken quick to heaven;
What will not hold perfection, let it burst;
What force hath any cannon, not being charg'd,
Or being not discharg'd? To have stuff and form,   35
And to lie idle, fearful, and unus'd,
Nor form nor stuff shows; happy Semele,
That died compress'd with glory! Happiness
Denies comparison of less or more,
And not at most, is nothing: like the shaft   40
Shot at the sun by angry Hercules,
And into shivers by the thunder broken,
Will I be if I burst; and in my heart
This shall be written: 'Yet 'twas high and right'.

Music again

Here too? They follow all my steps with music   45
As if my feet were numerous, and trod sounds
Out of the centre with Apollo's virtue,

That out of every thing his each part touch'd
Struck musical accents ; wheresoe'er I go,
They hide the earth from me with coverings rich,   50
To make me think that I am here in heaven.

Enter Picoté *in haste*

Pic. This way, your Highness.
Byr.   Come they ?
Pic.   Ay, my lord !
                                                   Exeunt

Enter the other Commissioners *of France*, Bellièvre, Brulart,
          [*with*] D'Aumale, Orange

Bel. My Lord d'Aumale, I am exceeding sorry
That your own obstinacy to hold out
Your mortal enmity against the King,   55
When Duke du Maine and all the faction yielded,
Should force his wrath to use the rites of treason
Upon the members of your senseless statue,
Your name and house, when he had lost your person,
Your love and duty.
Bru.   That which men enforce   60
By their own wilfulness, they must endure
With willing patience and without complaint.
D'Aum. I use not much impatience nor complaint,
Though it offends me much to have my name
So blotted with addition of a traitor,   65
And my whole memory with such despite
Mark'd and begun to be so rooted out.
Bru. It was despite that held you out so long,
Whose penance in the King was needful justice.
Bel. Come, let us seek our Duke, and take our leaves   70
Of th' Archduke's grace.   *Exeunt*

Enter Byron *and* Picoté [*above*]

Byr.   Here may we safely breathe ?
Pic. No doubt, my lord ; no stranger knows this way ;
Only the Archduke, and your friend, Count Mansfield,
Perhaps may make their general scapes to you
To utter some part of their private loves   75
Ere your departure.
Byr.   Then I well perceive
To what th' intention of his Highness tends ;
For whose, and others, here, most worthy lords,
I will become, with all my worth, their servant

In any office but disloyalty ;   80
But that hath ever show'd so foul a monster
To all my ancestors and my former life,
That now to entertain it I must wholly
Give up my habit in his contrary,
And strive to grow out of privation.   85
  Pic. My lord, to wear your loyal habit still,
When it is out of fashion, and hath done
Service enough, were rustic misery :
The habit of a servile loyalty
Is reckon'd now amongst privations,   90
With blindness, dumbness, deafness, silence, death ;
All which are neither natures by themselves
Nor substances, but mere decays of form,
And absolute decessions of nature ;
And so 'tis nothing, what shall you then lose ?   95
Your Highness hath a habit in perfection,
And in desert of highest dignities,
Which carve yourself, and be your own rewarder.
No true power doth admit privation
Adverse to him ; or suffers any fellow   100
Join'd in his subject ; you superiors,
It is the nature of things absolute
One to destroy another ; be your Highness
Like those steep hills that will admit no clouds,
No dews, nor least fumes bound about their brows,   105
Because their tops pierce into purest air,
Expert of humour ; or like air itself
That quickly changeth, and receives the sun
Soon as he riseth, everywhere dispersing
His royal splendour, girds it in his beams,   110
And makes itself the body of the light :
Hot, shining, swift, light, and aspiring things,
Are of immortal and celestial nature ;
Cold, dark, dull, heavy, of infernal fortunes
And never aim at any happiness :   115
Your Excellency knows that simple loyalty,
Faith, love, sincerity, are but words, no things,
Merely devis'd for form ; and as the Legate,
Sent from his Holiness to frame a peace
'Twixt Spain and Savoy, labour'd fervently,   120
For common ends, not for the Duke's particular,
To have him sign it ; he again endeavours,

Not for the Legate's pains, but his own pleasure,
To gratify him ; and being at last encounter'd,
Where the flood Ticin enters into Po,   125
They made a kind contention, which of them
Should enter th' other's boat ; one thrust the other ;
One leg was over, and another in ;
And with a fiery courtesy at last
Savoy leaps out into the Legate's arms,   130
And here ends all his love, and th' other's labour :
So shall these terms and impositions,
Express'd before, hold nothing in themselves
Really good, but flourishes of form ;
And further than they make to private ends   135
None wise, or free, their proper use intends.
  Byr. O, 'tis a dangerous and a dreadful thing
To steal prey from a lion, or to hide
A head distrustful in his open'd jaws ;
To trust our blood in others' veins, and hang   140
'Twixt heaven and earth in vapours of their breaths ;
To leave a sure pace on continuate earth,
And force a gate in jumps from tower to tower,
As they do that aspire from height to height :
The bounds of loyalty are made of glass,   145
Soon broke, but can in no date be repair'd ;
And as the Duke d'Aumale, now here in Court,
Flying his country, had his statue torn
Piece-meal with horses, all his goods confiscate,
His arms of honour kick'd about the streets,   150
His goodly house at Annet raz'd to th' earth,
And (for a strange reproach of his foul treason)
His trees about it cut off by their waists ;
So, when men fly the natural clime of truth,
And turn themselves loose out of all the bounds   155
Of justice and the straight way to their ends,
Forsaking all the sure force in themselves
To seek without them that which is not theirs,
The forms of all their comforts are distracted,
The riches of their freedoms forfeited,   160
Their human noblesse sham'd, the mansions
Of their cold spirits eaten down with cares,
And all their ornaments of wit and valour,
Learning, and judgment, cut from all their fruits.

[Enter the Archduke Albert]

Alb. O, here were now the richest prize in Europe,   165
Were he but taken in affection.   *[Embracing* Byron]
Would we might grow together, and be twins
Of either's fortune, or that, still embrac'd,
I were but ring to such a precious stone.

Byr. Your Highness' honours and high bounty shown me   170
Have won from me my voluntary power ;
And I must now move by your eminent will ;
To what particular objects if I know
By this man's intercession, he shall bring
My uttermost answer, and perform betwixt us   175
Reciprocal and full intelligence.

Alb. Even for your own deserved royal good
'Tis joyfully accepted ; use the loves
And worthy admirations of your friends,
That beget vows of all things you can wish,   180
And be what I wish : danger says, no more.   *Exit*

Enter Mansfield, *at another door*
Exit Picoté

Mans.   Your Highness makes the light of this Court stoop
With your so near departure ; I was forc'd
To tender to your Excellence in brief
This private wish, in taking of my leave,   185
That, in some army royal, old Count Mansfield
Might be commanded by your matchless valour
To the supremest point of victory ;
Who vows for that renown all prayer and service :
No more, lest I may wrong you.   *Exit* Mansfield
  Byr.   Thank your lordship.   190

Enter D'Aumale *and* Orange

D'Aum. All majesty be added to your Highness,
Of which I would not wish your breast to bear
More modest apprehension than may tread
The high gait of your spirit, and be known
To be a fit bound for your boundless valour.   195

  Or. So Orange wisheth, and to the deserts
Of your great actions their most royal crown.

Enter Picoté

  Pic. Away, my lord, the lords inquire for you.
                         Exit Byron [*and* Picoté]

Manet Orange, D'Aumale, Roiseau

Or. Would we might win his valour to our part.

D'Aum. 'Tis well prepar'd in his entreaty here,　　　　200
With all state's highest observations;
And to their form and words are added gifts.
He was presented with two goodly horses,
One of which two was the brave beast Pastrana,
With plate of gold, and a much prized jewel,　　　　205
Girdle and hangers set with wealthy stones,
All which were valued at ten thousand crowns;
The other lords had suits of tapestry,
And chains of gold; and every gentleman
A pair of Spanish gloves, and rapier blades:　　　　210
And here ends their entreaty, which I hope
Is the beginning of more good to us
Than twenty thousand times their gifts to them.

Enter [*below*] Albert, Byron, Bellièvre, Mansfield, *with others*

Alb. My lord, I grieve that all the setting forth
Of our best welcome made you more retired;　　　　215
Your chamber hath been more lov'd than our honours,
And therefore we are glad your time of parting
Is come to set you in the air you love:
Commend my service to his Majesty,
And tell him that this day of peace with him　　　　220
I'll hold as holy. All your pains, my lords,
I shall be always glad to gratify
With any love and honour your own hearts
Shall do me grace to wish express'd to you.　　　[*Exeunt*]

Rois. [*advancing*] Here hath been strange demeanour,　225
　　which shall fly
To the great author of this ambassy.　　　　　　[*Exit*]

FINIS ACTUS I

ACTUS II SCENA I

[*A Room in the House of* Nemours *at* Paris]

Enter Savoy, La Fin, Roncas, Rochette, Breton

Sav. Admit no entry, I will speak with none.
Good signior de la Fin, your worth shall find

That I will make a jewel for my cabinet
Of that the King, in surfeit of his store,
Hath cast out as the sweepings of his hall ;　　　5
I told him, having threaten'd you away,
That I did wonder this small time of peace
Could make him cast his armour so securely,
In such as you, and, as 'twere, set the head
Of one so great in counsels on his foot,　　　10
And pitch him from him with such guard[less] strength.

　La F.　He may, perhaps, find he hath pitch'd away
The axletree that kept him on his wheels.

　Sav.　I told him so, I swear, in other terms,
And not with too much note of our close loves,　　　15
Lest so he might have smok'd our practices.

　La F.　To choose his time, and spit his poison on me
Through th' ears and eyes of strangers !
　Sav.　　　　　　　　So I told him,
And more than that, which now I will not tell you :
It rests now then, noble and worthy friend,　　　20
That to our friendship we draw Duke Byron,
To whose attraction there is no such chain
As you can forge and shake out of your brain.

　La F.　I have devis'd the fashion and the weight ;
To valours hard to draw we use retreats ;　　　25
And to pull shafts home, with a good bow-arm
We thrust hard from us : since he came from Flanders
He heard how I was threaten'd with the King,
And hath been much inquisitive to know
The truth of all, and seeks to speak with me ;　　　30
The means he us'd, I answer'd doubtfully,
And with an intimation that I shunn'd him,
Which will, I know, put more spur to his charge ;
And if his haughty stomach be prepar'd
With will to any act for the aspiring　　　35
Of his ambitious aims, I make no doubt
But I shall work him to your Highness' wish.

　Sav.　But undertake it, and I rest assur'd :
You are reported to have skill in magic
And the events of things, at which they reach　　　40
That are in nature apt to overreach ;
Whom the whole circle of the present time,
In present pleasures, fortunes, knowledges,
Cannot contain ; those men, as broken loose

From human limits, in all violent ends   45
Would fain aspire the faculties of fiends;
And in such air breathe his unbounded spirits,
Which therefore well will fit such conjurations:
Attempt him then by flying, close with him,
And bring him home to us, and take my dukedom.   50
    La F.   My best in that, and all things, vows your [servant].
    Sav.   Thanks to my dear friend and the French Ulysses.

                                   Exit Savoy [*cum suis*]

                Enter Byron .

    Byr.   Here is the man.   My honour'd friend, La Fin !
Alone, and heavy countenanc'd ?   On what terms
Stood th' insultation of the King upon you ?   55
    La F.   Why do you ask ?
    Byr.   Since I would know the truth.
    La F.   And when you know it, what ?
    Byr.   I'll judge betwixt you.
And, as I may, make even th' excess of either.
    La F.   Alas ! my lord, not all your loyalty,
Which is in you more than hereditary,   60
Nor all your valour (which is more than human)
Can do the service you may hope on me
In sounding my displeased integrity;
Stand for the King as much in policy
As you have stirr'd for him in deeds of arms,   65
And make yourself his glory, and your country's,
Till you be suck'd as dry and wrought as lean
As my flay'd carcass; you shall never close
With me, as you imagine.
    Byr.   You much wrong me
To think me an intelligencing instrument.   70
    La F.   I know not how your so affected zeal
To be reputed a true-hearted subject
May stretch or turn you; I am desperate;
If I offend you, I am in your power;
I care not how I tempt your conquering fury,   75
I am predestin'd to too base an end
To have the honour of your wrath destroy me,
And be a worthy object for your sword.
I lay my hand and head too at your feet,
As I have ever, here I hold it still;   80
End me directly, do not go about.

Byr. How strange is this ! the shame of his disgrace
Hath made him lunatic.
      La F.   Since the King hath wrong'd me
He thinks I'll hurt myself ; no, no, my lord,
I know that all the kings in Christendom,   85
If they should join in my revenge, would prove
Weak foes to him, still having you to friend ;
If you were gone (I care not if you tell him)
I might be tempted then to right myself.   *Exit*
      Byr. He has a will to me, and dares not show it ;   90
His state decay'd, and he disgrac'd, distracts him.

                Redit La Fin

      La F. Change not my words, my lord ; I only said :
' I might be tempted then to right myself ' ;
Temptation to treason is no treason ;
And that word ' tempted ' was conditional too,   95
' If you were gone ' ; I pray inform the truth.   *Exiturus*
      Byr. Stay, injur'd man, and know I am your friend,
Far from these base and mercenary reaches ;
I am, I swear to you.
      La F.   You may be so ;
And yet you'll give me leave to be La Fin,   100
A poor and expuate humour of the Court ;
But what good blood came out with me, what veins
And sinews of the triumphs now it makes,
I list not vaunt ; yet will I now confess,
And dare assume it, I have power to add   105
To all his greatness, and make yet more fix'd
His bold security. Tell him this, my lord,
And this (if all the spirits of earth and air
Be able to enforce) I can make good ;
If knowledge of the sure events of things,   110
Even from the rise of subjects into kings ;
And falls of kings to subjects, hold a power
Of strength to work it, I can make it good ;
And tell him this too : if in midst of winter
To make black groves grow green, to still the thunder,   115
And cast out able flashes from mine eyes
To beat the lightning back into the skies,
Prove power to do it, I can make it good ;
And tell him this too : if to lift the sea

Up to the stars, when all the winds are still,   120
And keep it calm, when they are most enrag'd ;
To make earth's driest [plains] sweat humorous springs,
To make fix'd rocks walk and loose shadows stand,
To make the dead speak, midnight see the sun,
Mid-day turn mid-night, to dissolve all laws   125
Of nature and of order, argue power
Able to work all, I can make all good :
And all this tell the King.

 Byr.   'Tis more than strange,
To see you stand thus at the rapier's point
With one so kind and sure a friend as I.   130

 La F. Who cannot friend himself is foe to any,
And to be fear'd of all, and that is it
Makes me so scorn'd ; but make me what you can,
Never so wicked and so full of fiends,
I never yet was traitor to my friends :   135
The laws of friendship I have ever held,
As my religion ; and for other laws
He is a fool that keeps them with more care
Than they keep him safe, rich, and popular :
For riches, and for popular respects   140
Take them amongst ye, minions ; but for safety,
You shall not find the least flaw in my arms
To pierce or taint me ; what will great men be
To please the King and bear authority !   *Exit*

 Byr. How fit a sort were this to handsel Fortune !   145
And I will win it though I lose my self ;
Though he prove harder than Egyptian marble,
I'll make him malleable as th' Ophir gold :
I am put off from this dull shore of [ease]
Into industrious and high-going seas ;   150
Where, like Pelides in Scamander's flood,
Up to the ears in surges I will fight,
And pluck French Ilion underneath the waves !
If to be highest still, be to be best,
All works to that end are the worthiest :   155
Truth is a golden ball, cast in our way,
To make us stript by falsehood : and as Spain,
When the hot scuffles of barbarian arms
Smother'd the life of Don Sebastian,
To gild .the leaden rumour of his death   160
Gave for a slaughter'd body, held for his,

A hundred thousand crowns, caused all the state
Of superstitious Portugal to mourn
And celebrate his solemn funerals,
The Moors to conquest thankful feasts prefer,   165
And all made with the carcass of a Switzer :
So in the giantlike and politic wars
Of barbarous greatness, raging still in peace,
Shows to aspire just objects are laid on
With cost, with labour, and with form enough,   170
Which only makes our best acts brook the light,
And their ends had, we think we have their right ;
So worst works are made good with good success,
And so, for kings, pay subjects carcasses.   *Exit*

[SCENA II

A Room in the Court]

Enter Henry, Roiseau

  Hen.   Was he so courted ?
  Rois.   As a city dame,
Brought by her jealous husband to the Court,
Some elder courtiers entertaining him,
While others snatch a favour from his wife :
One starts from this door, from that nook another,   5
With gifts and junkets, and with printed phrase
Steal her employment, shifting place by place
Still as her husband comes : so Duke Byron
Was woo'd and worshipp'd in the Archduke's Court ;
And as th' assistants that your Majesty   10
Join'd in commission with him, or myself,
Or any other doubted eye appear'd,
He ever vanish'd ; and as such a dame,
As we compar'd with him before, being won
To break faith to her husband, lose her fame,   15
Stain both their progenies, and coming fresh
From underneath the burthen of her shame,
Visits her husband with as chaste a brow,
As temperate and confirm'd behaviour,
As she came quitted from confession :   20
So from his scapes would he present a presence,
The practice of his state adultery,

And guilt, that should a graceful bosom strike,
Drown'd in the set lake of a hopeless cheek.

   Hen. It may be he dissembled, or suppose 25
He be a little tainted, men whom virtue
Forms with the stuff of Fortune, great and gracious,
Must needs partake with Fortune in her humour
Of instability, and are like to shafts
Grown crook'd with standing, which to rectify 30
Must twice as much be bow'd another way.
He that hath borne wounds for his worthy parts,
Must for his worst be borne with : we must fit
Our government to men, as men to it :
In old time they that hunted savage beasts 35
Are said to clothe themselves in savage skins ;
They that were fowlers, when they went on fowling,
Wore garments made with wings resembling fowls ;
To bulls we must not show ourselves in red,
Nor to the warlike elephant in white. 40
In all things govern'd, their infirmities
Must not be stirr'd, nor wrought on ; Duke Byron
Flows with adust and melancholy choler,
And melancholy spirits are venomous,
Not to be touch'd, but as they may be cur'd : 45
I therefore mean to make him change the air,
And send him further from those Spanish vapours,
That still bear fighting sulphur in their breasts,
To breathe a while in temperate English air,
Where lips are spic'd with free and loyal counsels, 50
Where policies are not ruinous, but saving ;
Wisdom is simple, valour righteous,
Human, and hating facts of brutish forces ;
And whose grave natures scorn the scoffs of France,
The empty compliments of Italy, 55
The any-way encroaching pride of Spain,
And love men modest, hearty, just, and plain.

[Enter] Savoy, whispering with La Fin

   Sav. [*aside*] I'll sound him for Byron ; and what I find
In the King's depth, I'll draw up, and inform
In excitations to the Duke's revolt, 60
When next I meet with him.
   La F. [*aside*]   It must be done
With praising of the Duke ; from whom the King

Will take to give himself; which, told the Duke,
Will take his heart up into all ambition.
   Sav. [*aside*] I know it, politic friend, and 'tis my purpose.   65
Exit La Fin

Your Majesty hath miss'd a royal sight:
The Duke Byron on his brave beast Pastrana,
Who sits him like a full-sail'd Argosy
Danc'd with a lofty billow, and as snug
Plies to his bearer, both their motions mix'd;   70
And being consider'd in their site together,
They do the best present the state of man
In his first royalty ruling, and of beasts
In their first loyalty serving (one commanding,
And no way being mov'd; the other serving,   75
And no way being compell'd) of all the sights
That ever my eyes witness'd; and they make
A doctrinal and witty hieroglyphic
Of a blest kingdom: to express and teach
Kings to command as they could serve, and subjects   80
To serve as if they had power to command.
   Hen. You are a good old horseman, I perceive,
And still out all the use of that good part;
Your wit is of the true Pierian spring,
That can make anything of anything.   85
   Sav. So brave a subject as the Duke, no king
Seated on earth can vaunt of but your Highness,
So valiant, loyal, and so great in service.
   Hen. No question he sets valour in his height.
And hath done service to an equal pitch,   90
Fortune attending him with fit events,
To all his vent'rous and well-laid attempts.
   Sav. Fortune to him was Juno to Alcides;
For when or where did she but open way,
To any act of his? What stone took he   95
With her help, or without his own lost blood?
What fort won he by her, or was not forc'd?
What victory but 'gainst odds? On what commander
Sleepy or negligent did he ever charge?
What summer ever made she fair to him?   100
What winter not of one continued storm?
Fortune is so far from his creditress
That she owes him much, for in him her looks
Are lovely, modest, and magnanimous,

Constant, victorious ; and in his achievements   105
Her cheeks are drawn out with a virtuous redness,
Out of his eager spirit to victory,
And chaste contention to convince with honour ;
And, I have heard, his spirits have flow'd so high
In all his conflicts against any odds,   110
That, in his charge, his lips have bled with fervour.
How serv'd he at your famous siege of Dreux ?
Where the enemy, assur'd of victory,
Drew out a body of four thousand horse
And twice six thousand foot, and, like a crescent,   115
Stood for the signal ; you, that show'd yourself
A sound old soldier, thinking it not fit
To give your enemy the odds and honour
Of the first stroke, commanded de la Guiche
To let fly all his cannons, that did pierce   120
The adverse thickest squadrons, and had shot
Nine volleys ere the foe had once given fire.
Your troop was charg'd, and when your Duke's old father
Met with th' assailants, and their grove of reiters
Repuls'd so fiercely, made them turn their beards   125
And rally up themselves behind their troops,
Fresh forces, seeing your troops a little sever'd
From that part first assaulted, gave it charge,
Which then this Duke made good, seconds his father,
Beats through and through the enemy's greatest strength,   130
And breaks the rest like billows 'gainst a rock,
And there the heart of that huge battle broke.
    Hen.   The heart but now came on, in that strong body
Of twice two thousand horse, led by Du Maine ;
Which, if I would be glorious, I could say   135
I first encounter'd.
    Sav.   How did he take in
Beaune in view of that invincible army
Led by the Lord Great Constable of Castile,
Autun and Nuits ; in Burgundy chas'd away
Viscount Tavannes' troops before Dijon,   140
And puts himself in, and there that was won.
    Hen.   If you would only give me leave, my lord,
I would do right to him, yet must not give—
    Sav.   A league from Fountaine Françoise, when you sent
      him
To make discovery of the Castile army,   145

When he discern'd 'twas it, with wondrous wisdom
Join'd to his spirit, he seem'd to make retreat,
But when they press'd him, and the Baron of Lux,
Set on their charge so hotly that his horse
Was slain, and he most dangerously engag'd,   150
Then turn'd your brave Duke head, and, with such ease
As doth an echo beat back violent sounds
With their own forces, he (as if a wall
Start suddenly before them) pash'd them all
Flat as the earth, and there was that field won.   155
   Hen. Y'are all the field wide.
   Sav.   O, I ask you pardon,
The strength of that field yet lay in his back,
Upon the foe's part ; and what is to come
Of this your Marshal, now your worthy Duke,
Is much beyond the rest ; for now he sees   160
A sort of horse troops issue from the woods
In number near twelve hundred ; and retiring
To tell you that the entire army follow'd,
Before he could relate it, he was forc'd
To turn head and receive the main assault   165
Of five horse troops only with twenty horse ;
The first he met he tumbled to the earth,
And brake through all, not daunted with two wounds,
One on his head, another on his breast,
The blood of which drown'd all the field in doubt ; 170
Your Majesty himself was then engag'd,
Your power not yet arriv'd, and up you brought
The little strength you had (a cloud of foes,
Ready to burst in storms about your ears) ;
Three squadrons rush'd against you, and the first   175
You took so fiercely that you beat their thoughts
Out of their bosoms from the urged fight ;
The second all amazed you overthrew ;
The third dispers'd, with five and twenty horse ;
Left of the fourscore that pursu'd the chase :   180
And this brave conquest, now your Marshal seconds
Against two squadrons, but with fifty horse ;
One after other he defeats them both,
And made them run, like men whose heels were tripp'd,
And pitch their heads in their great general's lap ; 185
And him he sets on, as he had been shot
Out of a cannon ; beats him into rout,

And as a little brook being overrun
With a black torrent, that bears all things down
His fury overtakes, his foamy back   190
Loaded with cattle and with stacks of corn,
And makes the miserable plowman mourn ;
So was Du Maine surcharg'd, and so Byron
Flow'd over all his forces, every drop
Of his lost blood bought with a worthy man ;   195
And only with a hundred gentlemen
He won the place from fifteen hundred horse.
   Hen.   He won the place ?
   Sav.   On my word, so 'tis said !
   Hen.   Fie, you have been extremely misinform'd.
   Sav.   I only tell your Highness what I heard ;   200
I was not there ; and though I have been rude
With wonder of his valour, and presum'd
To keep his merit in his full career,
Not hearing you, when yours made such a thunder,
Pardon my fault, since 'twas t'extol your servant :   205
But is it not most true that, 'twixt ye both,
So few achiev'd the conquest of so many ?
   Hen.   It is a truth must make me ever thankful,
But not perform'd by him ; was not I there,
Commanded him, and in the main assault   210
Made him but second ?
   Sav.   He's the capital soldier
That lives this day in holy Christendom,
Except your Highness,—always except Plato.
   Hen.   We must not give to one to take from many :
For (not to praise our countrymen) here serv'd   215
The General, Mylor' Norris, sent from England,
As great a captain as the world affords,
One fit to lead and fight for Christendom,
Of more experience and of stronger brain,
As valiant for abiding, in command   220
(On any sudden, upon any ground,
And in the form of all occasions)
As ready and as profitably dauntless ;
And here was then another, Colonel Williams,
A worthy captain ; and more like the Duke,   225
Because he was less temperate than the General ;
And being familiar with the man you praise,
(Because he knew him haughty and incapable

Of all comparison) would compare with him,
And hold his swelling valour to the mark   230
Justice had set in him, and not his will :
And as in open vessels fill'd with water,
And on men's shoulders borne, they put treen cups
To keep the wild and slippery element
From washing over, follow all his sways   235
And tickle aptness to exceed his bounds,
And at the brim contain him ; so this knight
Swum in Byron, and held him but to right.
But leave these hot comparisons ; he's mine own,
And, than what I possess, I'll more be known.   240
    Sav. [*aside*]   All this shall to the Duke ; I fish'd for this.
                                             Exeunt

          FINIS ACTUS SECUNDI

ACTUS III   SCENA I

[A Room in Byron's *House]*

Enter La Fin, Byron *following, unseen*

   La F. [*aside*]   A feigned passion in his hearing now
(Which he thinks I perceive not), making conscience
Of the revolt that he hath urg'd to me,
(Which now he means to prosecute) would sound
How deep he stands affected with that scruple.—   5
As when the moon hath comforted the night
And set the world in silver of her light,
The planets, asterisms, and whole state of heaven,
In beams of gold descending, all the winds,
Bound up in caves, charg'd not to drive abroad   10
Their cloudy heads, an universal peace,
Proclaim'd in silence of the quiet earth ;
Soon as her hot and dry fumes are let loose,
Storms and clouds mixing suddenly put out
The eyes of all those glories, the creation   15
Tun'd in to Chaos ; and we then desire,
For all our joy of life, the death of sleep :
So when the glories of our lives, men's loves,
Clear consciences, our fames, and loyalties,

That did us worthy comfort, are eclips'd,   20
Grief and disgrace invade us ; and for all
Our night of life besides our misery craves
Dark earth would ope and hide us in our graves.
    Byr. [*advancing*]   How strange is this !
    La F.   What ! Did your Highness hear ?
    Byr.   Both heard and wonder'd that your wit and spirit,   25
And profit in experience of the slaveries
Impos'd on us in those mere politic terms
Of love, fame, loyalty, can be carried up,
To such a height of ignorant conscience,
Of cowardice, and dissolution   30
In all the free-born powers of royal man.
You, that have made way through all the guards
Of jealous state, and seen on both your sides
The pikes' points charging heaven to let you pass,
Will you, in flying with a scrupulous wing,   35
Above those pikes to heavenward, fall on them ?
This is like men that, spirited with wine,
Pass dangerous places safe, and die for fear
With only thought of them, being simply sober :
We must, in passing to our wished ends,   40
Through things call'd good and bad, be like the air
That evenly interpos'd betwixt the seas
And the opposed element of fire,
At either toucheth, but partakes with neither ;
Is neither hot nor cold, but with a slight   45
And harmless temper mix'd of both th' extremes.
    La F.   'Tis shrewd.
    Byr.   There is no truth of any good
To be discern'd on earth : and, by conversion,
Nought therefore simply bad ; but as the stuff
Prepar'd for arras pictures is no picture   50
Till it be form'd, and man hath cast the beams
Of his imaginous fancy through it,
In forming ancient kings and conquerors,
As he conceives they look'd and were attir'd,
Though they were nothing so : so all things here   55
Have all their price set down from men's conceits,
Which make all terms and actions good or bad,
And are but pliant and well-colour'd threads
Put into feigned images of truth ;
To which to yield and kneel as truth-pure kings,   60

That pull'd us down with clear truth of their gospel,
Were superstition to be hiss'd to hell.
    La F.   Believe it, this is reason.
    Byr.   'Tis the faith
Of reason and of wisdom.
    La F.   You persuade,
As if you could create : what man can shun   65
The searches and compressions of your Grace's ?
    Byr.   We must have these lures when we hawk for friends,
And wind about them like a subtle river
That, seeming only to run on his course,
Doth search yet as he runs, and still finds out   70
The easiest parts of entry on the shore ;
Gliding so slyly by, as scarce it touch'd,
Yet still eats something in it : so must those
That have large fields and currents to dispose.
Come, let us join our streams, we must run far,   75
And have but little time ; the Duke of Savoy
Is shortly to be gone, and I must needs
Make you well known to him.
    La F.   But hath your Highness
Some enterprise of value join'd with him ?
    Byr.   With him and greater persons !
    La F.   I will creep   80
Upon my bosom in your princely service.
Vouchsafe to make me known. I hear there lives not,
So kind, so bountiful, and wise a prince
But in your own excepted excellence.
    Byr.   He shall both know and love you : are you mine ?   85
    La F.   I take the honour of it, on my knee,
And hope to quite it with your Majesty.   *[Exeunt]*

[SCENA II

A Room in the Court]

Enter Savoy, Roncas, Rochette, Breton

    Sav.   La Fin is in the right, and will obtain ;
He draweth with his weight, and like a plummet
That sways a door, with falling off pulls after.
    Ron.   Thus will La Fin be brought a stranger to you
By him he leads ; he conquers that is conquer'd,   5

That's sought as hard to win, that sues to be won.

Sav.   But is my painter warn'd to take his picture,
When he shall see me and present La Fin ?

Roch.   He is, my lord, and, as your Highness will'd,
All we will press about him, and admire   10
The royal promise of his rare aspect,
As if he heard not.

Sav.   'Twill inflame him :
Such tricks the Archduke us'd t'extol his greatness,
Which compliments, though plain men hold absurd,
And a mere remedy for desire of greatness,   15
Yet great men use them as their state potatoes,
High cullises, and potions to excite
The lust of their ambition : and this Duke
You know is noted in his natural garb
Extremely glorious ; who will therefore bring   20
An appetite expecting such a bait :
He comes ; go instantly, and fetch the painter.

Enter Byron, La Fin

Byr.   All honour to your Highness !

Sav.   'Tis most true. [*embracing him*]
All honours flow to me, in you their ocean ;
As welcome, worthiest Duke, as if my marquisate   25
Were circled with you in these amorous arms.

Byr.   I sorrow, sir, I could not bring it with me
That I might so supply the fruitless compliment
Of only visiting your Excellence,
With which the King now sends me t'entertain you ;   30
Which, notwithstanding, doth confer this good
That it hath given me some small time to show
My gratitude for the many secret bounties
I have, by this your Lord Ambassador,
Felt from your Highness, and, in short, t'assure you   35
That all my most deserts are at your service.

Sav.   Had the King sent me by you half his kingdom,
It were not half so welcome.

Byr.   For defect
Of whatsoever in myself, my lord,
I here commend to your most princely service   40
This honour'd friend of mine.

Sav.   Your name, I pray you, sir ?

La F.   La Fin, my lord.

Sav.   La Fin ? [*To* Roncas] Is this the man,
That you so recommended to my love ?
  Ron.   The same, my lord.
  Sav.   Y'are, next my lord the Duke,
The most desir'd of all men. [*To* Byron] O my lord,   45
The King and I have had a mighty conflict
About your conflicts and your matchless worth
In military virtues ; which I put
In balance with the continent of France,
In all the peace and safety it enjoys,   50
And made even weight with all he could put in
Of all men's else and of his own deserts.
  Byr.   Of all men's else ? Would he weigh other men's
With my deservings ?
  Sav.   Ay, upon my life,
The English General, the Mylor' Norris,   55
That serv'd amongst you here, he parallel'd
With you at all parts, and in some preferr'd him ;
And Colonel Williams, a Welsh Colonel,
He made a man that at your most contain'd you :
Which the Welsh herald of their praise, the cuckoo,   60
Would scarce have put in his monology—
In jest and said with reverence to his merits.
  Byr.   With reverence ?   Reverence scorns him ; by the
      spoil
Of all her merits in me, he shall rue it.
Did ever Curtian Gulf play such a part ?   65
Had Curtius been so us'd, if he had brook'd
That ravenous whirlpool, pour'd his solid spirits
Through earth' dissolved sinews, stopp'd her veins,
And rose with saved Rome, upon his back ;
As I swum pools of fire and gulfs of brass   70
To save my country, thrust this venturous arm
Beneath her ruins, took her on my neck
And set her safe on her appeased shore ?
And opes the King a fouler bog than this,
In his so rotten bosom to devour   75
Him that devour'd what else had swallow'd him,
In a detraction so with spite embru'd,
And drown such good in such ingratitude ?
My spirit as yet, but stooping to his rest,
Shines hotly in him, as the sun in clouds   80
Purpled and made proud with a peaceful even :

But when I throughly set to him, his cheeks
Will, like those clouds, forego their colour quite,
And his whole blaze smoke into endless night.
   Sav. Nay, nay, we must have no such gall, my lord,   85
O'erflow our friendly livers ; my relation
Only delivers my inflamed zeal
To your religious merits ; which, methinks,
Should make your Highness canoniz'd a saint.
   Byr. What had his arms been, without my arm,   90
That with his motion made the whole field move ?
And this held up, we still had victory.
When overcharg'd with number, his few friends
Retir'd amaz'd, I set them on assur'd,
And what rude ruin seized on I confirm'd ;   95
When I left leading, all his army reel'd,
One fell on other foul, and as the Cyclop
That, having lost his eye, struck every way,
His blows directed to no certain scope,
Or as, the soul departed from the body,   100
The body wants coherence in his parts,
Cannot consist, but sever and dissolve ;
So, I remov'd once, all his armies shook,
Panted, and fainted, and were ever flying,
Like wandering pulses spers'd through bodies dying.   105
   Sav. It cannot be denied ; 'tis all so true
That what seems arrogance, is desert in you.
   Byr. What monstrous humours feed a prince's blood,
Being bad to good men, and to bad men good !
   Sav. Well, let these contradictions pass, my lord,   110
Till they be reconcil'd, or put in form,
By power given to your will, and you present
The fashion of a perfect government :
In mean space but a word, we have small time
To spend in private, which I wish may be   115
With all advantage taken : Lord La Fin—
   Ron. Is't not a face of excellent presentment ?
Though not so amorous with pure white and red,
Yet is the whole proportion singular.
   Roch. That ever I beheld !
   Bret.   It hath good lines,   120
And tracts drawn through it ; the [profile] rare.
   Ron. I heard the famous and right learned Earl
And Archbishop of Lyons, Pierre Pinac

(Who was reported to have wondrous judgment
In men's events and natures by their looks),   125
Upon his death-bed visited by this Duke,
He told his sister, when his Grace was gone,
That he had never yet observed a face
Of worse presage than this ; and I will swear
That, something seen in physiognomy,   130
I do not find in all the rules it gives
One slend'rest blemish tending to mishap,
But, on the opposite part, as we may see,
On trees late-blossom'd, when all frosts are past,
How they are taken, and what will be fruit :   135
So on this tree of sceptres I discern
How it is loaden with appearances,
Rules answering rules, and glances crown'd with glances.

                                  He snatches away the picture

    Byr.   What ! Does he take my picture ?
    Sav.   Ay, my lord.
    Byr. Your Highness will excuse me ; I will give you   140
My likeness put in statue, not in picture,
And by a statuary of mine own,
That can in brass express the wit of man,
And in his form make all men see his virtues :
Others that with much strictness imitate   145
The something-stooping carriage of my neck,
The voluble and mild radiance of mine eyes,
Never observe my masculine aspect
And lion-like instinct it shadoweth,
Which Envy cannot say is flattery :   150
And I will have my image promis'd you,
Cut in such matter as shall ever last,
Where it shall stand, fix'd with eternal roots
And with a most unmoved gravity ;
For I will have the famous mountain Oros,   155
That looks out of the duchy where I govern
Into your Highness' dukedom, first made yours,
And then with such inimitable art
Express'd and handled, chiefly from the place
Where most conspicuously he shows his face,   160
That, though it keep the true form of that hill
In all his longitudes and latitudes,
His height, his distances, and full proportion,
Yet shall it clearly bear my counterfeit.

Both in my face and all my lineaments ;   165
And every man shall say : This is Byron !
Within my left hand I will hold a city,
Which is the city Amiens, at whose siege
I served so memorably ; from my right
I'll pour an endless flood into a sea   170
Raging beneath me, which shall intimate
My ceaseless service drunk up by the King,
As th' ocean drinks up rivers and makes all
Bear his proud title : ivory, brass, and gold,
That thieves may purchase, and be bought and sold,   175
Shall not be us'd about me ; lasting worth
Shall only set the Duke of Byron forth.

    Sav. O that your statuary could express you
With any nearness to your own instructions !
That statue would I prize past all the jewels   180
Within my cabinet of Beatrice,
The memory of my grandame Portugal.
Most royal Duke, we cannot long endure
To be thus private ; let us then conclude
With this great resolution that your wisdom   185
Will not forget to cast a pleasing veil
Over your anger, that may hide each glance
Of any notice taken of your wrong,
And show yourself the more obsequious.
'Tis but the virtue of a little patience ;   190
There are so oft attempts made 'gainst his person,
That sometimes they may speed, for they are plants
That spring the more for cutting, and at last
Will cast their wished shadow, mark, ere long !

Enter Nemours, Soissons

See who comes here, my lord, [*aside*] as now no more,   195
Now must we turn our stream another way.—
My lord, I humbly thank his Majesty
That he would grace my idle time spent here
With entertainment of your princely person,
Which, worthily, he keeps for his own bosom.   200
My lord, the Duke Nemours, and Count Soissons !
Your honours have been bountifully done me
In often visitation : let me pray you
To see some jewels now, and help my choice
In making up a present for the King.   205

Nem. Your Highness shall much grace us.
Sav. 　　　　　　　　I am doubtful
That I have much incens'd the Duke Byron
With praising the King's worthiness in arms
So much past all men.
　　Sois. 　　　　　He deserves it highly.
　　　　Exit [Savoy *with the* Lords]. *Manet* Byron *and* La Fin
　　Byr. What wrongs are these, laid on me by the King, 210
To equal others' worths in war with mine !
Endure this, and be turn'd into his moil
To bear his sumptures ; honour'd friend, be true,
And we will turn these torrents. Hence, the King !
　　　　　　　　　　　　　　　　Exit La Fin

　　　Enter Henry, Epernon, Vitry, Janin.

　　Hen. Why suffer you that ill-aboding vermin　　　215
To breed so near your bosom ? Be assur'd
His haunts are ominous ; not the throats of ravens
Spent on infected houses, howls of dogs
When no sound stirs at midnight, apparitions,
And strokes of spirits clad in black men's shapes,　　220
Or ugly women's, the adverse decrees
Of constellations, nor security
In vicious peace, are surer fatal ushers
Of [feral] mischiefs and mortalities
Than this prodigious fiend is, where he fawns :　　225
La Fiend, and not La Fin, he should be call'd.
　　Byr. Be what he will, men in themselves entire
March safe with naked feet on coals of fire :
I build not outward, nor depend on props,
Nor choose my consort by the common ear,　　　230
Nor by the moonshine in the grace of kings ;
So rare are true deservers lov'd or known,
That men lov'd vulgarly are ever none,
Nor men grac'd servilely for being spots
In princes' trains, though borne even with their crowns : 235
The stallion, Power, hath such a besom tail
That it sweeps all from justice, and such filth
He bears out in it that men mere exempt
Are merely clearest ; men will shortly buy
Friends from the prison or the pillory　　　　240
Rather than Honour's markets. I fear none

But foul ingratitude and detraction
In all the brood of villany.
   Hen.   No ? not Treason ?
Be circumspect, for to a credulous eye
He comes invisible, veil'd with flattery ;   245
And flatterers look like friends, as wolves like dogs.
And as a glorious poem fronted well
With many a goodly herald of his praise,
So far from hate of praises to his face
That he prays men to praise him, and they ride   250
Before, with trumpets in their mouths, proclaiming
Life to the holy fury of his lines—
All drawn, as if with one eye he had leer'd
On his lov'd hand and led it by a rule,
That his plumes only imp the Muses' wings,   255
He sleeps with them, his head is napp'd with bays,
His lips break out with nectar, his tun'd feet
Are of the great last, the perpetual motion,—
And he puff'd with their empty breath believes
Full merit eas'd those passions of wind,   260
Which yet serve but to praise, and cannot merit,
And so his fury in their air expires :
So de la Fin and such corrupted heralds,
Hir'd to encourage and to glorify,
May force what breath they will into their cheeks 265
Fitter to blow up bladders than full men ;
Yet may puff men too with persuasions
That they are gods in worth and may rise kings
With treading on their noises ; yet the worthiest,
From only his own worth receives his spirit,   270
And right is worthy bound to any merit ;
Which right shall you have ever ; leave him then,
He follows none but mark'd and wretched men.
And now for England you shall go, my lord,
Our Lord Ambassador to that matchless Queen ; 275
You never had a voyage of such pleasure,
Honour, and worthy objects ; there's a Queen
Where Nature keeps her state, and State her Court,
Wisdom her study, Continence her fort ;
Where Magnanimity, Humanity,   280
Firmness in counsel and Integrity,
Grace to her poorest subjects, Majesty
To awe the greatest, have respects divine,

And in her each part, all the virtues shine.

Exit Henry [*cum suis*] : *manet* Byron

Byr. Enjoy your will awhile, I may have mine.   285
Wherefore, before I part to this ambassage,
I'll be resolv'd by a magician
That dwells hereby, to whom I'll go disguis'd
And show him my birth's figure, set before
By one of his profession, of the which   290
I'll crave his judgment, feigning I am sent
From some great personage, whose nativity
He wisheth should be censur'd by his skill.
But on go my plots, be it good or ill.   *Exit*

[SCENA III

The House of the Astrologer]

Enter La Brosse

La B. This hour by all rules of astrology
Is dangerous to my person, if not deadly.
How hapless is our knowledge to foretell,
And not be able to prevent a mischief :
O the strange difference 'twixt us and the stars ;   5
They work with inclinations strong and fatal,
And nothing know ; and we know all their working,
And nought can do, or nothing can prevent !
Rude ignorance is beastly, knowledge wretched ;
The heavenly Powers envy what they enjoin ;   10
We are commanded t'imitate their natures,
In making all our ends eternity,
And in that imitation we are plagued,
And worse than they esteem'd that have no souls
But in their nostrils, and like beasts expire,   15
As they do that are ignorant of arts,
By drowning their eternal parts in sense
And sensual affectations : while we live
Our good parts take away, the more they give.

[*Enter*] Byron *solus, disguised like a Carrier of Letters*

Byr. [*aside*] The forts that favourites hold in princes'
    hearts,   20
In common subjects' loves, and their own strengths,

Are not so sure and unexpugnable
But that the more they are presum'd upon,
The more they fail: daily and hourly proof
Tells us prosperity is at highest degree   25
The fount and handle of calamity :
Like dust before a whirlwind those men fly
That prostrate on the grounds of Fortune lie ;
And being great, like trees that broadest sprout,
Their own top-heavy state grubs up their root.   30
These apprehensions startle all my powers,
And arm them with suspicion gainst themselves.
In my late projects I have cast myself
Into the arms of others, and will see
If they will let me fall, or toss me up   35
Into th' affected compass of a throne.—
God save you, sir !
    La B.   Y'are welcome, friend ; what would you ?
    Byr. I would entreat you, for some crowns I bring,
To give your judgment of this figure cast,
To know, by his nativity there seen,   40
What sort of end the person shall endure
Who sent me to you and whose birth it is.
    La B. I'll herein do my best in your desire.
                        [He contemplates the figure]
The man is rais'd out of a good descent,
And nothing older than yourself, I think ;   45
Is it not you ?
    Byr.   I will not tell you that :
But tell me on what end he shall arrive.
    La B. My son, I see that he, whose end is cast
In this set figure, is of noble parts,
And by his military valour rais'd   50
To princely honours, and may be a king ;
But that I see a *Caput Algol* here
That hinders it, I fear.
    Byr.   A *Caput Algol* ?
What's that, I pray ?
    La B.   Forbear to ask me, son ;
You bid me speak what fear bids me conceal.   55.
    Byr. You have no cause to fear, and therefore speak.
    La B. You'll rather wish you had been ignorant,
Than be instructed in a thing so ill.
    Byr. Ignorance is an idle salve for ill ;

And therefore do not urge me to enforce   60
What I would freely know ; for by the skill
Shown in thy aged hairs I'll lay thy brain
Here scatter'd at my feet and seek in that
What safely thou must utter with thy tongue,
If thou deny it.
   La B.   Will you not allow me   65
To hold my peace ? What less can I desire ?
If not, be pleas'd with my constrained speech.
   Byr. Was ever man yet punish'd for expressing
What he was charg'd ? Be free, and speak the worst.
   La B. Then briefly this : the man hath lately done   70
An action that will make him lose his head.
   Byr. Curs'd be thy throat and soul, raven, screech-owl,
     hag !   [*Beating* La Brosse]
   La B. O, hold, for heaven's sake, hold !
   Byr.   Hold on, I will.
Vault and contractor of all horrid sounds,
Trumpet of all the miseries in hell,   75
Of my confusions, of the shameful end
Of all my services ; witch, fiend, accurs'd
For ever be the poison of thy tongue,
And let the black fume of thy venom'd breath
Infect the air, shrink heaven, put out the stars,   80
And rain so fell and blue a plague on earth,
That all the world may falter with my fall.
   La B. Pity my age, my lord.
   Byr.   Out, prodigy,
Remedy of pity, mine of flint,
Whence with my nails and feet I'll dig enough   85
Horror and savage cruelty to build
Temples to Massacre : dam of devils take thee !
Had'st thou no better end to crown my parts.
The bulls of Colchis, nor his triple neck,
That howls out earthquakes, the most mortal vapours   90
That ever stifled and struck dead the fowls,
That flew at never such a sightly pitch,
Could not have burnt my blood so.
   La B.   I told truth,
And could have flatter'd you.
   Byr.   O that thou had'st !
Would I had given thee twenty thousand crowns   95
That thou had'st flatter'd me ; there's no joy on earth,

Never so rational, so pure, and holy,
But is a jester, parasite, a whore,
In the most worthy parts, with which they please
A drunkenness of soul and a disease.   100
   La B. I knew you not.
   Byr.   Peace, dog of Pluto, peace!
Thou knew'st my end to come, not me here present:
Pox of your halting human knowledges!
O Death, how far off hast thou kill'd, how soon
A man may know too much, though never nothing!   105
Spite of the stars and all astrology
I will not lose my head; or if I do
A hundred thousand heads shall off before.
I am a nobler substance than the stars,
And shall the baser overrule the better?   110
Or are they better, since they are the bigger?
I have a will and faculties of choice,
To do, or not to do: and reason why
I do, or not do this: the stars have none;
They know not why they shine, more than this taper,   115
Nor how they work, nor what: I'll change my course,
I'll piece-meal pull the frame of all my thoughts,
And cast my will into another mould:
And where are all your *Caput Algols* then?
Your planets all, being underneath the earth   120
At my nativity, what can they do?
Malignant in aspects, in bloody houses?
Wild fire consume them! one poor cup of wine
More than I use, tha[n] my weak brain will bear,
Shall make them drunk and reel out of their spheres   125
For any certain act they can enforce.
O that mine arms were wings that I might fly,
And pluck out of their hearts my destiny!
I'll wear those golden spurs upon my heels,
And kick at fate; be free, all worthy spirits,   130
And stretch yourselves for greatness and for height,
Untruss your slaveries; you have height enough
Beneath this steep heaven to use all your reaches;
'Tis too far off to let you, or respect you.
Give me a spirit that on this life's rough sea   135
Loves t'have his sails fill'd with a lusty wind,
Even till his sail-yards tremble, his masts crack,
And his rapt ship run on her side so low

That she drinks water, and her keel plows air.
There is no danger to a man that knows   140
What life and death is ; there's not any law
Exceeds his knowledge ; neither is it lawful
That he should stoop to any other law.
He goes before them, and commands them all,
That to himself is a law rational.   145

Exit

ACTUS IV SCENA I

[A Room in the Court]

Enter D'Aumont, *with* Crequi

D'Aum.   The Duke of Byron is return'd from England,
And, as they say, was princely entertain'd,
School'd by the matchless queen there, who, I hear,
Spake most divinely ; and would gladly hear
Her speech reported.
   Creq.   I can serve your turn,   5
As one that speaks from others, not from her,
And thus it is reported at his parting.
' Thus, Monsieur Du Byron, you have beheld
. Our Court proportion'd to our little kingdom
In every entertainment ; yet our mind   10
To do you all the rites of your repair
Is as unbounded as the ample air.
What idle pains have you bestow'd to see
A poor old woman, who in nothing lives
More than in true affections borne your King,   15
And in the perfect knowledge she hath learn'd
Of his good knights and servants of your sort !
We thank him that he keeps the memory
Of us and all our kindness ; but must say
That it is only kept, and not laid out   20
To such affectionate profit as we wish,
Being so much set on fire with his deserts
That they consume us, not to be restor'd
By your presentment of him, but his person :
And we had [not] thought that he whose virtues fly   25

So beyond wonder and the reach of thought,
Should check at eight hours' sail, and his high spirit,
That stoops to fear, less than the poles of heaven,
Should doubt an under-billow of the sea,
And, being a sea, be sparing of his streams :   30
And I must blame all you that may advise him,
That, having help'd him through all martial dangers,
You let him stick at the kind rites of peace,
Considering all the forces I have sent,
To set his martial seas up in firm walls   35
On both his sides for him to pass at pleasure,
Did plainly open him a guarded way
And led in nature to this friendly shore.
But here is nothing worth his personal sight,
Here are no walled cities ; for that Crystal   40
Sheds, with his light, his hardness and his height
About our thankful person and our realm,
Whose only aid we ever yet desired.
And now I see the help we sent to him,
Which should have swum to him in our own blood,   45
Had it been needful (our affections
Being more given to his good than he himself),
Ends in the actual right it did his state,
And ours is slighted ; all our worth is made
The common stock and bank, from whence are serv'd   50
All men's occasions ; yet, thanks to Heaven,
Their gratitudes are drawn dry, not our bounties.
And you shall tell your King that he neglects
Old friends for new, and sets his soothed ease
Above his honour ; marshals policy   55
In rank before his justice, and his profit
Before his royalty ; his humanity gone,
To make me no repayment of mine own '
    D'Aum.   What answered the Duke ?
    Creq.   In this sort.
' Your Highness' sweet speech hath no sharper end   60
Than he would wish his life, if he neglected
The least grace you have nam'd ; but to his wish
Much power is wanting : the green roots of war
Not yet so close cut up, but he may dash
Against their relics to his utter ruin,   65
Without more near eyes fix'd upon his feet,
Than those that look out of his country's soil.

And this may well excuse his personal presence,
Which yet he oft hath long'd to set by yours,
That he might imitate the majesty,   70
Which so long peace hath practis'd, and made full
In your admir'd appearance, to illustrate
And rectify his habit in rude war.
And his will to be here must needs be great,
Since Heaven hath thron'd so true a royalty here,   75
That he thinks no king absolutely crown'd
Whose temples have not stood beneath this sky,
And whose height is not harden'd with these stars,
Whose influences, for this altitude
Distill'd and wrought in with this temperate air   80
And this division of the element,
Have with your reign brought forth more worthy spirits
For counsel, valour, height of wit and art,
Than any other region of the earth,
Or were brought forth to all your ancestors.   85
And as a cunning orator reserves
His fairest similes, best-adorning figures,
Chief matter, and most moving arguments
For his conclusion ; and doth then supply
His ground-streams laid before, glides over them,   90
Makes his full depth seen through ; and so takes up
His audience in applauses past the clouds :
So in your government, conclusive Nature
(Willing to end her excellence in earth
When your foot shall be set upon the stars)   95
Shows all her sovereign beauties, ornaments,
Virtues, and raptures ; overtakes her works
In former empires, makes them but your foils ;
Swells to her full sea, and again doth drown
The world in admiration of your crown '.   100
   D'Aum.   He did her, at all parts, confessed right.
   Creq.   She took it yet but as a part of courtship,
And said ' he was the subtle orator
To whom he did too gloriously resemble
Nature in her and in her government '.   105
He said ' he was no orator, but a soldier,
More than this air in which you breathe hath made me,
My studious love of your rare government,
And simple truth, which is most eloquent ;
Your Empire is so amply absolute   110

That even your theatres show more comely rule,
True noblesse, royalty, and happiness
Than others' Courts : you make all state before
Utterly obsolete ; all to come, twice sod.
And therefore doth my royal Sovereign wish   115
Your years may prove as vital as your virtues,
That (standing on his turrets this way turn'd,
Ord'ring and fixing his affairs by yours)
He may at last, on firm grounds, pass your seas,
And see that maiden-sea of majesty,   120
In whose chaste arms so many kingdoms lie '.
    D'Aum.   When came she to her touch of his ambition ?
    Creq.   In this speech following, which I thus remember :
' If I hold any merit worth his presence,
Or any part of that your courtship gives me,   125
My subjects have bestow'd it ; some in counsel,
In action some, and in obedience all ;
For none knows with such proof as you, my lord,
How much a subject may renown his prince,
And how much princes of their subjects hold :   130
In all the services that ever subject
Did for his sovereign, he that best deserv'd
Must, in comparison, except Byron ;
And to win this prize clear, without the maims
Commonly given men by ambition   135
When all their parts lie open to his view,
Shows continence, past their other excellence ;
But for a subject to affect a kingdom,
Is like the camel that of Jove begg'd horns ;
And such mad-hungry men as well may eat   140
Hot coals of fire to feed their natural heat :
For to aspire to competence with your King,
What subject is so gross and giantly ?
He having now a Dauphin born to him,
Whose birth, ten days before, was dreadfully   145
Usher'd with earthquakes in most parts of Europe ;
And that gives all men cause enough to fear
All thought of competition with him.
Commend us, good my lord, and tell our brother
How much we joy in that his royal issue,   150
And in what prayers we raise our hearts to heaven,
That in more terror to his foes and wonder
He may drink earthquakes, and devour the thunder.

So we admire your valour and your virtues,
And ever will contend to win their honour'.   155
Then spake she to Crequi and Prince d'Auvergne,
And gave all gracious farewells; when Byron
Was thus encounter'd by a Councillor
Of great and eminent name and matchless merit:
'I think, my lord, your princely Dauphin bears   160
Arion on his cradle through your kingdom,
In the sweet music joy strikes from his birth'.
He answer'd: 'And good right; the cause commands it'.
'But', said the other, 'had we a fift Henry
To claim his old right, and one man to friend   165
(Whom you well know, my lord), that for his friendship
Were promised the vice-royalty of France,
We would not doubt of conquest, in despite
Of all those windy earthquakes'.   He replied:
'Treason was never guide to English conquests,   170
And therefore that doubt shall not fright our Dauphin;
Nor would I be the friend to such a foe
For all the royalties in Christendom'.
'Fix there your foot', said he, 'I only give
False fire, and would be loath to shoot you off: 175
He that wins empire with the loss of faith
Out-buys it, and will bankrout; you have laid
A brave foundation by the hand of virtue;
Put not the roof to fortune: foolish statuaries,
That under little saints suppose great bases   180
Make less to sense the saints; and so, where Fortune
Advanceth vile minds to states great and noble,
She much the more exposeth them to shame,
Not able to make good and fill their bases
With a conformed structure: I have found   185
(Thanks to the Blesser of my search), that counsels
Held to the line of justice still produce
The surest states, and greatest, being sure;
Without which fit assurance, in the greatest—
As you may see a mighty promontory   190
More digg'd and under-eaten than may warrant
A safe supportance to his hanging brows;
All passengers avoid him, shun all ground
That lies within his shadow, and bear still
A flying eye upon him: so great men,   195
Corrupted in their grounds, and building out

Too swelling fronts for their foundations,
When most they should be propp'd are most forsaken ;
And men will rather thrust into the storms
Of better-grounded states than take a shelter   200
Beneath their ruinous and fearful weight ;
Yet they so oversee their faulty bases,
That they remain securer in conceit :
And that security doth worse presage
Their near destructions than their eaten grounds ;   205
And therefore heaven itself is made to us
A perfect hieroglyphic to express
The idleness of such security,
And the grave labour of a wise distrust,
In both sorts of the all-inclining stars,   210
Where all men note this difference in their shining,
As plain as they distinguish either hand,
The fixed stars waver, and the erring stand '.
   D'Aum. How took he this so worthy admonition ?
   Creq. ' Gravely applied ', said he, ' and like the man, 215
Whom, all the world says, overrules the stars ;
Which are divine books to us, and are read
By understanders only, the true objects
And chief companions of the truest men ;
And, though I need it not, I thank your counsel,   220
That never yet was idle, but, spherelike,
Still moves about and is the continent
To this blest isle '.

*   *   *   *   *

ACTUS V SCENA I

[*A Room in the Court*]

Enter Byron, D'Auvergne, La Fin.

   Byr. The circle of this ambassy is clos'd,
For which I long have long'd for mine own ends,
To see my faithful, and leave courtly friends ;
To whom I came, methought, with such a spirit,
As you have seen a lusty courser show   5

That hath been long time at his manger tied,
High fed, alone, and when, his headstall broken,
He runs his prison, like a trumpet neighs,
Cuts air in high curvets, and shakes his head,
With wanton stoppings, 'twixt his forelegs, mocking   10
The heavy centre, spreads his flying crest,
Like to an ensign, hedge and ditches leaping,
Till in the fresh meat, at his natural food,
He sees free fellows, and hath met them free.
And now, good friend, I would be fain inform'd,   15
What our right princely lord, the Duke of Savoy
Hath thought on, to employ my coming home.
   La F. To try the King's trust in you, and withal
How hot he trails on our conspiracy,
He first would have you beg the government,   20
Of the important citadel of Bourg,
Or to place in it any you shall name ;
Which will be wondrous fit to march before
His other purposes, and is a fort
He rates in love above his patrimony ;   25
To make which fortress worthy of your suit,
He vows, if you obtain it, to bestow
His third fair daughter on your Excellence,
And hopes the King will not deny it you.
   Byr. Deny it me ? Deny me such a suit ?   30
Who will he grant, if he deny it me ?
   La. F. He'll find some politic shift to do't, I fear.
   Byr. What shift, or what evasion can he find ?
What one patch is there in all Policy's shop,
That botcher-up of kingdoms, that can mend   35
The brack betwixt us, any way denying ?
   D'Auv. That's at your peril.
   Byr.   Come, he dares not do't.
   D'Auv. Dares not ? Presume not so ; you know, good
    Duke,
That all things he thinks fit to do, he dares.
   Byr. By heaven, I wonder at you ; I will ask it   40
As sternly, and secure of all repulse,
As th' ancient Persians did when they implored
Their idol, fire, to grant them any boon ;
With which they would descend into a flood,
And threaten there to quench it, if they fail'd   45
Of that they ask'd it.

La F.   Said like your King's king ;
Cold hath no act in depth, nor are suits wrought,
Of any high price, that are coldly sought ;
I'll haste, and with your courage comfort Savoy.
                                     Exit La Fin
D'Auv. I am your friend, my lord, and will deserve   50
That name, with following any course you take ;
Yet, for your own sake, I could wish your spirit
Would let you spare all broad terms of the King ;
Or, on my life, you will at last repent it.
    Byr. What can he do ?
    D'Auv.   All that you cannot fear.   55
    Byr. You fear too much ; be by when next I see him,
And see how I will urge him in this suit ;
He comes : mark you, that think he will not grant it.

        Enter Henry, Epernon, Soissons, Janin

I am become a suitor to your Highness.
    Hen. For what, my lord, 'tis like you shall obtain.   60
    Byr. I do not much doubt that ; my services,
I hope, have more strength in your good conceit
Than to receive repulse in such requests.
    Hen. What is it ?
    Byr. That you would bestow **on** one whom I shall name 65
The keeping of the citadel of Bourg.
    Hen. Excuse me, sir, I must not grant you that.
    Byr. Not grant me that !
    Hen.   It is not fit I should :
You are my governor in Burgundy,
And province governors, that command in chief,   70
Ought not to have the charge of fortresses ;
Besides, it is the chief key of my kingdom,
That opens towards Italy, and must therefore
Be given to one that hath immediately
Dependence on us.
    Byr.   These are wondrous reasons :   75
Is not a man depending on his merits
As fit to have the charge of such a key
As one that merely hangs upon your humours ?
    Hen. Do not enforce your merits so yourself ;
It takes away their lustre and reward.   80
    Byr. But you will grant my suit ?

Hen.   I swear I cannot,
Keeping the credit of my brain and place.
   Byr. Will you deny me, then ?
   Hen.   I am enforc'd :
I have no power, more than yourself, in things
That are beyond my reason.
   Byr.   Than myself ?   85
That's a strange slight in your comparison ;
Am I become th' example of such men
As have least power ?   Such a diminutive ?
I was comparative in the better sort ;
And such a King as you would say, I cannot   90
Do such or such a thing, were I as great
In power as he ; even that indefinite ' he '
Express'd me full : this moon is strangely chang'd.
   Hen. How can I help it ?   Would you have a king
That hath a white beard have so green a brain ?   95
   Byr. A plague of brain ! What doth this touch your brain ?
You must give me more reason, or I swear—
   Hen. Swear ? What do you swear ?
   Byr.   I swear you wrong me,
And deal not like a king, to jest and slight
A man that you should curiously reward ;   100
Tell me of your grey beard ! It is not grey
With care to recompense me, who eas'd your care.
   Hen. You have been recompens'd from head to foot.
   Byr. With a distrusted dukedom. Take your dukedom,
Bestow'd on me, again ; it was not given   105
For any love, but fear and force of shame.
   Hen. Yet 'twas your honour ; which, if you respect not,
Why seek you this addition ?
   Byr.   Since this honour
Would show you lov'd me, too, in trusting me ;
Without which love and trust honour is shame,   110
A very pageant and a property :
Honour, with all his adjuncts, I deserve ;
And you quit my deserts with your grey beard.
   Hen. Since you expostulate the matter so,
I tell you plain another reason is,   115
Why I am mov'd to make you this denial,
That I suspect you to have had intelligence
With my vow'd enemies.
   Byr.   Misery of virtue,

Ill is made good with worse! This reason pours
Poison for balm into the wound you made;   120
You make me mad, and rob me of my soul,
To take away my tried love and my truth.
Which of my labours, which of all my wounds,
Which overthrow, which battle won for you,
Breeds this suspicion? Can the blood of faith   125
(Lost in all these to find it proof and strength)
Beget disloyalty? All my rain is fall'n
Into the horse-fair, springing pools, and mire,
And not in thankful grounds or fields of fruit:
Fall then before us, O thou flaming Crystal,   130
That art the uncorrupted register
Of all men's merits, and remonstrate here
The fights, the dangers, the affrights and horrors,
Whence I have rescu'd this unthankful King;
And show, commix'd with them, the joys, the glories   135
Of his state then, then his kind thoughts of me,
Then my deservings, now my infamy:
But I will be mine own king; I will see
That all your chronicles be fill'd with me,
That none but I and my renowned sire   140
Be said to win the memorable fields
Of Arques and Dieppe; and none but we of all
Kept you from dying there in an hospital;
None but myself that won the day at Dreux
(A day of holy name, and needs no night);   145
Nor none but I at Fountaine Françoise burst
The heart-strings of the Leaguers; I alone
Took Amiens in these arms, and held her fast
In spite of all the pitchy fires she cast,
And clouds of bullets pour'd upon my breast,   150
Till she show'd yours, and took her natural form;
Only myself (married to victory)
Did people Artois, Douai, Picardy,
Béthune and Saint-Paul, Bapaume and Courcelles,
With her triumphant issue.

Hen.   Ha, ha, ha!   *Exit* 155
        Byron *drawing and is held by* D'Auvergne
D'Auv. O hold, my lord; for my sake, mighty spirit!
                    Exit [Byron *followed by* D'Auvergne]

[SCENA II

Another Room in the Court]

Enter Byron, D'Auvergne *following unseen*

Byr. Respect, Revenge; Slaughter, repay for laughter.
What's grave in earth, what awful, what abhorr'd,
If my rage be ridiculous ? I will make it
The law and rule of all things serious.
So long as idle and ridiculous King[s]   5
Are suffer'd, sooth'd, and wrest all right to safety,
So long is Mischief gathering massacres
For their curs'd kingdoms, which I will prevent.
Laughter ? I'll fright it from him, far as he
Hath cast irrevocable shame ; which ever   10
Being found is lost, and, lost, returneth never ;
Should kings cast off their bounties with their dangers ?
He that can warm at fires where Virtue burns,
Hunt pleasure through her torments, nothing feel
Of all his subjects suffer ; but, long hid   15
In wants and miseries, and having pass'd
Through all the gravest shapes of worth and honour,
For all heroic fashions to be learn'd
By those hard lessons show an antic vizard—
Who would not wish him rather hew'd to nothing   20
Than left so monstrous ? Slight my services ?
Drown the dead noises of my sword in laughter ?
(My blows as but the passages of shadows,
Over the highest and most barren hills)
And use me like no man, but as he took me   25
Into a desert, gash'd with all my wounds
Sustain'd for him, and buried me in flies ?
Forth, Vengeance, then, and open wounds in him
Shall let in Spain and Savoy.
                Offers to draw and D'Auvergne *again holds him*
   D'Auv.   O my lord,
This is too large a licence given your fury ;   30
Give time to it ; what reason suddenly
Cannot extend, respite doth oft supply.
   Byr. While respite holds revenge the wrong redoubles,
And so the shame of sufferance ; it torments me
To think what I endure at his shrunk hands,   35
That scorns the gift of one poor fort to me,

That have subdu'd for him (O injury !)
Forts, cities, countries, ay, and yet my fury—

                    [*Exiturus. Enter* Henry]

Hen.   Byron ?
D'Auv.   My lord, the King calls !
Hen.   Turn, I pray.
How now, from whence flow these distracted faces ?   40
From what attempt return they, as disclaiming
Their late heroic bearer ? What, a pistol ?
Why, good my lord, can mirth make you so wrathful ?

   Byr.   Mirth ? 'Twas Mockery, a contempt, a scandal
To my renown for ever ; a repulse   45
As miserably cold as Stygian water,
That from sincere earth issues, and doth break
The strongest vessels, not to be contain'd
But in the tough hoof of a patient ass.

   Hen.   My lord, your judgment is not competent   50
In this dissension ; I may say of you
As Fame says of the ancient Eleans
That in th' Olympian contentions
They ever were the justest arbitrators,
If none of them contended, nor were parties :   55
Those that will moderate disputations well,
Must not themselves affect the coronet ;
For as the air contain'd within our ears,
If it be not in quiet, nor refrains
Troubling our hearing with offensive sounds   60
(But our affected instrument of hearing,
Replete with noise and singings in itself)
It faithfully receives no other voices ;
So of all judgments, if within themselves
They suffer spleen and are tumultuous,   65
They cannot equal differences without them ;
And this wind, that doth sing so in your ears,
I know is no disease bred in yourself,
But whisper'd in by others ; who in swelling
Your veins with empty hope of much, yet able   70
To perform nothing, are like shallow streams
That make themselves so many heavens to sight,
Since you may see in them the moon and stars,
The blue space of the air, as far from us,
To our weak senses, in those shallow streams,   75
As if they were as deep as heaven is high ;

Yet with your middle finger only sound them,
And you shall pierce them to the very earth ;
And therefore leave them and be true to me,
Or you'll be left by all ; or be like one   80
That in cold nights will needs have all the fire,
And there is held by others, and embrac'd
Only to burn him ; your fire will be inward,
Which not another deluge can put out.

              Byron *kneels while the* King *goes on*
O Innocence, the sacred amulet   85
Gainst all the poisons of infirmity,
Of all misfortune, injury, and death,
That makes a man in tune still in himself,
Free from the hell to be his own accuser,
Ever in quiet, endless joy enjoying,   90
No strife nor no sedition in his powers,
No motion in his will against his reason,
No thought gainst thought, nor (as 'twere in the confines
Of wishing and repenting) doth possess
Only a wayward and tumultuous peace,   95
But (all parts in him friendly and secure,
Fruitful of all best things in all worst seasons)
He can with every wish be in their plenty ;
When the infectious guilt of one foul crime
Destroys the free content of all our time.   100
    Byr. 'Tis all acknowledg'd, and, though all too late,
Here the short madness of my anger ends :
If ever I did good I lock'd it safe
In you, th' impregnable defence of goodness ;
If ill, I press it with my penitent knees   105
To that unsounded depth whence nought returneth.
    Hen. 'Tis music to mine ears ; rise then, for ever
Quit of what guilt soever till this hour,
And nothing touch'd in honour or in spirit,
Rise without flattery, rise by absolute merit.   110

          Enter Epernon, *to the* King, Byron, *etc.*

    Ep. Sir, if it please you to be taught any courtship take
you to your stand; Savoy is at it with three mistresses at
once; he loves each of them best, yet all differently.
    Hen. For the time he hath been here, he hath talked a
volume greater than the Turk's Alcoran; stand up close; his 115
lips go still.   [*Retiring with* Byron *and the* Lords]

Enter Savoy *with three* Ladies

Sav. Excuse me, excuse me ; the King has ye all.

1st Lady. True sir, in honourable subjection.

2nd Lady. To the which we are bound by our loyalty.

Sav. Nay your excuse, your excuse ! Intend me for affec- 120
tion ; you are all bearers of his favours, and deny him not
your opposition by night.

3rd Lady. You say rightly in that, for therein we oppose
us to his command.

1st Lady. In the which he never yet pressed us.   125

2nd Lady. Such is the benediction of our peace.

Sav. You take me still in flat misconstruction, and conceive not by me.

1st Lady. Therein we are strong in our own purposes ; for
it were something scándalous for us to conceive by you.   130

2nd Lady. Though there might be question made of your
fruitfulness, yet dry weather in harvest does no harm.

Hen. [*aside*] They will talk him into Savoy ; he begins to
hunt down.

Sav. As the King is, and hath been, a most admired and 135
most unmatchable soldier, so hath he been, and is, a sole
excellent and unparalleled courtier.

Hen. [*aside*] *Pauvre ami, merci !*

1st Lady. Your Highness does the King but right, sir.

2nd Lady. And heaven shall bless you for that justice 140
with plentiful store of want in ladies' affections.

Sav. You are cruel, and will not vouchsafe me audience
to any conclusion.

1st Lady. Beseech your Grace conclude, that we may
present our curtsies to you and give you the adieu.   145

Sav. It is said the King will bring an army into Savoy.

2nd Lady. Truly we are not of his council of war.

Sav. Nay, but vouchsafe me—

3rd Lady. Vouchsafe him, vouchsafe him, else there 's no
play in't.   150

1st Lady. Well, I vouchsafe your Grace.

Sav. Let the King bring an army into Savoy, and I'll
find him sport for forty years.

Hen. [*aside*] Would I were sure of that ! I should then
have a long age, and a merry.   155

1st Lady. I think your Grace would play with his army at
balloon.

2nd Lady. My faith, and that's a martial recreation !

3rd Lady. It is next to impious courting.

Sav. I am not he that can set my squadrons overnight, by 160
midnight leap my horse, curry seven miles, and by three leap
my mistress ; return to mine army again, and direct as I were
infatigable ; I am no such tough soldier.

1st Lady. Your disparity is believed, sir.

2nd Lady. And 'tis a piece of virtue to tell true.   165

3rd Lady. God's me, the King !   [*Discovering* Henry]

Sav. Well, I have said nothing that may offend.

1st Lady. 'Tis hoped so.

2nd Lady. If there be any mercy in laughter.

Sav. I'll take my leave. [*To* Henry]   170
After the tedious stay my love hath made,
Most worthy to command our earthly zeal,
I come for pardon, and to take my leave ;
Affirming, though I reap no other good
By this my voyage but t'have seen a prince   175
Of greatness in all grace so past report,
I nothing should repent me ; and to show
Some token of my gratitude, I have sent
Into your treasury the greatest jewels
In all my cabinet of Beatrice,   180
And of my late deceased wife, th' Infanta,
Which are two basins and their ewers of crystal,
Never yet valu'd for their workmanship,
Nor the exceeding riches of their matter.
And to your stable, worthy Duke of Byron,   185
I have sent in two of my fairest horses.

Byr. Sent me your horses ! Upon what desert ?
I entertain no presents but for merits,
Which I am far from at your Highness' hands,
As being of all men to you the most stranger ;   190
There is as ample bounty in refusing
As in bestowing, and with this I quit you.

Sav. Then have I lost nought but my poor goodwill.

Hen. Well, cousin, I with all thanks welcome that,
And the rich arguments with which you prove it,   195
Wishing I could to your wish welcome you.
Draw, for your Marquisate, the articles
Agreed on in our composition,
And it is yours ; but where you have propos'd
(In your advices) my design for Milan,   200
I will have no war with the King of Spain

Unless his hopes prove weary of our peace;
And, princely cousin, it is far from me
To think your wisdom needful of my counsel,
Yet love oft-times must offer things unneedful;   205
And therefore I would counsel you to hold
All good terms with his Majesty of Spain:
If any troubles should be stirr'd betwixt you,
I would not stir therein, but to appease them;
I have too much care of my royal word   210
To break a peace so just and consequent,
Without force of precedent injury;
Endless desires are worthless of just princes,
And only proper to the swinge of tyrants.

    Sav. At all parts spoke like the Most Christian King.   215
I take my humblest leave, and pray your Highness
To hold me as your servant and poor kinsman,
Who wisheth no supremer happiness
Than to be yours. To you, right worthy princes,
I wish for all your favours pour'd on me   220
The love of all these ladies mutually,
And, so they please their lords, that they may please
Themselves by all means. And be you assur'd,
Most lovely princesses, as of your lives,
You cannot be true women if true wives.   *Exit* 225

    Hen. Is this he, Epernon, that you would needs persuade
us courted so absurdly?

    Ep. This is even he, sir, howsoever he hath studied his
parting courtship.

    Hen. In what one point seemed he so ridiculous as you   230
would present him?

    Ep. Behold me, sir, I beseech you behold me; I appear to
you as the great Duke of Savoy with these three ladies.

    Hen. Well, sir, we grant your resemblance.

    Ep. He stole a carriage, sir, from Count d'Auvergne here.   235

    D'Auv. From me, sir?

    Ep. Excuse me, sir, from you, I assure you: here, sir, he
lies at the Lady Antoinette, just thus, for the world, in the
true posture of Count d'Auvergne.

    D'Auv. Y'are exceeding delightsome.   240

    Hen. Why is not that well? It came in with the organ
hose.

    Ep. Organ hose? A pox on't! Let it pipe itself into
contempt; he hath stolen it most feloniously, and it graces
him like a disease.   245

Hen.　I think he stole it from D'Auvergne indeed.

Ep.　Well, would he had robbed him of all his other diseases ! He were then the soundest lord in France.

D'Auv.　As I am, sir, I shall stand all weathers with you.

Ep.　But, sir, he has praised you above th' invention 250 of rhymers.

Hen.　Wherein, or how ?

Ep.　He took upon him to describe your victories in war, and where he should have said you were the most absolute soldier in Christendom (no ass could have missed it), he 255 delivered you for as pretty a fellow of your hands as any was in France.

Hen.　Marry, God dild him !

Ep.　A pox on him !

Hen.　Well, to be serious, you know him well　　　260
To be a gallant courtier : his great wit
Can turn him into any form he lists,
More fit to be avoided than deluded.
For my Lord Duke of Byron here well knows
That it infecteth, where it doth affect,　　　265
And where it seems to counsel, it conspires.
With him go all our faults, and from us fly,
With all his counsel, all conspiracy.

FINIS ACTUS QUINTI ET ULTIMI

THE TRAGEDY OF CHARLES
DUKE OF BYRON

The Tragedy of Charles Duke of Byron

DRAMATIS PERSONAE

Henry IV, *King of France*
The Infant Dauphin
The Duke *of* Byron
D'Auvergne
The Spanish Ambassador
La Fin
The Vidame *of Chartres, his nephew*

Epernon,
Soissons,
Montigny,
D'Escures, } *French Nobles*

Harlay,
Potier,
Fleury, } *Judges*

Bellièvre, *the Chancellor*
Janin,   a *Minister of Henry*
Prâlin,
Vitry, } *Captains of the Guard*
La Brunel, *a Captain under* Byron

Varennes, *Lieutenant of* Byron's Guard
A Bishop
A Captain of Byron's *Guard*
A Messenger
The Hangman
A Soldier

The Nurse *of the Dauphin*
A Lady
Byron's Sister

In the Masque
Marie de Medici, *Queen of France*
Mademoiselle d'Entragues, *the King's Mistress*
Cupid
Four Ladies

Torch-bearers, Ushers, Soldiers, Guards

ACTUS I SCENA I

[A Room in the Court]

Henry, the Vidame, D'Escures, Epernon, Janin

Hen. Byron fall'n in so trait'rous a relapse,
Alleged for our ingratitude ! What offices,
Titles of honour, and what admiration
Could France afford him that it pour'd not on ?
When he was scarce arriv'd at forty years,   5
He ran through all chief dignities of France.
At fourteen years of age he was made Colonel
To all the Suisses serving then in Flanders ;
Soon after he was Marshal of the camp,
And, shortly after, Marshal General ;   10
He was received High Admiral of France
In that our Parliament we held at Tours,
Marshal of France in that we held at Paris.
And at the siege of Amiens he acknowledg'd
None his superior but ourself, the King ;   15
Though I had there the Princes of the blood,
I made him my Lieutenant-General,
Declar'd him jointly the prime Peer of France,
And raised his barony into a duchy.
   Jan. And yet, my lord, all this could not allay   20
The fatal thirst of his ambition ;
For some have heard him say he would not die
Till on the wings of valour he had reach'd
One degree higher ; and had seen his head
Set on the royal quarter of a crown :   25
Yea, at so unbeliev'd a pitch he aim'd
That he hath said his heart would still complain
Till he aspir'd the style of Sovereign.
And from what ground, my lord, rise all the levies
Now made in Italy ? From whence should spring   30

The warlike humour of the Count Fuentes,
The restless stirrings of the Duke of Savoy,
The discontent the Spaniard entertain'd,
With such a threatening fury, when he heard
The prejudicial conditions   35
Propos'd him in the treaty held at Vervins,
And many other braveries this way aiming,
But from some hope of inward aid from hence ?
And that all this directly aims at you
Your Highness hath by one intelligence   40
Good cause to think ; which is your late advice
That the sea army, now prepar'd at Naples,
Hath an intended enterprise on Provence ;
Although the cunning Spaniard gives it out
That all is for Algier.

    Hen.   I must believe   45
That, without treason bred in our own breasts,
Spain's affairs are not in so good estate,
To aim at any action against France ;
And if Byron should be their instrument,
His alter'd disposition could not grow   50
So far wide in an instant ; nor resign
His valour to these lawless resolutions
Upon the sudden ; nor without some charms
Of foreign hopes and flatteries sung to him :
But far it flies my thoughts that such a spirit,   55
So active, valiant, and vigilant,
Can see itself transform'd with such wild furies,
And like a dream it shows to my conceits,
That he who by himself hath won such honour,
And he to whom his father left so much,   60
He that still daily reaps so much from me,
And knows he may increase it to more proof
From me than any other foreign king,
Should quite against the stream of all religion,
Honour, and reason, take a course so foul,   65
And neither keep his oath, nor save his soul.
Can the poor keeping of a citadel,
Which I denied to be at his disposure,
Make him forego the whole strength of his honours ?
It is impossible ; though the violence   70
Of his hot spirit made him make attempt
Upon our person for denying him,

Yet well I found his loyal judgment serv'd
To keep it from effect : besides, being offer'd
Two hundred thousand crowns in yearly pension,   75
And to be General of all the forces
The Spaniards had in France, they found him still
As an unmatch'd Achilles in the wars,
So a most wise Ulysses to their words,
Stopping his ears at their enchanted sounds ;   80
And plain he told them that although his blood,
Being mov'd, by nature were a very fire
And boil'd in apprehension of a wrong,
Yet should his mind hold such a sceptre there
As would contain it from all act and thought   85
Of treachery or ingratitude to his prince.
Yet do I long, methinks, to see La Fin,
Who hath his heart in keeping ; since his state,
Grown to decay and he to discontent,
Comes near the ambitious plight of Duke Byron.   90
My Lord Vidame, when does your lordship think
Your uncle of La Fin will be arriv'd ?
    Vid. I think, my lord, he now is near arriving,
For his particular journey and devotion
Vow'd to the holy Lady of Loretto,   95
Was long since past and he upon return.
    Hen. In him, as in a crystal that is charm'd,
I shall discern by whom and what designs
My rule is threaten'd ; and that sacred power
That hath enabled this defensive arm   100
(When I enjoy'd but an unequal nook
Of that I now possess) to front a king
Far my superior, and from twelve set battles
March home a victor—ten of them obtain'd,
Without my personal service—will not see   105
A trait'rous subject foil me, and so end
What his hand hath with such success begun.

    Enter a Lady *and a* Nurse *bringing the* Dauphin

    Ep. See the young Dauphin brought to cheer your
        Highness.
    Hen. My royal blessing and the King of Heaven
Make thee an aged and a happy king :   110
Help, nurse, to put my sword into his hand.

Hold, boy, by this ; and with it may thy arm
Cut from thy tree of rule all trait'rous branches
That strive to shadow and eclipse thy glories ;
Have thy old father's Angel for thy guide,   115
Redoubled be his spirit in thy breast
(Who, when this state ran like a turbulent sea
In civil hates and bloody enmity,
Their wraths and envies, like so many winds,
Settled and burst), and like the halcyon's birth,   120
Be thine to bring a calm upon the shore,
In which the eyes of war may ever sleep
As overmatch'd with former massacres,
When guilty [lust] made noblesse feed on noblesse—
All the sweet plenty of the realm exhausted—   125
When the nak'd merchant was pursu'd for spoil,
When the poor peasants frighted neediest thieves
With their pale leanness (nothing left on them
But meagre carcases sustain'd with air,
Wand'ring like ghosts affrighted from their graves),   130
When with the often and incessant sounds
The very beasts knew the alarum bell,
And, hearing it, ran bellowing to their home :
From which unchristian broils and homicides
Let the religious sword of justice free   135
Thee and thy kingdoms govern'd after me.
O heaven ! Or if th' unsettled blood of France
With ease and wealth renew her civil furies,
Let all my powers be emptied in my son
To curb and end them all, as I have done.   140
Let him by virtue quite [cut] off from Fortune
Her feather'd shoulders and her winged shoes,
And thrust from her light feet her turning stone
That she may ever tarry by his throne.
And of his worth let after ages say   145
(He fighting for the land and bringing home
Just conquests, loaden with his enemies' spoils),
His father pass'd all France in martial deeds,
But he his father twenty times exceeds.   [*Exeunt*]

[SCENA II

At Dijon]

Enter the Duke of Byron, D'Auvergne, *and* La Fin

Byr.   My dear friends, D'Auvergne and La Fin,
We need no conjurations to conceal
Our close intendments to advance our states
Even with our merits, which are now neglected;
Since Bretagne is reduc'd, and breathless War   5
Hath sheath'd his sword and wrapp'd his ensigns up,
The King hath now no more use of my valour,
And therefore I shall now no more enjoy
The credit that my service held with him—
My service that hath driven through all extremes,   10
Through tempests, droughts, and through the deepest floods,
Winters of shot, and over rocks so high
That birds could scarce aspire their ridgy tops.
The world is quite inverted, Virtue thrown
At Vice's feet, and sensual Peace confounds   15
Valour and cowardice, fame and infamy;
The rude and terrible age is turn'd again,
When the thick air hid heaven, and all the stars
Were drown'd in humour, tough and hard to pierce;
When the red sun held not his fixed place,   20
Kept not his certain course, his rise and set,
Nor yet distinguish'd with his definite bounds,
Nor in his firm conversions were discern'd
The fruitful distances of time and place
In the well-varied seasons of the year;   25
When th' incompos'd incursions of floods
Wasted and eat the earth, and all things show'd
Wild and disorder'd: nought was worse than now.
We must reform and have a new creation
Of state and government, and on our Chaos   30
Will I sit brooding up another world.
I, who through all the dangers that can siege
The life of man have forc'd my glorious way
To the repairing of my country's ruins,
Will ruin it again to re-advance it.   35
Roman Camillus sav'd the state of Rome
With far less merit than Byron hath France;
And how short of this is my recompence.

The King shall know I will have better price
Set on my services, in spite of whom   40
I will proclaim and ring my discontents
Into the farthest ear of all the world.
   La F. How great a spirit he breathes! How learn'd,
    how wise!
But, worthy Prince, you must give temperate air
To your unmatch'd and more than human wind,   45
Else will our plots be frost-bit in the flower.
   D'Auv. Betwixt ourselves we may give liberal vent
To all our fiery and displeas'd impressions;
Which nature could not entertain with life
Without some exhalation; a wrong'd thought   50
Will break a rib of steel.
   Byr.   My princely friend,
Enough of these eruptions; our grave counsellor
Well knows that great affairs will not be forg'd
But upon anvils that are lin'd with wool;
We must ascend to our intentions' top   55
Like clouds, that be not seen till they be up.
   La F. O, you do too much ravish and my soul
Offer to music in your numerous breath,
Sententious, and so high it wakens death:
It is for these parts that the Spanish King   60
Hath sworn to win them to his side
At any price or peril, that great Savoy
Offers his princely daughter and a dowry
Amounting to five hundred thousand crowns,
With full transport of all the sovereign rights   65
Belonging to the State of Burgundy;
Which marriage will be made the only cement
T'effect and strengthen all our secret treaties.
Instruct me therefore, my assured Prince,
Now I am going to resolve the King   70
Of his suspicions, how I shall behave me.
   Byr. Go, my most trusted friend, with happy feet;
Make me a sound man with him; go to Court
But with a little train, and be prepar'd
To hear, at first, terms of contempt and choler,   75
Which you may easily calm, and turn to grace,
If you beseech his Highness to believe
That your whole drift and course for Italy
(Where he hath heard you were) was only made

Out of your long well-known devotion   80
To our right holy Lady of Loretto,
As you have told some of your friends in Court,
And that in passing Milan and Turin
They charg'd you to propound my marriage
With the third daughter of the Duke of Savoy ;   85
Which you have done, and I rejected it,
Resolv'd to build upon his royal care
For my bestowing, which he lately vow'd.
 La F. O, you direct, as if the God of light
Sat in each nook of you and pointed out   90
The path of empire, charming all the dangers,
On both sides arm'd, with his harmonious finger.
 Byr. Besides, let me entreat you to dismiss
All that have made the voyage with your lordship,
But specially the curate, and to lock   95
Your papers in some place of doubtless safety,
Or sacrifice them to the God of fire,
Considering worthily that in your hands
I put my fortunes, honour, and my life.
 La F. Therein the bounty that your Grace hath shown me 100
I prize past life and all things that are mine,
And will undoubtedly preserve and tender
The merit of it, as my hope of heaven.
 Byr. I make no question ; farewell, worthy friend.
         Exit [Byron *with the others*]

[SCENA III

A Room in the Court]

Henry, Chancellor, La Fin, D'Escures, Janin ; Henry
   having many papers in his hand

 Hen. Are these proofs of that purely Catholic zeal
That made him wish no other glorious title
Than to be call'd the Scourge of Huguenots ?
 Chan. No question, sir, he was of no religion ;
But, upon false grounds by some courtiers laid,   5
Hath oft been heard to mock and jest at all.
 Hen. Are not his treasons heinous ?
 All.   Most abhorr'd.
 Chan. All is confirm'd that you have heard before,
And amplified with many horrors more.

Hen. Good de la Fin, you were our golden plummet   10
To sound this gulf of all ingratitude ;
In which you have with excellent desert
Of loyalty and policy express'd
Your name in action ; and with such appearance
Have prov'd the parts of his ingrateful treasons   15
That I must credit more than I desir'd.
　　La F. I must confess, my lord, my voyages
Made to the Duke of Savoy and to Milan
Were with endeavour that the wars return'd
Might breed some trouble to your Majesty,   20
And profit those by whom they were procur'd ;
But since in their designs your sacred person
Was not excepted, which I since have seen,
It so abhorr'd me that I was resolv'd
To give you full intelligence thereof ;   25
And rather choos'd to fail in promises
Made to the servant than infringe my fealty
Sworn to my royal Sovereign and master.
　　Hen. I am extremely discontent to see
This most unnatural conspiracy ;   30
And would not have the Marshal of Byron
The first example of my forced justice ;
Nor that his death should be the worthy cause
That my calm reign (which hitherto hath held
A clear and cheerful sky above the heads   35
Of my dear subjects) should so suddenly
Be overcast with clouds of fire and thunder ;
Yet on submission, I vow still his pardon.
　　Jan. And still our humble counsels, for his service,
Would so resolve you, if he will employ   40
His honour'd valour as effectually
To fortify the state against your foes
As he hath practis'd bad intendments with them.
　　Hen. That vow shall stand, and we will now address
Some messengers to call him home to Court,   45
Without the slend'rest intimation
Of any ill we know ; we will restrain
(With all forgiveness, if he will confess)
His headlong course to ruin ; and his taste
From the sweet poison of his friendlike foes :   50
Treason hath blister'd heels ; dishonest things
Have bitter rivers, though delicious springs.

D'Escures, haste you unto him and inform,
That having heard by sure intelligence
Of the great levies made in Italy   55
Of arms and soldiers, I am resolute,
Upon my frontiers to maintain an army,
The charge whereof I will impose on him ;
And to that end expressly have commanded
De Vic, our Lord Ambassador in Suisse,   60
To demand levy of six thousand men,
Appointing them to march where Duke Byron
Shall have directions ; wherein I have follow'd
The counsel of my Constable, his gossip ;
Whose lik'd advice I made him know by letters,   65
Wishing to hear his own from his own mouth,
And by all means conjure his speediest presence ;
Do this with utmost haste.
    D'Es.   I will, my lord.
                             Exit D'Escures
    Hen. My good Lord Chancellor, of many pieces,
More than is here, of his conspiracies   70
Presented to us by our friend La Fin,
You only shall reserve these seven-and-twenty,
Which are not those that [most] conclude against him,
But mention only him, since I am loth
To have the rest of the conspirators known.   75
    Chan. My lord, my purpose is to guard all these
So safely from the sight of any other
That in my doublet I will have them sew'd,
Without discovering them to mine own eyes
Till need or opportunity requires.   80
    Hen. You shall do well, my lord, they are of weight ;
But I am doubtful that his conscience
Will make him so suspicious of the worst
That he will hardly be induc'd to come.
    Jan. I much should doubt that too, but that I hope   85
The strength of his conspiracy as yet
Is not so ready that he dare presume
By his refusal to make known so much
Of his disloyalty.
    Hen.   I yet conceive
His practices are turn'd to no bad end ;   90
And, good La Fin, I pray you write to him
To hasten his repair, and make him sure

That you have satisfied me to the full
For all his actions, and have utter'd nought
But what might serve to banish bad impressions.   95
  La F. I will not fail, my lord.
  Hen.   Convey your letters
By some choice friend of his, or by his brother ;
And for a third excitement to his presence,
Janin, yourself shall go, and with the power
That both the rest employ to make him come,   100
Use you the strength of your persuasions.
  Jan. I will, my lord, and hope I shall present him.

                                           Exit Janin

            *   *   *   *   *

[ACTUS II

A Room in the Court]

  Enter Epernon, Soissons, Vitry, Prâlin, etc. [*to the* King]

  Ep. Will't please your Majesty to take your place ?
The Masque is coming.
  Hen.   Room, my lords ; stand close.

Music and a song above, and Cupid *enters with a table written
    hung about his neck ; after him two torch-bearers ; after
    them* Marie, D'Entragues, *and four ladies more with their
    torch-bearers, etc.*
    Cupid *speaks.*

  Cup. My lord, these nymphs, part of the scatter'd train
Of friendless Virtue (living in the woods
Of shady Arden, and of late not hearing   5
The dreadful sounds of war, but that sweet Peace,
Was by your valour lifted from her grave,
Set on your royal right hand, and all Virtues
Summon'd with honour and with rich rewards
To be her handmaids) : these, I say, the Virtues,   10
Have put their heads out of their caves and coverts,
To be your true attendants in your Court :
In which desire I must relate a tale
Of kind and worthy emulation
'Twixt these two Virtues, leaders of the train,   15
This on the right hand is Sophrosyne,
Or Chastity, this other Dapsile,

Or Liberality ; their emulation
Begat a jar, which thus was reconcil'd.
I (having left my Goddess mother's lap,　　　　20
To hawk and shoot at birds in Arden groves)
Beheld this princely nymph with much affection,
Left killing birds, and turn'd into a bird,
Like which I flew betwixt her ivory breasts
As if I had been driven by some hawk　　　　25
To sue to her for safety of my life ;
She smil'd at first, and sweetly shadow'd me
With soft protection of her silver hand ;
Sometimes she tied my legs in her rich hair,
And made me (past my nature, liberty)　　　　30
Proud of my fetters. As I pertly sat,
On the white pillows of her naked breasts,
I sung for joy ; she answer'd note for note,
Relish for relish, with such ease and art
In her divine division, that my tunes　　　　35
Show'd like the God of shepherds' to the Sun's,
Compar'd with hers ; asham'd of which disgrace,
I took my true shape, bow, and all my shafts,
And lighted all my torches at her eyes ;
Which set about her in a golden ring,　　　　40
I follow'd birds again from tree to tree,
Kill'd and presented, and she kindly took.
But when she handled my triumphant bow,
And saw the beauty of my golden shafts,
She begg'd them of me ; I, poor boy, replied　　　　45
I had no other riches, yet was pleas'd
To hazard all and stake them gainst a kiss
At an old game I us'd, call'd penny-prick.
She, privy to her own skill in the play,
Answer'd my challenge ; so I lost my arms,　　　　50
And now my shafts are headed with her looks ;
One of which shafts she put into my bow,
And shot at this fair nymph, with whom before,
I told your Majesty she had some jar.
The nymph did instantly repent all parts　　　　55
She play'd in urging that effeminate war,
Lov'd and submitted ; which submission
This took so well that now they both are one ;
And as for your dear love their discords grew,
So for your love they did their loves renew.　　　　60

And now to prove them capable of your Court
In skill of such conceits and qualities
As here are practis'd, they will first submit
Their grace in dancing to your Highness' doom,
And p[r]ay the press to give their measures room.   65

Music, dance, etc., which done Cupid *speaks*

If this suffice for one Court compliment
To make them gracious and entertain'd,
Behold another parcel of their courtship,
Which is a rare dexterity in riddles,
Shown in one instance, which is here inscrib'd.   70
Here is a riddle, which if any knight
At first sight can resolve, he shall enjoy
This jewel here annex'd ; which, though it show
To vulgar eyes no richer than a pebble,
And that no lapidary nor great man   75
Will give a sou for it, 'tis worth a kingdom ;
For 'tis an artificial stone compos'd
By their great mistress, Virtue, and will make
Him that shall wear it live with any little
Suffic'd and more content than any king.   80
If he that undertakes cannot resolve it,
And that these nymphs can have no harbour here
(It being consider'd that so many Virtues
Can never live in Court), he shall resolve
To leave the Court and live with them in Arden.   85
  Ep. Pronounce the riddle ; I will undertake it.
  Cup. 'Tis this, sir.
What's that a fair lady most of all likes,
Yet ever makes show she least of all seeks :
That's ever embrac'd and affected by her,   90
Yet never is seen to please or come nigh her :
Most serv'd in her night-weeds, does her good in a corner :
But a poor man's thing, yet doth richly adorn her :
Most cheap and most dear, above all worldly pelf,
That is hard to get in, but comes out of itself ?
  Ep. Let me peruse it, Cupid.   95
  Cup.   Here it is.
  Ep. Your riddle is good fame.
  Cup. Good fame ? How make you that good ?
  Ep. Good fame is that a good lady most likes, I am sure.

Cup. That's granted.　　　　　　　　　　　　　　100

Ep. ' Yet ever makes show she least of all seeks ' : for she
likes it only for virtue, which is not glorious.

Hen. That holds well.

Ep. 'Tis ' ever embrac'd and affected by her ', for she
must persevere in virtue or fame vanishes ; ' yet never is seen 105
to please or come nigh her ', for fame is invisible.

Cup. Exceeding right !

Ep. ' Most served in her night-weeds ', for ladies that
most wear their night-weeds come least abroad, and they that
come least abroad serve fame most, according to this : *Non* 110
forma, sed fama, in publicum exire debet.

Hen. 'Tis very substantial.

Ep. ' Does her good in a corner '—that is, in her most
retreat from the world comforts her ; ' but a poor man's
thing ' : for every poor man may purchase it, ' yet doth richly 115
adorn ' a lady.

Cup. That all must grant.

Ep. ' Most cheap,' for it costs nothing ; 'and most dear',
for gold cannot buy it ; ' above all worldly pelf ', for that's
transitory, and fame eternal. 'It is hard to get in'; that 120
is, hard to get ; ' but comes out of itself ', for when it is
virtuously deserved with the most inward retreat from
the world, it comes out in spite of it. And so, Cupid, your
jewel is mine.

Cup. It is : and be the virtue of it yours.
We'll now turn to our dance, and then attend　　　　125
Your Highness' will, as touching our resort,
If Virtue may be entertain'd in Court.

Hen. This show hath pleased me well for that it figures
The reconcilement of my Queen and mistress :
Come, let us in and thank them, and prepare　　　　130
To entertain our trusty friend Byron.　　　*Exeunt*

FINIS ACTUS SECUNDI

ACTUS III SCENA I

[At Dijon]

Enter Byron, D'Auvergne

Byr. Dear friend, we must not be more true to kings
Than kings are to their subjects ; there are schools
Now broken ope in all parts of the world,

First founded in ingenious Italy,
Where some conclusions of estate are held   5
That for a day preserve a prince, and ever
Destroy him after ; from thence men are taught
To glide into degrees of height by craft,
And then lock in themselves by villany :
But God (who knows kings are not made by art,   10
But right of Nature, nor by treachery propp'd,
But simple virtue) once let fall from heaven
A branch of that green tree, whose root is yet
Fast fix'd above the stars ; which sacred branch
We well may liken to that laurel spray   15
That from the heavenly eagle's golden seres
Fell in the lap of great Augustus' wife ;
Which spray, once set, grew up into a tree
Whereof were garlands made, and emperors
Had their estates and foreheads crown'd with them ; 20
And as the arms of that tree did decay
The race of great Augustus wore away ;
Nero being last of that imperial line,
The tree and Emperor together died.
Religion is a branch, first set and blest   25
By Heaven's high finger in the hearts of kings,
Which whilom grew into a goodly tree ;
Bright angels sat and sung upon the twigs,
And royal branches for the heads of kings
Were twisted of them ; but since squint-eyed Envy 30
And pale Suspicion dash'd the heads of kingdoms
One gainst another, two abhorred twins,
With two foul tails, stern War and Liberty,
Enter'd the world. The tree that grew from heaven
Is overrun with moss ; the cheerful music   35
That heretofore hath sounded out of it
Begins to cease ; and as she casts her leaves,
By small degrees the kingdoms of the earth
Decline and wither ; and look, whensoever
That the pure sap in her is dried-up quite,   40
The lamp of all authority goes out,
And all the blaze of princes is extinct.
Thus, as the poet sends a messenger
Out to the stage to show the sum of all
That follows after, so are kings' revolts   45
And playing both ways with religion

Fore-runners of afflictions imminent,
Which (like a Chorus) subjects must lament.

 D'Auv. My lord, I stand not on these deep discourses
To settle my course to your fortunes ; mine   50
Are freely and inseparably link'd,
And to your love, my life.

 Byr.   Thanks, princely friend ;
And whatsoever good shall come of me,
Pursu'd by all the Catholic Princes' aids
With whom I join, and whose whole states propos'd 55
To win my valour, promise me a throne,
All shall be, equal with myself, thine own.

[Enter La Brunel]

 La Brun. My lord, here is D'Escures, sent from the King,
Desires access to you.

 Byr.   Attend him in.

Enter D'Escures

 D'Es. Health to my lord the Duke !

 Byr.   Welcome, D'Escures ! 60
In what health rests our royal Sovereign ?

 D'Es. In good health of his body, but his mind
Is something troubled with the gathering storms
Of foreign powers, that, as he is inform'd,
Address themselves into his frontier towns ;   65
And therefore his intent is to maintain
The body of an army on those parts,
And yield their worthy conduct to your valour.

 Byr. From whence hears he that any storms are rising ?

 D'Es. From Italy ; and his intelligence   70
No doubt is certain, that in all those parts
Levies are hotly made ; for which respect,
He sent to his ambassador, de Vic,
To make demand in Switzerland for the raising
With utmost diligence of six thousand men,   75
All which shall be commanded to attend
On your direction, as the Constable,
Your honour'd gossip, gave him in advice,
And he sent you by writing ; of which letters
He would have answer and advice from you   80
By your most speedy presence.

 Byr.   This is strange,

That when the enemy is t'attempt his frontiers
He calls me from the frontiers ; does he think
It is an action worthy of my valour
To turn my back to an approaching foe ?   85
    D'Es.   The foe is not so near but you may come,
And take more strict directions from his Highness
Than he thinks fit his letters should contain,
Without the least attainture of your valour.
And therefore, good my lord, forbear excuse,   90
And bear yourself on his direction,
Who, well you know, hath never made design
For your most worthy service where he saw
That anything but honour could succeed.
    Byr.   I will not come, I swear.
    D'Es.   I know your Grace   95
Will send no such unsavoury reply.
    Byr.   Tell him that I beseech his Majesty
To pardon my repair till th' end be known
Of all these levies now in Italy.
    D'Es.   My lord, I know that tale will never please him, 100
And wish you, as you love his love and pleasure,
To satisfy his summons speedily,
And speedily I know he will return you.
    Byr.   By heaven, it is not fit, if all my service
Makes me know anything : beseech him, therefore,   105
To trust my judgment in these doubtful charges,
Since in assur'd assaults it hath not fail'd him.
    D'Es.   I would your lordship now would trust his judg-
        ment.
    Byr.   God's precious, y'are importunate past measure,
And, I know, further than your charge extends.   110
I'll satisfy his Highness, let that serve ;
For by this flesh and blood, you shall not bear
Any reply to him but this from me.
    D'Es.   'Tis nought to me, my lord ; I wish your good,
And for that cause have been importunate.   115
                                   Exit D'Escures
    La Brun.   By no means go, my lord ; but, with distrust
Of all that hath been said or can be sent,
Collect your friends, and stand upon your guard ;
The King's fair letters and his messages
Are only golden pills, and comprehend   120
Horrible purgatives.

Byr.   I will not go,
For now I see th' instructions lately sent me
That something is discover'd are too true,
And my head rules none of those neighbour nobles
That every pursuivant brings beneath the axe :   125
If they bring me out, they shall see I'll hatch
Like to the blackthorn, that puts forth his leaf,
Not with the golden fawnings of the sun,
But sharpest showers of hail, and blackest frosts :
Blows, batteries, breaches, showers of steel and blood,   130
Must be his downright messengers for me,
And not the mizzling breath of policy ;
He, he himself, made passage to his crown
Through no more armies, battles, massacres
Than I will ask him to arrive at me.   135
He takes on him my executions ;
And on the demolitions, that this arm
Hath shaken out of forts and citadels,
Hath he advanc'd the trophies of his valour ;
Where I, in those assumptions, may scorn   140
And speak contemptuously of all the world,
For any equal yet I ever found ;
And in my rising, not the Sirian star
That in the Lion's mo[n]th undaunted shines,
And makes his brave ascension with the sun,   145
Was of th' Egyptians with more zeal beheld,
And made a rule to know the circuit
And compass of the year, than I was held
When I appear'd from battle, the whole sphere
And full sustainer of the state we bear ;   150
I have Alcides-like gone under th' earth,
And on these shoulders borne the weight of France :
And for the fortunes of the thankless King,
My father, all know, set him in his throne,
And, if he urge me, I may pluck him out.   155

Enter Messenger

Mes. Here is the President Janin, my lord,
Sent from the King, and urgeth quick access.
Byr. Another pursuivant, and one so quick ?
He takes next course with me to make him stay :
But let him in, let's hear what he importunes.   160

[*Exit* La Brunel], *enter* Janin

Jan.   Honour and loyal hopes to Duke Byron!
Byr.   No other touch me : say how fares the King?
Jan.   Fairly, my lord ; the cloud is yet far off
That aims at his obscuring, and his will
Would gladly give the motion to your powers   165
That should disperse it ; but the means himself
Would personally relate in your direction.
Byr.   Still on that haunt?
Jan.   Upon my life, my lord,
He much desires to see you ; and your sight
Is now grown necessary to suppress   170
(As with the glorious splendour of the sun)
The rude winds that report breathes in his ears,
Endeavouring to blast your loyalty.
Byr.   Sir, if my loyalty stick in him no faster
But that the light breath of report may loose it,   175
So I rest still unmov'd, let him be shaken.
Jan.   But these aloof abodes, my lord, bewray,
That there is rather firmness in your breath
Than in your heart.   Truth is not made of glass,
That with a small touch it should fear to break,   180
And therefore should not shun it ; believe me
His arm is long, and strong ; and it can fetch
Any within his will, that will not come :
Not he that surfeits in his mines of gold,
And for the pride thereof compares with God,   185
Calling (with almost nothing different)
His powers invincible, for omnipotent,
Can back your boldest fort gainst his assaults :
It is his pride, and vain ambition,
That hath but two stairs in his high designs—   190
The lowest, envy, and the highest, blood—
That doth abuse you, and gives minds too high
Rather a will by giddiness to fall
Than to descend by judgment.
Byr.   I rely
On no man's back nor belly ; but the King   195
Must think that merit, by ingratitude crack'd,
Requires a firmer cementing than words.
And he shall find it a much harder work,
To solder broken hearts than shiver'd glass.

Jan. My lord, 'tis better hold a Sovereign's love   200
By bearing injuries, than by laying out
Stir his displeasure ; princes' discontents,
Being once incens'd, are like the flames of Etna,
Not to be quench'd, nor lessen'd ; and, be sure,
A subject's confidence in any merit   205
Against his Sovereign, that makes him presume
To fly too high, approves him like a cloud
That makes a show as it did hawk at kingdoms,
And could command all rais'd beneath his vapour :
When suddenly, the fowl that hawk'd so fair,   210
Stoops in a puddle, or consumes in air.

Byr. I fly with no such aim, nor am oppos'd
Against my Sovereign ; but the worthy height
I have wrought by my service I will hold,
Which, if I come away, I cannot do ;   215
For if the enemy should invade the frontier,
Whose charge to guard is mine, with any spoil,
Although the King in placing of another
Might well excuse me, yet all foreign kings,
That can take note of no such secret quittance,   220
Will lay the weakness here, upon my wants ;
And therefore my abode is resolute,

Jan. I sorrow for your resolution,
And fear your dissolution will succeed.

Byr. I must endure it.

Jan.   Fare you well, my lord !   225

                                    Exit Janin

Enter La Brunel

Byr. Farewell to you !
Captain, what other news ?

La Brun.   La Fin salutes you. [*Giving letters*]

Byr. Welcome, good friend ; I hope your wish'd arrival
Will give some certain end to our designs.

La Brun. I know not that, my lord ; reports are rais'd   230
So doubtful and so different, that the truth
Of any one can hardly be assur'd.

Byr. Good news, D'Auvergne ; our trusty friend La Fin
Hath clear'd all scruple with his Majesty,
And utter'd nothing but what serv'd to clear   235
All bad suggestions.

La Brun.   So he says, my lord ;

But others say La Fin's assurances
Are mere deceits, and wish you to believe
That, when the Vidame, nephew to La Fin,
Met you at Autun to assure your doubts   240
His uncle had said nothing to the King
That might offend you, all the journey's charge
The King defray'd ; besides, your truest friends
Will'd me to make you certain that your place
Of government is otherwise dispos'd ;   245
And all advise you, for your latest hope,
To make retreat into the Franche-Comté.

    Byr. I thank them all, but they touch not the depth
Of the affairs betwixt La Fin and me,
Who is return'd contented to his house,   250
Quite freed of all displeasure or distrust ;
And therefore, worthy friends, we'll now to Court.

    D'Auv. My lord, I like your other friends' advices
Much better than La Fin's ; and on my life
You cannot come to Court with any safety.   255

    Byr. Who shall infringe it ? I know all the Court
Have better apprehension of my valour
Than that they dare lay violent hands on me ;
If I have only means to draw this sword,
I shall have power enough to set me free   260
From seizure by my proudest enemy.

                Exit [Byron *with the others*]

[SCENA II

A Room in the Court]

Enter Epernon, Vitry, Prâlin

    Ep. He will not come, I dare engage my hand.
    Vit. He will be fetch'd then, I'll engage my head.
    Prâ. Come, or be fetch'd, he quite hath lost his honour
In giving these suspicions of revolt
From his allegiance ; that which he hath won   5
With sundry wounds, and peril of his life,
With wonder of his wisdom and his valour,
He loseth with a most enchanted glory,
And admiration of his pride and folly.
    Vit. Why, did you never see a fortunate man   10

Suddenly rais'd to heaps of wealth and honour.
Nor any rarely great in gifts of nature
(As valour, wit, and smooth use of the tongue
Set strangely to the pitch of popular likings),
But with as sudden falls the rich and honour'd   15
Were overwhelm'd by poverty and shame,
Or had no use of both above the wretched ?

   Ep.   Men ne'er are satisfied with that they have ;
But as a man match'd with a lovely wife
When his most heavenly theory of her beauties   20
Is dull'd and quite exhausted with his practice,
He brings her forth to feasts, where he, alas !
Fails to his viands with no thought like others
That think him blest in her ; and they, poor men,
Court, and make faces, offer service, sweat   25
With their desires' contention, break their brains
For jests and tales, sit mute and lose their looks
(Far out of wit, and out of countenance) :
So all men else do, what they have, transplant,
And place their wealth in thirst of what they want.   30

   Enter Henry, Chancellor, *the* Vidame, D'Escures, Janin

   Hen.   He will not come : I must both grieve and wonder,
That all my care to win my subjects' love
And in one cup of friendship to commix
Our lives and fortunes, should leave out so many
As give a man (contemptuous of my love   35
And of his own good in the kingdom's peace)
Hope, in a continuance so ungrateful,
To bear out his designs in spite of me.
How should I better please all than I do ?
When they suppos'd I would have given some   40
Insolent garrisons, others citadels,
And to all sorts increase of miseries,
Province by province I did visit all
Whom those injurious rumours had dis[m]ay'd,
And show'd them how I never sought to build   45
More forts for me than were within their hearts,
Nor use more stern constraints than their good wills
To succour the necessities of my crown ;
That I desir'd to add to their contents
By all occasions rather than subtract ;   50

Nor wish'd I that my treasury should flow
With gold that swum in, in my subjects' tears;
And then I found no man that did not bless
My few years' reign, and their triumphant peace;
And do they now so soon complain of ease?   55
He will not come!

Enter Byron, D'Auvergne, brother, *with others*

Ep.   O madness, he is come!
Chan. The Duke is come, my lord.
Hen.   Oh sir, y'are welcome,
And fitly, to conduct me to my house.
Byr. I must beseech your Majesty's excuse,
That, jealous of mine honour, I have us'd   60
Some of mine own commandment in my stay,
And came not with your Highness' soonest summons.
Hen. The faithful servant, right in Holy Writ,
That said he would not come and yet he came:
But come you hither, I must tell you now   65
Not the contempt you stood to in your stay,
But the bad ground that bore up your contempt,
Makes you arrive at no port but repentance,
Despair, and ruin.
Byr.   Be what port it will,
At which your will will make me be arrived,   70
I am not come to justify myself,
To ask you pardon, nor accuse my friends.
Hen. If you conceal my enemies, you are one;
And then my pardon shall be worth your asking,
Or else your head be worth my cutting off.   75
Byr. Being friend and worthy fautor of myself,
I am no foe of yours, nor no impairer,
Since he can no way worthily maintain
His prince's honour that neglects his own;
And if your will have been, to my true reason,   80
(Maintaining still the truth of loyalty)
A check to my free nature and mine honour,
And that on your free justice I presum'd
To cross your will a little, I conceive
You will not think this forfeit worth my head.   85
Hen. Have you maintain'd your truth of loyalty,
When, since I pardon'd foul intentions

(Resolving to forget eternally
What they appear'd in, and had welcom'd you
As the kind father doth his riotous son),　　　　　90
I can approve facts fouler than th' intents
Of deep disloyalty and highest treason ?

　Byr.　May this right hand be thunder to my breast,
If I stand guilty of the slend'rest fact
Wherein the least of those two can be proved,　　95
For could my tender conscience but have touch'd
At any such unnatural relapse,
I would not with this confidence have run
Thus headlong in the furnace of a wrath
Blown and thrice kindled, having way enough　　100
In my election both to shun and slight it.

　Hen.　Y'are grossly and vaingloriously abus'd ;
There is no way in Savoy nor in Spain
To give a fool that hope of your escape ;
And had you not, even when you did, arrived,　　105
With horror to the proudest hope you had
I would have fetch'd you.

　Byr.　　　　　　　You must then have us'd
A power beyond my knowledge, and a will
Beyond your justice. For a little stay
More than I us'd would hardly have been worthy　　110
Of such an open expedition ;
In which to all the censures of the world
My faith and innocence had been foully foil'd ;
Which, I protest by heaven's bright witnesses
That shine far, far, from mixture with our fears,　　115
Retain as perfect roundness as their spheres.

　Hen.　'Tis well, my lord ; I thought I could have frighted
Your firmest confidence : some other time
We will, as now in private, sift your actions,
And pour more than you think into the sieve,　　120
Always reserving clemency and pardon
Upon confession, be you ne'er so foul.
Come, let's clear up our brows : shall we to tennis ?

　Byr.　Ay, my lord, if I may make the match.
The Duke Epernon and myself will play　　125
With you and Count Soissons.

　Ep.　　　　　　　I know, my lord,
You play well, but you make your matches ill.

　Hen.　Come, 'tis a match　　　　　　*Exit*

Byr. [*To* Epernon]   How like you my arrival ?

Ep.   I'll tell you as your friend in your ear.

You have given more preferment to your courage   130
Than to the provident counsels of your friends.

D'Auv.   I told him so, my lord, and much was griev'd
To see his bold approach, so full of will.

Byr.   Well, I must bear it now, though but with th' head,
The shoulders bearing nothing.

Ep.   By Saint John,   135
'Tis a good headless resolution.   *Exeunt*

ACTUS IV SCENA I

[*A Room in the Court*]

Byron, D'Auvergne

Byr.   O the most base fruits of a settled peace !
In men I mean, worse than their dirty fields,
Which they manure much better than themselves :
For them they plant and sow, and ere they grow
Weedy and chok'd with thorns, they grub and proin,   5
And make them better than when cruel war
Frighted from thence the sweaty labourer ;
But men themselves, instead of bearing fruits,
Grow rude and foggy, overgrown with weeds,
Their spirits and freedoms smother'd in their ease ;   10
And as their tyrants and their ministers
Grow wild in prosecution of their lusts,
So they grow prostitute, and lie, like whores,
Down, and take up, to their abhorr'd dishonours ;
The friendless may be injur'd and oppress'd,   15
The guiltless led to slaughter, the deserver
Given to the beggar, right be wholly wrong'd,
And wrong be only honour'd, till the strings
Of every man's heart crack ; and who will stir
To tell authority that it doth err ?   20
All men cling to it, though they see their bloods
In their most dear associates and allies,
Pour'd into kennels by it, and who dares
But look well in the breast whom that impairs ?
How all the Court now looks askew on me !   25
Go by without saluting, shun my sight,

Which, like a March sun, agues breeds in them,
From whence of late 'twas health to have a beam.
   D'Auv. Now none will speak to us ; we thrust ourselves
Into men's companies, and offer speech   30
As if not made for their diverted ears,
Their backs turn'd to us, and their words to others.
And we must, like obsequious parasites,
Follow their faces, wind about their persons
For looks and answers, or be cast behind,   35
No more view'd than the wallet of their faults.

Enter Soissons

   Byr. Yet here's one views me, and I think will speak.
   Sois. My lord, if you respect your name and race,
The preservation of your former honours,
Merits, and virtues, humbly cast them all   40
At the King's mercy ; for beyond all doubt
Your acts have thither driven them ; he hath proofs
So pregnant and so horrid, that to hear them
Would make your valour in your very looks
Give up your forces, miserably guilty ;   45
But he is most loath (for his ancient love
To your rare virtues, and in their impair,
The full discouragement of all that live
To trust or favour any gifts in nature)
T'expose them to the light, when darkness may   50
Cover her own brood, and keep still in day
Nothing of you but that may brook her brightness :
You know what horrors these high strokes do bring
Rais'd in the arm of an incensed king.
   Byr. My lord, be sure the King cannot complain   55
Of anything in me but my true service,
Which, in so many dangers of my death,
May so approve my spotless loyalty
That those quite opposite horrors you assure
Must look out of his own ingratitude,   60
Or the malignant envies of my foes,
Who pour me out in such a Stygian flood,
To drown me in myself, since their deserts
Are far from such a deluge, and in me
Hid like so many rivers in the sea.   65
   Sois. You think I come to sound you : fare you well.
Exit

Enter Chancellor, Epernon, Janin, *the* Vidame, Vitry, Prâlin,
whispering by couples, etc.

D'Auv. See, see, not one of them will cast a glance
At our eclipsed faces.

Byr.   They keep all
To cast in admiration on the King ;
For from his face are all their faces moulded.   70

D'Auv.   But when a change comes we shall see them all
Chang'd into water, that will instantly
Give look for look, as if it watch'd to greet us ;
Or else for one they'll give us twenty faces,
Like to the little specks on sides of glasses.   75

Byr. Is't not an easy loss to lose their looks
Whose hearts so soon are melted ?

D'Auv.   But methinks,
Being courtiers, they should cast best looks on men
When they thought worst of them.

Byr.   O no, my lord !
They ne'er dissemble but for some advantage ;   80
They sell their looks and shadows, which they rate
After their markets, kept beneath the State ;
Lord, what foul weather their aspects do threaten !
See in how grave a brake he sets his vizard ;
Passion of nothing, see, an excellent gesture !   85
Now courtship goes a-ditching in their foreheads,
And we are fall'n into those dismal ditches.
Why even thus dreadfully would they be rapt,
If the King's butter'd eggs were only spilt.

Enter Henry

Hen.   Lord Chancellor !
Chan.   Ay, my lord !
Hen.   And Lord Vidame !   90
          Exit [Henry *with the* Chancellor *and the* Vidame]

Byr. And not Byron ? Here's a prodigious change !
D'Auv. He cast no beam on you.
Byr.   Why, now you see
From whence their countenances were copied.

Enter the Captain of Byron's guard, *with a letter*

D'Auv. See, here comes some news, I believe, my lord.
Byr. What says the honest Captain of my guard ?   95

Cap. I bring a letter from a friend of yours.

Byr. 'Tis welcome, then.

D'Auv.   Have we yet any friends?

Cap. More than ye would, I think; I never saw
Men in their right minds so unrighteous
In their own causes.

Byr. [*showing the letter*] See what thou hast brought.   100
He wills us to retire ourselves my lord,
And makes as if it were almost too late.
What says my captain? Shall we go, or no?

Cap. I would your dagger's point had kiss'd my heart,
When you resolv'd to come.

Byr.   I pray thee, why?   105

Cap. Yet doth that senseless apoplexy dull you?
The devil or your wicked angel blinds you,
Bereaving all your reason of a man,
And leaves you but the spirit of a horse
In your brute nostrils, only power to dare.   110

Byr. Why, dost thou think my coming here hath brought
    me
To such an unrecoverable danger?

Cap. Judge by the strange ostents that have succeeded
Since your arrival; the kind fowl, the wild duck,
That came into your cabinet so beyond   115
The sight of all your servants, or yourself,
That flew about, and on your shoulder sat,
And which you had so fed and so attended
For that dumb love she show'd you, just as soon
As you were parted, on the sudden died.   120
And to make this no less than an ostent,
Another, that hath fortun'd since, confirms it:
Your goodly horse, Pastrana, which the Archduke
Gave you at Brussels, in the very hour
You left your strength, fell mad, and kill'd himself;   125
The like chanc'd to the horse the Great Duke sent you;
And, with both these, the horse the Duke of Lorraine
Sent you at Vimy, made a third presage
Of some inevitable fate that touch'd you,
Who, like the other, pin'd away and died.   130

Byr. All these together are indeed ostentful,
Which, by another like, I can confirm:
The matchless Earl of Essex, whom some make
(In their most sure divinings of my death)

A parallel with me in life and fortune,   135
Had one horse, likewise, that the very hour
He suffer'd death (being well the night before),
Died in his pasture. Noble, happy beasts,
That die, not having to their wills to live ;
They use no deprecations nor complaints,   140
Nor suit for mercy ; amongst them, the lion
Serves not the lion, nor the horse the horse,
As man serves man : when men show most their spirits
In valour, and their utmost dares to do
They are compar'd to lions, wolves, and boars ;   145
But, by conversion, none will say a lion
Fights as he had the spirit of a man.
Let me then in my danger now give cause
For all men to begin that simile.
For all my huge engagement I provide me   150
This short sword only, which, if I have time
To show my apprehender, he shall use
Power of ten lions if I get not loose.   [*Exeunt*]

[SCENA II

Another Room in the Court]

Enter Henry, Chancellor, *the* Vidame, Janin, Vitry, Prâlin

Hen. What shall we do with this unthankful man ?
Would he of one thing but reveal the truth,
Which I have proof of, underneath his hand,
He should not taste my justice. I would give
Two hundred thousand crowns that he would yield   5
But such means for my pardon as he should ;
I never lov'd man like him ; would have trusted
My son in his protection, and my realm :
He hath deserv'd my love with worthy service,
Yet can he not deny but I have thrice   10
Sav'd him from death ; I drew him off the foe
At Fountaine Françoise, where he was engag'd,
So wounded, and so much amaz'd with blows,
That, as I play'd the soldier in his rescue,
I was enforc'd to play the Marshal   15
To order the retreat, because he said
He was not fit to do it, nor to serve me.

Chan. Your Majesty hath us'd your utmost means
Both by your own persuasions and his friends
To bring him to submission, and confess   20
With some sign of repentance his foul fault ;
Yet still he stands prefract and insolent.
You have, in love and care of his recovery,
Been half in labour to produce a course
And resolution that were fit for him ;   25
And since so amply it concerns your crown,
You must by law cut off what by your grace
You cannot bring into the state of safety.
     Jan. Begin at th' end, my lord, and execute,
Like Alexander with Parmenio.   30
Princes, you know, are masters of their laws,
And may resolve them to what forms they please,
So all conclude in justice ; in whose stroke
There is one sort of manage for the great,
Another for inferior : the great mother   35
Of all productions, grave Necessity,
Commands the variation ; and the profit,
So certainly foreseen, commends the example.
     Hen. I like not executions so informal,
For which my predecessors have been blam'd :   40
My subjects and the world shall know my power
And my authority by law's usual course
Dares punish, not the devilish heads of treason,
But their confederates, be they ne'er so dreadful.
The decent ceremonies of my laws   45
And their solemnities shall be observed
With all their sternness and severity.
     Vit. Where will your Highness have him apprehended ?
     Hen. Not in the Castle, as some have advis'd,
But in his chamber.
     Prâ.   Rather in your own,   50
Or coming out of it ; for 'tis assur'd
That any other place of apprehension
Will make the hard performance end in blood.
     Vit. To shun this likelihood, my lord, 'tis best
To make the apprehension near your chamber ;   55
For all respect and reverence given the place,
More than is needful to chastise the person
And save the opening of too many veins,
Is vain and dangerous.

Hen.   Gather you your guard,
And I will find fit time to give the word   60
When you shall seize on him and on D'Auvergne.
    Vit. We will be ready to the death, my lord.
                              Exeunt [all but Henry]
    Hen. O Thou that govern'st the keen swords of kings,
Direct my arm in this important stroke,
Or hold it being advanc'd ; the weight of blood,   65
Even in the basest subject, doth exact
Deep consultation in the highest king ;
For in one subject death's unjust affrights,
Passions, and pains, though he be ne'er so poor,
Ask more remorse than the voluptuous spleens   70
Of all kings in the world deserve respect :
He should be born grey-headed that will bear
The sword of empire ; judgment of the life,
Free state, and reputation of a man,
If it be just and worthy, dwells so dark   75
That it denies access to sun and moon ;
The soul's eye sharpen'd with that sacred light
Of whom the sun itself is but a beam,
Must only give that judgment. O how much
Err those kings, then, that play with life and death, 80
And nothing put into their serious states
But humour and their lusts, for which alone
Men long for kingdoms ; whose huge counterpoise
In cares and dangers could a fool comprise,
He would not be a king, but would be wise.   85

Enter Byron *talking with the* Queen, Epernon, D'Entragues,
        D'Auvergne, *with another lady*, [Montigny *and*] *others
        attending.*

Here comes the man, with whose ambitious head
(Cast in the way of treason) we must stay
His full chase of our ruin and our realm ;
This hour shall take upon her shady wings
His latest liberty and life to hell.   90
    D'Auv. [*aside to* Byron] We are undone !
                              [*Exit* D'Auvergne]
    Queen.   What's that ?
    Byr.   I heard him not.
    Hen. Madam, y'are honour'd much that Duke Byron
Is so observant : some to cards with him ;

You four, as now you come, sit to primero ;
And I will fight a battle at the chess.　　　　　　95
　　Byr.　A good safe fight, believe me ; other war
Thirsts blood and wounds ; and, his thirst quench'd, is thank-
　　　less.
　　　[Byron, *The* Queen, Epernon *and* Montigny *play at cards*]
　　Ep.　Lift, and then cut.
　　Byr.　　　　　　　　　　　'Tis right the end of lifting ;
When men are lifted to their highest pitch,
They cut off those that lifted them so high.　　　　100
　　Queen.　Apply you all these sports so seriously ?
　　Byr.　They first were from our serious acts devis'd,
The best of which are to the best but sports
(I mean by best the greatest), for their ends,
In men that serve them best, are their own pleasures.　　105
　　Queen.　So in those best men's services their ends
Are their own pleasures.　Pass !
　　Byr.　　　　　　　　　　I vie't.
　　Hen. [*aside*].　　　　　　　　　I see't,
And wonder at his frontless impudence.
　　　　　　　　　　　　　　　Exit Henry.
　　Chan. [*To the* Queen]　How speeds your Majesty ?
　　Queen.　　　　　　　　Well ; the Duke instructs me
With such grave lessons of mortality　　　　　110
Forc'd out of our light sport that, if I lose,
I cannot but speed well.
　　Byr.　　　　　　Some idle talk,
For courtship' sake, you know, does not amiss.
　　Chan.　Would we might hear some of it,
　　Byr.　　　　　　　　　　That you shall ;
I cast away a card now, makes me think　　　　115
Of the deceased worthy King of Spain.
　　Chan.　What card was that ?
　　Byr.　　　　　　　The King of Hearts, my lord ;
Whose name yields well the memory of that king,
Who was indeed the worthy king of hearts,
And had both of his subjects' hearts and strangers'　　120
Much more than all the kings of Christendom.
　　Chan.　He won them with his gold.
　　Byr.　　　　　　　　He won them chiefly
With his so general piety and justice ;
And as the little, yet great, Macedon
Was said with his humane philosophy　　　　125

To teach the rapeful Hyrcans marriage,
And bring the barbarous Sogdians to nourish,
Not kill their aged parents as before ;
Th' incestuous Persians to reverence.
Their mothers, not to use them as their wives ;   130
The Indians to adore the Grecian gods ;
The Scythians to inter, not eat their parents ;
So he, with his divine philosophy
(Which I may call his, since he chiefly us'd it)
In Turkey, India, and through all the world,   135
Expell'd profane idolatry, and from earth
Rais'd temples to the Highest : whom with the Word
He could not win, he justly put to sword.
    Chan.   He sought for gold and empire.
    Byr.   'Twas religion,
And her full propagation, that he sought ;   140
If gold had been his end, it had been hoarded,
When he had fetch'd it in so many fleets,
Which he spent not on Median luxury,
Banquets, and women, Calydonian wine,
Nor dear Hyrcanian fishes, but employ'd it   145
To propagate his empire ; and his empire
Desir'd t' extend so that he might withal
Extend religion through it, and all nations
Reduce to one firm constitution
Of piety, justice, and one public weal ;   150
To which end he made all his matchless subjects
Make tents their castles and their garrisons ;
True Catholics, countrymen and their allies ;
Heretics, strangers and their enemies.
There was in him the magnanimity—   155
    Mont.   To temper your extreme applause, my lord,
Shorten and answer all things in a word,
The greatest commendation we can give
To the remembrance of that king deceas'd
Is that he spar'd not his own eldest son,   160
But put him justly to a violent death,
Because he sought to trouble his estates.
    Byr.   Is't so ?
    Chan. [*aside to* Montigny.   That bit, my lord, upon my
      life ;
'Twas bitterly replied, and doth amaze him.

The King *suddenly enters, having determined what to do*

Hen. It is resolv'd ; a work shall now be done,   165
Which, while learn'd Atlas shall with stars be crown'd,
While th' Ocean walks in storms his wavy round,
While moons, at full, repair their broken rings,
While Lucifer foreshows Aurora's springs,
And Arctos sticks above the earth unmov'd,   170
Shall make my realm be blest, and me belov'd.
Call in the Count d'Auvergne.

Enter D'Auvergne

                    A word, my lord !
Will you become as wilful as your friend,
And draw a mortal justice on your heads,
That hangs so black and is so loath to strike ?   175
If you would utter what I know you know
Of his inhuman treason, one strong bar
Betwixt his will and duty were dissolv'd,
For then I know he would submit himself.
Think you it not as strong a point of faith   180
To rectify your loyalties to me,
As to be trusty in each other's wrong ?
Trust that deceives ourselves i[s] treachery,
And truth, that truth conceals, an open lie.

D'Auv. My lord, if I could utter any thought   185
Instructed with disloyalty to you,
And might light any safety to my friend,
Though mine own heart came after, it should out.

Hen. I know you may, and that your faiths affected
To one another are so vain and false   190
That your own strengths will ruin you : ye contend
To cast up rampires to you in the sea,
And strive to stop the waves that run before you.

D'Auv. All this, my lord, to me is [mystery].

Hen. It is ? I'll make it plain enough, believe me !   195
Come, my Lord Chancellor, let us end our mate.

Enter Varennes, *whispering to* Byron

Var. You are undone, my lord.   *Exit*
Byr.   Is it possible ?
Queen. Play, good my lord : whom look you for ?
Ep.   Your mind
Is not upon your game.

Byr.   Play, pray you play !
Hen. Enough, 'tis late, and time to leave our play   200
On all hands ; all forbear the room ! [*Exeunt all but* Byron
   and Henry] My lord,
Stay you with me ; yet is your will resolved
To duty and the main bond of your life ?
I swear, of all th' intrusions I have made
Upon your own good and continu'd fortunes,   205
This is the last ; inform me yet the truth,
And here I vow to you (by all my love,
By all means shown you even to this extreme,
When all men else forsake you) you are safe.
What passages have slipp'd 'twixt Count Fuentes,   210
You, and the Duke of Savoy ?
Byr.   Good my lord,
This nail is driven already past the head,
You much have overcharg'd an honest man ;
And I beseech you yield my innocence justice,
But with my single valour, gainst them all   215
That thus have poisoned your opinion of me,
And let me take my vengeance by my sword ;
For I protest I never thought an action
More than my tongue hath utter'd.
Hen.   Would 'twere true !
And that your thoughts and deeds had fell no fouler.   220
But you disdain submission, not rememb'ring,
That (in intents urg'd for the common good)
He that shall hold his peace, being charg'd to speak,
Doth all the peace and nerves of empire break ;
Which on your conscience lie. Adieu, good-night ! *Exit* 225
Byr. Kings hate to hear what they command men speak ;
Ask life, and to desert of death ye yield :
Where medicines loathe, it irks men to be heal'd.

Enter Vitry, *with two or three of the* Guard, Epernon, *the*
   Vidame, *following.* Vitry *lays hand on* Byron's *sword.*

Vit. Resign your sword, my lord ; the King commands it.
Byr. Me to resign my sword ? What king is he   230
Hath us'd it better for the realm than I ?
My sword, that all the wars within the length,
Breadth, and the whole dimensions of great France,
Hath sheath'd betwixt his hilt and horrid point,

And fix'd ye all in such a flourishing peace !   235
My sword, that never enemy could enforce,
Bereft me by my friends ! Now, good my lord,
Beseech the King I may resign my sword
To his hand only.

Enter Janin

    Jan. [*To Vitry*] You must do your office,
The King commands you.
    Vit.   'Tis in vain to strive,   240
For I must force it.
    Byr.   Have I ne'er a friend,
That bears another for me ? All the guard ?
What, will you kill me, will you smother here
His life that can command and save in field.
A hundred thousand lives ? For manhood sake   245
Lend something to this poor forsaken hand ;
For all my service let me have the honour
To die defending of my innocent self,
And have some little space to pray to God.

Enter Henry

    Hen. Come, you are an atheist, Byron, and a traitor   250
Both foul and damnable. Thy innocent self !
No leper is so buried quick in ulcers
As thy corrupted soul. Thou end the war,
And settle peace in France ! What war hath rag'd
Into whose fury I have not expos'd   255
My person [with] as free a spirit as thine ?
Thy worthy father and thyself combin'd
And arm'd in all the merits of your valours,
Your bodies thrust amidst the thickest fights,
Never were bristled with so many battles,   260
Nor on the foe have broke such woods of lances
As grew upon my thigh, and I have marshall'd—
I am asham'd to brag thus ; [but] where Envy
And Arrogance their opposite bulwark raise,
Men are allow'd to use their proper praise.   265
Away with him.   *Exit Henry*
    Byr.   Away with him ? Live I,
And hear my life thus slighted ? Cursed man,
That ever the intelligencing lights

Betray'd me to men's whorish fellowships,
To princes' Moorish slaveries, to be made   270
The anvil on which only blows and wounds
Were made the seed and wombs of others' honours ;
A property for a tyrant to set up
And puff down with the vapour of his breath.
Will you not kill me ?

   Vit.   No, we will not hurt you ;   275
We are commanded only to conduct you
Into your lodging.

     Byr.   To my lodging ? Where ?
     Vit. Within the Cabinet of Arms, my lord.
     Byr. What, to a prison ? Death ! I will not go.
     Vit. We'll force you then.
     Byr.   And take away my sword ; 280
A proper point of force ; ye had as good
Have robb'd me of my soul, slaves of my stars
Partial and bloody ! O that in mine eyes
Were all the sorcerous poison of my woes
That I might witch ye headlong from your height,   285
And trample out your execrable light.

     Vit. Come, will you go, my lord ?   This rage is vain.
     Byr. And so is all your grave authority ;
And that all France shall feel before I die.
Ye see all how they use good Catholics !   290

                    [*Exit* Byron *guarded*]

     Ep. Farewell for ever ! So have I discern'd
An exhalation that would be a star
Fall, when the sun forsook it, in a sink.
Sho[w]s ever overthrow that are too large,
And hugest cannons burst with overcharge.   295

      Enter D'Auvergne, Prâlin, *following with a* Guard

     Prâ. My lord, I have commandment from the King
To charge you go with me, and ask your sword.

     D'Auv. My sword ? Who fears it ? It was ne'er the
     death
Of any but wild boars. I prithee take it ;
Hadst thou advertis'd this when last we met,   300
I had been in my bed, and fast asleep
Two hours ago ; lead, I'll go where thou wilt.

                       Exit [*guarded*]

Vid.   See how he bears his cross with his small strength
On easier shoulders than the other Atlas.

   Ep.   Strength to aspire is still accompanied   305
With weakness to endure ; all popular gifts
Are colours [that] will bear no vinegar,
And rather to adverse affairs betray
Thine arm against them : his state still is best
That hath most inward worth ; and that's best tried   310
That neither glories, nor is glorified.   *Exeunt*

ACTUS V SCENA I

[*The Council Chamber*]

Enter Henry, Soissons, Janin, D'Escures, *cum aliis*

   Hen.   What shall we think, my lords, of these new forces
That from the King of Spain hath pass'd the Alps ?
For which, I think, his Lord Ambassador
Is come to Court to get their pass for Flanders ?

   Jan.   I think, my lord, they have no end for Flanders ;   5
Count Maurice being already enter'd Brabant
To pass to Flanders, to relieve Ostend,
And th' Archduke full prepar'd to hinder him ;
And sure it is that they must measure forces,
Which (ere this new force could have pass'd the Alps)   10
Of force must be encounter'd.

   Sois.   'Tis unlikely
That their march hath so large an aim as Flanders.

   D'Es.   As these times sort, they may have shorter reaches,
That would pierce further.

   Hen.   I have been advertis'd
How Count Fuentes (by whose means this army   15
Was lately levied, and whose hand was strong
In thrusting on Byron's conspiracy)
Hath caus'd these cunning forces to advance
With colour only to set down in Flanders ;
But hath intentional respect to favour   20
And count'nance his false partisans in Bresse
And friends in Burgundy, to give them heart
For the full taking of their hearts from me.
Be as it will ; we shall prevent their worst ;
And therefore call in Spain's Ambassador.   25

Enter Ambassador *with others*

What would the Lord Ambassador of Spain ?
  Amb. First, in my master's name, I would beseech
Your Highness' hearty thought that his true hand,
Held in your vow'd amities, hath not touch'd
At any least point in Byron's offence, 30
Nor once had notice of a crime so foul ;
Whereof, since he doubts not you stand resolv'd,
He prays your league's continuance in this favour,
That the army he hath rais'd to march for Flanders
May have safe passage by your frontier towns, 35
And find the river free that runs by Rhone.
  Hen. My lord, my frontiers shall not be disarm'd,
Till, by arraignment of the Duke of Byron,
My scruples are resolv'd, and I may know
In what account to hold your master's faith 40
For his observance of the league betwixt us.
You wish me to believe that he is clear
From all the projects caus'd by Count Fuentes,
His special agent ; but where deeds pull down,
Words may repair no faith. I scarce can think 45
That his gold was so bounteously employ'd
Without his special counsel and command :
These faint proceedings in our royal faiths,
Make subjects prove so faithless ; if, because
We sit above the danger of the laws, 50
We likewise lift our arms above their justice,
And that our heavenly Sovereign bounds not us
In those religious confines out of which
Our justice and our true laws are inform'd,
In vain have we expectance that our subjects 55
Should not as well presume to offend their earthly,
As we our heavenly Sovereign ; and this breach
Made in the forts of all society,
Of all celestial, and humane respects,
Makes no strengths of our bounties, counsels, arms, 60
Hold out against their treasons ; and the rapes
Made of humanity and religion,
In all men's more than Pagan liberties,
Atheisms, and slaveries, will derive their springs
From their base precedents, copied out of kings. 65
But all this shall not make me break the commerce

Authoris'd by our treaties ; let your army
Take the directest pass ; it shall go safe.
  Amb. So rest your Highness ever, and assur'd
That my true Sovereign loathes all opposite thoughts.   70
                      [*Exit the* Ambassador]
  Hen. [*To* Janin] Are our despatches made to all the
    kings,
Princes, and potentates of Christendom,
Ambassadors and province governors,
T'inform the truth of this conspiracy ?
  Jan. They all are made, my lord ; and some give out   75
That 'tis a blow given to religion,
To weaken it, in ruining of him
That said he never wish'd more glorious title
Than to be call'd the Scourge of Huguenots.
  Sois. Others that are like favourers of the fault,   80
Said 'tis a politic advice from England
To break the sacred javelins both together.
  Hen. Such shut their eyes to truth ; we can but set
His lights before them, and his trumpet sound
Close to their ears ; their partial wilfulness,   85
In resting blind and deaf, or in perverting
What their most certain senses apprehend,
Shall nought discomfort our impartial justice,
Nor clear the desperate fault that doth enforce it.
                         Enter Vitry
  Vit. The Peers of France, my lord, refuse t'appear   90
At the arraignment of the Duke Byron.
  Hen. The Court may yet proceed ; and so command it.
'Tis not their slackness to appear shall serve
To let my will t'appear in any fact
Wherein the boldest of them tempts my justice   95
I am resolv'd, and will no more endure
To have my subjects make what I command
The subject of their oppositions,
Who evermore slack their allegiance,
As kings forbear their penance. How sustain   100
Your prisoners their strange durance ?
  Vit.   One of them,
Which is the Count d'Auvergne, hath merry spirits,
Eats well and sleeps, and never can imagine
That any place where he is, is a prison ;
Where, on the other part, the Duke Byron,   105

Enter'd his prison as into his grave,
Rejects all food, sleeps not, nor once lies down ;
Fury hath arm'd his thoughts so thick with thorns
That rest can have no entry : he disdains
To grace the prison with the slend'rest show   110
Of any patience, lest men should conceive
He thought his sufferance in the [least] sort fit ;
And holds his bands so worthless of his worth
That he impairs it to vouchsafe to them
The [least] part of the peace that freedom owes it ;   115
That patience therein is a willing slavery,
And like the camel stoops to take the load :
So still he walks ; or rather as a bird,
Enter'd a closet, which unwares is made
His desperate prison, being pursu'd, amaz'd   120
And wrathful beats his breast from wall to wall,
Assaults the light, strikes down himself, not out,
And being taken, struggles, gasps, and bites,
Takes all his taker's strokings to be strokes,
Abhorreth food, and with a savage will   125
Frets, pines, and dies for former liberty :
So fares the wrathful Duke ; and when the strength
Of these dumb rages break out into sounds,
He breathes defiance to the world, and bids us
Make ourselves drunk with the remaining blood   130
Of five and thirty wounds receiv'd in fight
For us and ours, for we shall never brag
That we have made his spirits check at death.
This rage in walks and words ; but in his looks
He comments all and prints a world of books.   135
    Hen.   Let others learn by him to curb their spleens,
Before they be curb'd, and to cease their grudges.
Now I am settled in my sun of height,
The circular splendour and full sphere of state
Take all place up from envy : as the sun   140
At height and passive o'er the crowns of men,
His beams diffus'd, and down-right pour'd on them,
Cast but a little or no shade at all :
So he that is advanc'd above the heads
Of all his emulators with high light   145
Prevents their envies, and deprives them quite.

                                          Exeunt

[SCENA II

The Golden Chamber in the Palace of Justice]

Enter the Chancellor, Harlay, Potier, Fleury, *in scarlet gowns,*
　　La Fin, D'Escures, *with other officers of state*

Chan.　I wonder at the prisoner's so long stay.
　Har.　I think it may be made a question
If his impatience will let him come.
　Pot.　Yes, he is now well stay'd : time and his judgment,
Have cast his passion and his fever off.　　　　　　　　5
　Fleu.　His fever may be past, but for his passions,
I fear me we shall find it spic'd too hotly
With his old powder.
　D'Es.　　　　　　He is sure come forth ;
The carosse of the Marquis of Rosny
Conducted him along to th' Arsenal　　　　　　　　10
Close to the river-side ; and there I saw him
Enter a barge cover'd with tapestry,
In which the King's guards waited and receiv'd him.
Stand by there, clear the place !
　Chan.　　　　　　　　The prisoner comes.
My Lord La Fin, forbear your sight awhile ;　　　　　15
It may incense the prisoner, who will know,
By your attendance near us, that your hand
Was chief in his discovery ; which, as yet,
I think he doth not doubt.
　La F.　　　　　　　I will forbear
Till your good pleasures call me.　　　　*Exit* La Fin
　Har.　　　　　　　　When he knows,　　　20
And sees La Fin accuse him to his face,
The Court I think will shake with his distemper.

Enter Vitry, Byron, *with others and a* guard

　Vit.　You see, my lord, 'tis in the Golden Chamber.
　Byr.　The Golden Chamber ! Where the greatest kings
Have thought them honour'd to receive a place,　　25
And I have had it ; am I come to stand
In rank and habit here of men arraign'd,
Where I have sat assistant, and been honour'd
With glorious title of the chiefest virtuous ;
Where the King's chief Solicitor hath said　　　　30
There was in France no man that ever liv'd

Whose parts were worth my imitation ;
That, but mine own worth, I could imitate none :
And that I made myself inimitable
To all that could come after ; whom this Court   35
Hath seen to sit upon the flower-de-luce
In recompence of my renowned service.
Must I be sat on now by petty judges ?
These scarlet robes, that come to sit and fight
Against my life, dismay my valour more   40
Than all the bloody cassocks Spain hath brought
To field against it.
    Vit.   To the bar, my lord !
              He salutes and stands to the bar
    Har. Read the indictment !
    Chan.   Stay, I will invert,
For shortness' sake, the form of our proceedings
And out of all the points the process holds,
Collect five principal, with which we charge you.   45
    1. First you conferr'd with one, call'd Picoté,
At Orleans born, and into Flanders fled,
To hold intelligence by him with the Archduke,
And for two voyages to that effect,   50
Bestow'd on him five hundred fifty crowns.
    2. Next you held treaty with the Duke of Savoy,
Without the King's permission ; offering him
All service and assistance gainst all men,
In hope to have in marriage his third daughter.   55
    3. Thirdly, you held intelligence with the Duke,
At taking in of Bourg and other forts ;
Advising him, with all your prejudice,
Gainst the King's army and his royal person.
    4. The fourth is, that you would have brought the King, 60
Before Saint Katherine's fort, to be there slain ;
And to that end writ to the Governor,
In which you gave him notes to know his Highness.
    5. Fifthly, you sent La Fin to treat with Savoy
And with the Count Fuentes of more plots,   65
Touching the ruin of the King and realm.
    Byr. All this, my lord, I answer, and deny.
And first for Picoté : he was my prisoner,
And therefore I might well confer with him ;
But that our conference tended to the Archduke   70
Is nothing so : I only did employ him

To Captain La Fortune, for the reduction
Of Seurre to the service of the King,
Who us'd such speedy diligence therein,
That shortly 'twas assur'd his Majesty.   75
     2. Next, for my treaties with the Duke of Savoy,
Roncas, his secretary, having made
A motion to me for the Duke's third daughter,
I told it to the King, who having since
Given me the understanding by La Force   80
Of his dislike, I never dream'd of it.
     3. Thirdly, for my intelligence with the Duke,
Advising him against his Highness' army :
Had this been true I had not undertaken
Th' assault of Bourg against the King's opinion,   85
Having assistance but by them about me ;
And, having won it for him, had not been
Put out of such a government so easily.
     4. Fourthly, for my advice to kill the King ;
I would beseech his Highness' memory   90
Not to let slip that I alone dissuaded
His viewing of that fort, informing him
It had good mark-men, and he could not go
But in exceeding danger ; which advice
Diverted him, the rather since I said   95
That if he had desire to see the place
He should receive from me a plot of it,
Offering to take it with five hundred men,
And I myself would go to the assault.
     5. And lastly, for intelligences held   100
With Savoy and Fuentes, I confess
That being denied to keep the citadel,
Which with incredible peril I had got,
And seeing another honour'd with my spoils,
I grew so desperate that I found my spirit   105
Enrag'd to any act, and wish'd myself
Cover'd with blood.
     Chan.   With whose blood ?
     Byr.   With mine own ;
Wishing to live no longer, being denied,
With such suspicion of me and set will
To rack my furious humour into blood.   110
And for two months' space I did speak and write
More than I ought, but have done ever well ;

And therefore your informers have been false,
And, with intent to tyrannize, suborn'd.
 Fleu. What if our witnesses come face to face, 115
And justify much more than we allege ?
 Byr. They must be hirelings, then, and men corrupted.
 Pot. What think you of La Fin !
 Byr.   I hold La Fin
An honour'd gentleman, my friend and kinsman.
 Har. If he then aggravate what we affirm   120
With greater accusations to your face,
What will you say ?
 Byr.   I know it cannot be.
 Chan. Call in my Lord La Fin.
 Byr.   Is he so near,
And kept so close from me ? Can all the world
Make him a treacher ?

Enter La Fin

 Chan.   I suppose, my lord,   125
You have not stood within, without the ear
Of what hath here been urg'd against the Duke ;
If you have heard it, and upon your knowledge
Can witness all is true upon your soul,
Utter your knowledge.
 La F.   I have heard, my lord, 130
All that hath pass'd here, and, upon my soul,
(Being charg'd so urgently in such a Court)
Upon my knowledge I affirm all true ;
And so much more as, had the prisoner lives
As many as his years, would make all forfeit. 135
 Byr. O all ye virtuous Powers in earth and heaven
That have not put on hellish flesh and blood,
From whence these monstrous issues are produc'd,
That cannot bear, in execrable concord
And one prodigious subject, contraries ;   140
Nor as the isle that, of the world admir'd,
Is sever'd from the world, can cut yourselves
From the consent and sacred harmony
Of life, yet live ; of honour, yet be honour'd ;
As this extravagant and errant rogue,   145
From all your fair decorums and just laws
Finds power to do, and like a loathsome wen
Sticks to the face of nature and this Court :

Thicken this air, and turn your plaguy rage
Into a shape as dismal as his sin ;   150
And with some equal horror tear him off
From sight and memory : let not such a Court,
To whose fame all the kings of Christendom
Now laid their ears, so crack her royal trump,
As to sound through it that here vaunted justice   155
Was got in such an incest. Is it justice
To tempt and witch a man to break the law,
And by that witch condemn him ? Let me draw
Poison into me with this cursed air
If he bewitch'd me and transform'd me not ;   160
He bit me by the ear, and made me drink
Enchanted waters ; let me see an image
That utter'd these distinct words : *Thou shalt die,
O wicked king* ; and if the Devil gave him
Such power upon an image, upon me   165
How might he tyrannize that by his vows
And oaths so Stygian had my nerves and will
In more awe than his own ? What man is he
That is so high but he would higher be ?
So roundly sighted, but he may be found   170
To have a blind side, which by craft pursu'd,
Confederacy, and simply trusted treason,
May wrest him past his Angel and his reason ?
     Chan.   Witchcraft can never taint an honest mind.
     Har.   True gold will any trial stand untouch'd. 175
     Pot.   For colours that will stain when they are tried,
The cloth itself is ever cast aside.
     Byr.   Sometimes the very gloss in anything
Will seem a stain ; the fault, not in the light,
Nor in the guilty object, but our sight.   180
My gloss, rais'd from the richness of my stuff,
Had too much splendour for the owly eye
Of politic and thankless royalty ;
I did deserve too much ; a pleurisy
Of that blood in me is the cause I die.   185
Virtue in great men must be small and slight,
For poor stars rule where she is exquisite.
'Tis tyrannous and impious policy
To put to death by fraud and treachery ;
Sleight is then royal when it makes men live   190
And if it urge faults, urgeth to forgive.

He must be guiltless that condemns the guilty.
Like things do nourish like, and not destroy them,
Minds must be sound that judge affairs of weight,
And seeing hands cut corrosives from your sight.   195
A lord, intelligencer! Hangman-like?
Thrust him from human fellowship to the deserts,
Blow him with curses; shall your Justice call
Treachery her father? Would you wish her weigh
My valour with the hiss of such a viper?   200
What I have done to shun the mortal shame
Of so unjust an opposition,
My envious stars cannot deny me this,
That I may make my judges witnesses,
And that my wretched fortunes have reserv'd   205
For my last comfort: ye all know, my lords,
This body, gash'd with five and thirty wounds,
Whose life and death you have in your award,
Holds not a vein that hath not open'd been,
And which I would not open yet again   210
For you and yours; this hand, that writ the lines
Alleg'd against me, hath enacted still
More good than there it only talk'd of ill.
I must confess my choler hath transferr'd
My tender spleen to all intemperate speech,   215
But reason ever did my deeds attend
In worth of praise, and imitation.
Had I borne any will to let them loose,
I could have flesh'd them with bad services
In England lately, and in Switzerland;   220
There are a hundred gentlemen by name
Can witness my demeanour in the first,
And in the last ambassage I adjure
No other testimonies than the Seigneurs
De Vic and Sillery, who amply know   225
In what sort and with what fidelity
I bore myself to reconcile and knit
In one desire so many wills disjoin'd,
And from the King's allegiance quite withdrawn.
My acts ask'd many men, though done by one;   230
And I were but one I stood for thousands,
And still I hold my worth, though not my place:
Nor slight me, judges, though I be but one.
One man, in one sole expedition,

Reduc'd into th' imperial power of Rome   235
Armenia, Pontus, and Arabia,
Syria, Albania, and Iberia,
Conquer'd th' Hyrcanians, and to Caucasus
His arm extended ; the Numidians
And Afric to the shores meridional   240
His power subjected ; and that part of Spain
Which stood from those parts that Sertorius rul'd,
Even to the Atlantic sea he conquered.
Th' Albanian kings he from [their] kingdoms chas'd,
And at the Caspian sea their dwellings plac'd ;   245
Of all the earth's globe, by power and his advice,
The round-eyed Ocean saw him victor thrice.
And what shall let me, but your cruel doom,
To add as much to France as he to Rome.
And, to leave Justice neither sword nor word   250
To use against my life, this senate knows
That what with one victorious hand I took
I gave to all your uses with another ;
With this I took and propp'd the falling kingdom,
And gave it to the King ; I have kept   255
Your laws of state from fire, and you yourselves
Fix'd in this high tribunal, from whose height
The vengeful Saturnals of the League
Had hurl'd ye headlong ; do ye then return
This retribution ? Can the cruel King,   260
The kingdom, laws, and you, all sav'd by me,
Destroy their saver ? What, ay me ! I did
Adverse to this, this damn'd enchanter did,
That took into his will my motion ;
And being bankrout both of wealth and worth,   265
Pursu'd with quarrels and with suits in law,
Fear'd by the kingdom, threaten'd by the King,
Would raise the loathed dunghill of his ruins
Upon the monumental heap of mine !
Torn with possessed whirlwinds may he die,   270
And dogs bark at his murtherous memory.
   Chan. My lord, our liberal sufferance of your speech
Hath made it late, and for this session
We will dismiss you ; take him back, my lord !
                            Exit Vitry *and* Byron
Har. You likewise may depart.   *Exit* La Fin
Chan.   What resteth now   275

To be decreed gainst this great prisoner ?
A mighty merit and a monstrous crime
Are here concurrent ; what by witnesses
His letters and instructions we have prov'd,
Himself confesseth, and excuseth all   280
With witchcraft and the only act of thought.
For witchcraft, I esteem it a mere strength
Of rage in him, conceiv'd gainst his accuser,
Who, being examin'd, hath denied it all.
Suppose it true, it made him false ; but wills   285
And worthy minds witchcraft can never force.
And for his thoughts that brake not into deeds,
Time was the cause, not will ; the mind's free act
In treason still is judg'd as th' outward fact.
If his deserts have had a wealthy share   290
In saving of our land from civil furies,
Manlius had so that sav'd the Capitol ;
Yet for his after traitorous factions
They threw him headlong from the place he sav'd.
My definite sentence, then, doth this import :   295
That we must quench the wild-fire with his blood
In which it was so traitorously inflam'd ;
Unless with it we seek to incense the land.
The King can have no refuge for his life,
If his be quitted ; this was it that made   300
Louis th' Eleventh renounce his countrymen,
And call the valiant Scots out of their kingdom
To use their greater virtues and their faiths
Than his own subjects in his royal guard.
What then conclude your censures ?
    Omnes.   He must die.   305
    Chan.   Draw then his sentence formally, and send him ;
And so all treasons in his death attend him.   *Exeunt*

[SCENA III

Byron's *Cell in the Bastile*]

Enter Byron, Epernon, Soissons, Janin, *the* Vidame, D'Escures

    Vid.   I·joy you had so good a day, my lord.
    Byr.   I won it from them all ; the Chancellor
I answer'd to his uttermost improvements ;

I mov'd my other judges to lament
My insolent misfortunes, and to loathe　　　　　　　　5
The pocky soul and state-bawd, my accuser.
I made reply to all that could be said,
So eloquently and with such a charm
Of grave enforcements, that methought I sat
Like Orpheus casting reins on savage beasts;　　　10
At the arm's end, as 'twere, I took my bar
And set it far above the high tribunal,
Where, like a cedar on Mount Lebanon,
I grew, and made my judges show like box-trees;
And box-trees right their wishes would have made them,　15
Whence boxes should have grown, till they had strook
My head into the budget; but, alas!
I held their bloody arms with such strong reasons,
And, by your leave, with such a jerk of wit,
That I fetch'd blood upon the Chancellor's cheeks.　　20
Methinks I see his countenance as he sat,
And the most lawyerly delivery
Of his set speeches; shall I play his part?
　　Ep.　For heaven's sake, good my lord!
　　Byr.　　　　　　　　　　　　I will, i' faith!
'Behold a wicked man, a man debauch'd,　　　　　　25
A man contesting with his King, a man
On whom, my lord, we are not to connive,
Though we may condole; a man
That, *læsa majestate*, sought a lease
Of *plus quam satis*. A man that *vi et armis*　　　30
Assail'd the King, and would *per fas et nefas*
Aspire the kingdom'. Here was lawyer's learning!
　　Ep.　He said not this, my lord, that I have heard.
　　Byr.　This, or the like, I swear! I pen no speeches.
　　Sois.　Then there is good hope of your wish'd acquittal.　35
　　Byr.　Acquittal? They have reason; were I dead
I know they cannot all supply my place.
Is't possible the King should be so vain
To think he can shake me with fear of death?
Or make me apprehend that he intends it?　　　　　40
Thinks he to make his firmest men his clouds?
The clouds, observing their aërial natures,
Are borne aloft, and then, to moisture [c]hang'd,
Fall to the earth; where being made thick and cold,
They lose both all their heat and levity;　　　　　45

Yet then again recovering heat and lightness,
Again they are advanc'd, and by the sun
Made fresh and glorious ; and since clouds are rapt
With these uncertainties, now up, now down,
Am I to flit so with his smile or frown ?   50
 Ep.   I wish your comforts and encouragements
May spring out of your safety ; but I hear
The King hath reason'd so against your life,
And made your most friends yield so to his reasons
That your estate is fearful.
 Byr.   Yield t' his reasons ?   55
O how friends' reasons and their freedoms stretch
When Power sets his wide tenters to their sides !
How like a cure, by mere opinion,
It works upon our blood ! Like th' ancient gods
Are modern kings, that liv'd past bounds themselves,   60
Yet set a measure down to wretched men ;
By many sophisms they made good deceit,
And, since they pass'd in power, surpass'd in right ;
When kings' wills pass, the stars wink and the sun
Suffers eclipse ; rude thunder yields to them   65
His horrid wings, sits smooth as glass eng[l]az'd ;
And lightning sticks 'twixt heaven and earth amaz'd :
Men's faiths are shaken, and the pit of Truth
O'erflows with darkness, in which Justice sits,
And keeps her vengeance tied to make it fierce ;   70
And when it comes, th' increased horrors show,
Heaven's plague is sure, though full of state, and slow.
 Sister. (*Within.*) O my dear lord and brother ! O the Duke !
 Byr.   What sounds are these, my lord ? Hark, hark, me-
  thinks
I hear the cries of people !
 Ep.   'Tis for one,   75
Wounded in fight here at Saint Anthony's gate :
 Byr.   'Sfoot, one cried ' the Duke ' ! I pray harken
Again, or burst yourselves with silence—no !
What countryman's the common headsman here ?
 Sois.   He's a Burgonian.
 Byr.   The great devil he is !   80
The bitter wizard told me a Burgonian
Should be my headsman—strange concurrences.
'Sdeath, who's here ?

Enter four Ushers *bare*, Chancellor, Harlay, Potier, Fleury,
Vitry, Prâlin, *with others*

O then I am but dead,
Now, now ye come all to pronounce my sentence.
I am condemn'd unjustly ; tell my kinsfolks   85
I die an innocent ; if any friend
Pity the ruin of the State's sustainer,
Proclaim my innocence ; ah, Lord Chancellor,
Is there no pardon, will there come no mercy ?
Ay, put your hat on, and let me stand bare.   90
Show yourself right a lawyer.
   Chan.   I am bare ;
What would you have me do ?
   Byr.   You have not done
Like a good Justice, and one that knew
He sat upon the precious blood of virtue ;
Y'ave pleas'd the cruel King, and have not borne   95
As great regard to save as to condemn ;
You have condemn'd me, my Lord Chancellor,
But God acquits me ; He will open lay
All your close treasons against Him to colour
Treasons laid to His truest images ;   100
And you, my lord, shall answer this injustice
Before his judgment-seat : to which I summon
In one year and a day your hot appearance.
I go before, by men's corrupted dooms ;
But they that caus'd my death shall after come   105
By the immaculate justice of the Highest.
   Chan. Well, good my lord, commend your soul to Him
And to His mercy ; think of that, I pray !
   Byr. Sir, I have thought of it, and every hour
Since my affliction ask'd on naked knees   110
Patience to bear your unbeliev'd injustice :
But you, nor none of you, have thought of Him
In my eviction : y'are come to your benches
With plotted judgments ; your link'd ears so loud
Sing with prejudicate winds that nought is heard   115
Of all poor prisoners urge gainst your award.
   Har. Passion, my lord, transports your bitterness
Beyond all colour and your proper judgment :
No man hath known your merits more than I,
And would to God your great misdeeds had been   120

As much undone as they have been conceal'd ;
The cries of them for justice, in desert,
Have been so loud and piercing that they deafen'd
The ears of Mercy ; and have labour'd more
Your judges to compress than to enforce them.   125
    Pot.   We bring you here your sentence ; will you read it ?
    Byr.   For Heaven's sake, shame to use me with such rigour ;
I know what it imports, and will not have
Mine ear blown into flames with hearing it.
[*To* Fleury] Have you been one of them that have condemn'd
    me ?   130
    Fleu.   My lord, I am your orator ; God comfort you !
    Byr.   Good sir, my father lov'd you so entirely
That if you have been one, my soul forgives you.
It is the King (most childish that he is,
That takes what he hath given) that injures me :   135
He gave grace in the first draught of my fault,
And now restrains it : grace again I ask ;
Let him again vouchsafe it : send to him,
A post will soon return : the Queen of England
Told me that if the wilful Earl of Essex   140
Had us'd submission, and but ask'd her mercy,
She would have given it past resumption.
She like a gracious princess did desire
To pardon him, even as she pray'd to God
He would let down a pardon unto her ;   145
He yet was guilty, I am innocent :
He still refus'd grace, I importune it.
    Chan.   This ask'd in time, my lord, while he besought it,
And ere he had made his severity known,
Had with much joy to him, I know, been granted.   150
    Byr.   No, no, his bounty then was misery,
To offer when he knew 'twould be refus'd ;
He treads the vulgar path of all advantage,
And loves men for his vices, not for their virtues.
My service would have quicken'd gratitude   155
In his own death, had he been truly royal ;
It would have stirr'd the image of a king
Into perpetual motion to have stood
Near the conspiracy restrain'd at Mantes,
And in a danger, that had then the wolf   160
To fly upon his bosom, had I only held
Intelligence with the conspirators,

Who stuck at no check but my loyalty,
Nor kept life in their hopes but in my death.
The siege of Amiens would have soften'd rocks,   165
Where, cover'd all in showers of shot and fire,
I seem'd to all men's eyes a fighting flame
With bullets cut in fashion of a man,
A sacrifice to valour, impious king!
Which he will needs extinguish with my blood.   170
Let him beware: justice will fall from heaven
In the same form I served in that siege,
And by the light of that he shall discern
What good my ill hath brought him; it will nothing
Assure his state; the same quench he hath cast   175
Upon my life, shall quite put out his fame.
This day he loseth what he shall not find
By all days he survives, so good a servant,
Nor Spain so great a foe; with whom, alas!
Because I treated am I put to death?   180
'Tis but a politic gloze; my courage rais'd me,
For the dear price of five and thirty scars,
And that hath ruin'd me, I thank my stars.
Come, I'll go where ye will, ye shall not lead me.

                                        [*Exit* Byron]

  Chan. I fear his frenzy; never saw I man   185
Of such a spirit so amaz'd at death.
  Har. He alters every minute: what a vapour
The strongest mind is to a storm of crosses!

                                        Exeunt
  Manent Epernon, Soissons, Janin, *the* Vidame, D'Escures

  Ep. Oh of what contraries consists a man!
Of what impossible mixtures! Vice and virtue,   190
Corruption, and eternnesse, at one time,
And in one subject, let together loose!
We have not any strength but weakens us,
No greatness but doth crush us into air.
Our knowledges do light us but to err,   195
Our ornaments are burthens, our delights
Are our tormenters, fiends that, rais'd in fears,
At parting shake our roofs about our ears.
  Sois. O Virtue, thou art now far worse than Fortune;
Her gifts stuck by the Duke when thine are vanish'd,   200
Thou brav'st thy friend in need: Necessity,

That used to keep thy wealth, Contempt, thy love,
Have both abandon'd thee in his extremes,
Thy powers are shadows, and thy comfort, dreams.
    Vid.   O real Goodness, if thou be a power,   205
And not a word alone, in human uses,
Appear out of this angry conflagration,
Where this great captain, thy late temple, burns,
And turn his vicious fury to thy flame
From all earth's hopes mere gilded with thy fame :   210
Let Piety enter with her willing cross,
And take him on it ; ope his breast and arms,
To all the storms Necessity can breathe,
And burst them all with his embraced death.
    Jan.   Yet are the civil tumults of his spirits   215
Hot and outrageous : not resolv'd, alas,
(Being but one man [under] the kingdom's doom)
He doubts, storms, threatens, rues, complains, implores ;
Grief hath brought all his forces to his looks,
And nought is left to strengthen him within,   220
Nor lasts one habit of those griev'd aspects ;
Blood expels paleness, paleness blood doth chase,
And sorrow errs through all forms in his face.
    D'Es.   So furious is he, that the politic law
Is much to seek, how to enact her sentence :   225
Authority back'd with arms, though he unarm'd,
Abhors his fury, and with doubtful eyes
Views on what ground it should sustain his ruins ;
And as a savage boar that (hunted long,
Assail'd and set up) with his only eyes   230
Swimming in fire, keeps off the baying hounds,
Though sunk himself, yet holds his anger up,
And snows it forth in foam ; holds firm his stand,
Of battailous bristles ; feeds his hate to die,
And whets his tusks with wrathful majesty :   235
So fares the furious Duke, and with his looks
Doth teach Death horrors ; makes the hangman learn
New habits for his bloody impudence,
Which now habitual horror from him drives,
Who for his life shuns death, by which he lives.   240
                                                   [Exeunt]

[SCENA IV

The Courtyard of the Bastile. A Scaffold]

Enter Chancellor, Harlay, Potier, Fleury, Vitry, [Prâlin]

Vit. Will not your lordship have the Duke distinguish'd
From other prisoners, where the order is
To give up men condemn'd into the hands
Of th' executioner ? He would be the death
Of him that he should die by, ere he suffer'd   5
Such an abjection.
   Chan.   But to bind his hands
I hold it passing needful.
   Har.   'Tis my lord,
And very dangerous to bring him loose.
   Prâ. You will in all despair and fury plunge him,
If you but offer it.   10
   Pot.   My lord, by this
The prisoner's spirit is something pacified,
And 'tis a fear that th' offer of those bands
Would breed fresh furies in him and disturb
The entry of his soul into her peace.
   Chan. I would not that, for any possible danger   15
That can be wrought by his unarmed hands,
And therefore in his own form bring him in.

Enter Byron, *a* Bishop *or two, with all the guards, soldiers with
muskets*

Byr. Where shall this weight fall ? On what region
Must this declining prominent pour his load ?
I'll break my blood's high billows 'gainst my stars.   20
Before this hill be shook into a flat,
All France shall feel an earthquake ; with what murmur,
This world shrinks into chaos !
   [*Bishop.*]   Good, my lord,
Forego it willingly ; and now resign
Your sensual powers entirely to your soul.   25
   Byr. Horror of death ! Let me alone in peace.
And leave my soul to me, whom it concerns ;
You have no charge of it ; I feel her free :
How she doth rouse and like a falcon stretch
Her silver wings, as threatening Death with death ;   30
At whom I joyfully will cast her off.

I know this body but a sink of folly,
The ground-work and rais'd frame of woe and frailty,
The bond and bundle of corruption,
A quick corse, only sensible of grief,   35
A walking sepulchre, or household thief,
A glass of air, broken with less than breath,
A slave bound face to face to Death till death :
And what said all you more ? I know, besides,
That life is but a dark and stormy night   40
Of senseless dreams, terrors, and broken sleeps ;
A tyranny, devising pains to plague
And make man long in dying, racks his death ;
And Death is nothing ; what can you say more ?
I [being] a [large] globe, and a little earth,   45
Am seated like earth, betwixt both the heavens,
That if I rise, to heaven I rise ; if fall,
I likewise fall to heaven ; what stronger faith
Hath any of your souls ? What say you more ?
Why lose I time in these things ? Talk of knowledge !   50
It serves for inward use. I will not die
Like to a clergyman ; but like the captain
That pray'd on horseback, and with sword in hand,
Threaten'd the sun, commanding it to stand ;
These are but ropes of sand.
    Chan.   Desire you then   55
To speak with any man ?
    Byr. I would speak with La Force and Saint Blancart.
    [*Vit.* They are not in the city.]
    Byr.   Do they fly me ?
Where is Prevost, Controller of my house ?
    Prâ. Gone to his house i' th' country three days since. 60
    Byr. He should have stay'd here ; he keeps all my blanks.
Oh all the world forsakes me ! Wretched world,
Consisting most of parts that fly each other,
A firmness breeding all inconstancy,
A bond of all disjunction ; like a man   65
Long buried, is a man that long hath liv'd ;
Touch him, he falls to ashes : for one fault,
I forfeit all the fashion of a man.
Why should I keep my soul in this dark light,
Whose black beams lighted me to lose my self ?   70
When I have lost my arms, my fame, my mind,
Friends, brother, hopes, fortunes, and even my fury ?

O happy were the man could live alone,
To know no man, nor be of any known!

   Har. My lord, it is the manner once again   75
To read the sentence.

   Byr.   Yet more sentences?
How often will ye make me suffer death,
As ye were proud to hear your powerful dooms!
I know and feel you were the men that gave it,
And die most cruelly to hear so often   80
My crimes and bitter condemnation urg'd!
Suffice it I am brought here and obey,
And that all here are privy to the crimes.

   Chan. It must be read, my lord, no remedy.

   Byr. Read, if it must be, then, and I must talk.   85

   Har. [*reads the sentence*] '*The process being extraordinarily
made and examined by the Court and Chambers assembled*——'

   Byr. Condemn'd for depositions of a witch,
The common deposition, and her whore
To all whorish perjuries and treacheries!   90
Sure he call'd up the devil in my spirits,
And made him to usurp my faculties:
Shall I be cast away now he's cast out?
What justice is in this? Dear countrymen,
Take this true evidence betwixt heaven and you,   95
And quit me in your hearts.

   Chan. Go on.

   Har. [*reading*] '*Against Charles Gontaut of Byron, Knight
of both the Orders, Duke of Byron, Peer and Marshal of France,
Governor of Burgundy, accused of treason, a sentence was given* 100
*the twenty-second of this month, condemning the said Duke of
Byron of high treason, for his direct conspiracies against the
King's person, enterprises against his state*——'

   Byr. That is most false! Let me for ever be
Depriv'd of heaven, as I shall be of earth,   105
If it be true; know, worthy countrymen,
These two and twenty months I have been clear
Of all attempts against the King and state.

   Har. [*reading*] '*Treaties and treacheries with his enemies,
being Marshal of the King's army; for reparation of which* 110
*crimes they deprived him of all his estates, honours, and dignities,
and condemned him to lose his head upon a scaffold at the
Grève*——

   Byr. The Grève? Had that place stood for my dispatch

I had not yielded ; all your forces should not
Stir me one foot, wild horses should have drawn   115
My body piecemeal ere you all had brought me.
  Har. [*reading*] ' *Declaring all his goods, moveable and im-
moveable, whatsoever, to be confiscate to the King ; the Seigneury
of Byron to lose the title of Duchy and Peer for ever* '.
  Byr. Now is your form contented ?
  Chan.   Ay, my lord,   120
And I must now entreat you to deliver
Your order up ; the King demands it of you.
  Byr. And I restore it, with my vow of safety
In that world where both he and I are one,
I never brake the oath I took to take it.   125
  Chan. Well, now, my lord, we'll take our latest leaves,
Beseeching Heaven to take as clear from you
All sense of torment in your willing death,
All love and thought of what you must leave here,
As when you shall aspire heaven's highest sphere.   130
  Byr. Thanks to your lordship, and let me pray too
That you will hold good censure of my life,
By the clear witness of my soul in death,
That I have never pass'd act gainst the King ;
Which, if my faith had let me undertake,   135
[He] had been three years since amongst the dead.
  Har. Your soul shall find his safety in her own.
Call the executioner ! [*Exeunt the* Chancellor *and* Harlay.]
  Byr.   Good sir, I pray
Go after and beseech the Chancellor
That he will let my body be interr'd   140
Amongst my predecessors at Byron.
  D'Es. I go, my lord.   *Exit*
  Byr.   Go, go ! Can all go thus,
And no man come with comfort ? Farewell, world !
He is at no end of his actions blest
Whose ends will make him greatest, and not best ;   145
They tread no ground, but ride in air on storms
That follow state, and hunt their empty forms ;
Who see not that the valleys of the world
Make even right with the mountains, that they grow
Green and lie warmer, and ever peaceful are,   150
When clouds spit fire at hills and burn them bare ;

Not valleys' part, but we should imitate streams,
That run below the valleys and do yield
To every molehill, every bank embrace
That checks their currents, and when torrents come,   155
That swell and raise them past their natural height,
How mad they are, and troubled! Like low [streams]
With torrents crown'd, are men with diadems.

 Vit. My lord, 'tis late; will't please you to go up?
 Byr. Up? 'Tis a fair preferment—ha, ha, ha!   160
There should go shouts to upshots; not a breath
Of any mercy yet? Come, since we must;

       [He mounts the scaffold]

    [Enter the Hangman]

Who's this?
 Prâ.   The executioner, my lord.
 Byr. Death, slave, down, or by the blood that moves
  me
I'll pluck thy throat out! Go, I'll call you straight.   165
Hold, boy, and this!

    [Casting his handkerchief and doublet to a boy]
 Hangman.   Soft, boy, I'll bar you that!
 Byr. Take this, then; yet, I pray thee that again.
I do not joy in sight of such a pageant
As presents Death; though this life have a curse,
'Tis better than another that is worse.   170

     [He blindfolds his own eyes]
 [Bishop.] My lord, now you are blind to this world's sight,
Look upward to a world of endless light.
 Byr. Ay, ay, you talk of upward still to others,
And downwards look with headlong eyes yourselves.
Now come yòu up, sir; *[To the* Executioner] but not touch
 me yet;   175
Where shall I be now?
 Hangman.   Here, my lord!
 Byr.   Where's that?
 Hangman. There, there, my lord!
 Byr.   And where, slave, is that there?
Thou seest I see not, yet speak['st] as I saw.
Well, now is't fit?
 Hangman.   Kneel, I beseech your Grace,
That I may do mine office with most order.   180
 Byr. Do it, and if at one blow thou art short,

Give one and thirty, I'll endure them all.
Hold, stay a little! Comes there yet no mercy?
High Heaven curse these exemplary proceedings,
When justice fails, they sacrifice our example.   185
   Hangman. Let me beseech you I may cut your hair.
   Byr. Out, ugly image of my cruel justice!
Yet wilt thou be before me? Stay my will,
Or, by the will of Heaven, I'll strangle thee!
   Vit. My lord, you make too much of this your body.   190
Which is no more your own.
   Byr.   Nor is it yours;
I'll take my death with all the horrid rites
And representments of the dread it merits;
Let tame nobility and numbed fools
That apprehend not what they undergo,   195
Be such exemplary and formal sheep.
I will not have him touch me till I will;
If you will needs rack me beyond my reason,
Hell take me but I'll strangle half that's here,
And force the rest to kill me! I'll leap down,   200
If but once more they tempt me to despair.
You wish my quiet, yet give cause of fury:
Think you to set rude winds upon the sea,
Yet keep it calm, or cast me in a sleep
With shaking of my chains about mine ears?   205
O honest soldiers, [*To the* Guard] you have seen me free
From any care of many thousand deaths,
Yet of this one the manner doth amaze me.
View, view this wounded bosom! How much bound
Should that man make me that would shoot it through.   210
Is it not pity I should lose my life
By such a bloody and infamous stroke?
   Soldier. Now by thy spirit, and thy better Angel,
If thou wert clear, the continent of France
Would shrink beneath the burthen of thy death   215
Ere it would bear it.
   Vit.   Who's that?
   Soldier.   I say well,
And clear your justice: here is no ground shrinks;
If he were clear it would; and I say more,
Clear, or not clear, if he with all his foulness
Stood here in one scale, and the King's chief minion   220
Stood in another place; put here a pardon,

Here lay a royal gift, this, this, in merit
Should hoise the other minion into air.
   Vit.   Hence with that frantic!
     Byr.   This is some poor witness
That my desert might have outweigh'd my forfeit: 225
But danger haunts desert when he is greatest;
His hearty ills are prov'd out of his glances,
And kings' suspicions needs no balances;
So here's a most decretal end of me:
Which, I desire, in me may end my wrongs.   230
Commend my love, I charge you, to my brothers,
And by my love and misery command them
To keep their faiths that bind them to the King,
And prove no stomachers of my misfortunes,
Nor come to Court till time hath eaten out   235
The blots and scars of my opprobrious death;
And tell the Earl, my dear friend of D'Auvergne,
That my death utterly were free from grief
But for the sad loss of his worthy friendship;
And if I had been made for longer life   240
I would have more deserv'd him in my service,
Beseeching him to know I have not us'd
One word in my arraignment that might touch him;
Had I no other want than so ill meaning.
And so farewell for ever! Never more   245
Shall any hope of my revival see me;
Such is the endless exile of dead men.
Summer succeeds the Spring; Autumn the Summer;
The frosts of Winter the fall'n leaves of Autumn:
All these and all fruits in them yearly fade,   250
And every year return: but cursed man
Shall never more renew his vanish'd face.
Fall on your knees then, statists, ere ye fall,
That you may rise again: knees bent too late,
Stick you in earth like statues: see in me   255
How you are pour'd down from your clearest heavens;
Fall lower yet, mix'd with th' unmoved centre,
That your own shadows may no longer mock ye.
Strike, strike, O strike; fly, fly, commanding soul,
And on thy wings for this thy body's breath,   260
Bear the eternal victory of Death!

FINIS

THE TRAGEDY OF CHABOT
ADMIRAL OF FRANCE

DRAMATIS PERSONAE

Francis I, *King of France*

Philip Chabot, *Admiral of France*

Montmorency, *Lord High Constable*

Poyet, *Lord Chancellor*

The Treasurer

The Secretary

The Proctor-General, *or* Advocate

Two Judges

A Notary

The Father-in-law *of Chabot*

Asall, *a gentleman-in-waiting*

Allegre, *a servant of Chabot*

A Courtier

The Captain of the Guard

Officers, Ushers, Guards, Petitioners, *and* Courtiers

The Queen

The Wife *of Chabot*

The Tragedy of Chabot
Admiral of France

ACTUS PRIMUS

[SCENA I

A Room in the Court]

Enter Asall *and* Allegre

As. Now Philip Chabot, Admiral of France,
The great and only famous favourite
To Francis, first of that imperial name,
Hath found a fresh competitor in glory
(Duke Montmorency, Constable of France)   5
Who drinks as deep as he of the stream royal,
And may in little time convert the strength
To raise his spring, and blow the other's fall.
Al. The world would wish it so, that will not patiently
Endure the due rise of a virtuous man.   10
As. If he be virtuous, what is the reason
That men affect him not ? Why is he lost
To th' general opinion, and become
Rather their hate than love ?
Al.   I wonder you
Will question it ; ask a ground or reason   15
Of men bred in this vile, degenerate age !
The most men are not good, and it agrees not
With impious natures to allow what's honest ;
'Tis an offence enough to be exalted
To regal favours ; great men are not safe   20
In their own vice where good men by the hand
Of kings are planted to survey their workings.
What man was ever fix'd i' th' sphere of honour,
And precious to his sovereign, whose actions,
Nay, very soul, was not expos'd to every   25
Common and base dissection ? And not only
That which in Nature hath excuse, and in
Themselves is privileg'd by name of frailty,

But even virtues are made crimes, and doom'd
To th' fate of treason.

As.   A bad age the while!   30
I ask your pardon, sir, but thinks your judgment
His love to justice and corruption's hate
Are true and hearty?

Al.   Judge yourself, by this
One argument, his hearty truth to all;
For in the heart hath anger his wisest seat,   35
And gainst unjust suits such brave anger fires him
That when they seek to pass his place and power,
(Though mov'd and urg'd by the other minion,
Or by his greatest friends, and even the King
Lead them to his allowance with his hand,   40
First given in bill assign'd) even then his spirit,
In nature calm as any summer's evening,
Puts up his whole powers like a winter's sea,
His blood boils over, and his heart even cracks
At the injustice, and he tears the bill,   45
And would do, were he for't to be torn in pieces.

As. 'Tis brave, I swear!

Al.   Nay, it is worth your wonder,
That I must tell you further, there's no needle
In a sun-dial, plac'd upon his steel
In such a tender posture that doth tremble,   50
The timely dial being held amiss,
And will shake ever till you hold it right,
More tender than himself in anything
That he concludes in justice for the state:
For, as a fever held him, he will shake   55
When he is signing any things of weight,
Lest human frailty should misguide his justice.

As. You have declar'd him a most noble justicer.

Al. He truly weighs and feels, sir, what a charge
The subjects' livings are (being even their lives   60
Laid on the hand of power), which abus'd,
Though seen blood flow not from the justice-seat,
'Tis in true sense as grievous and horrid.

As. It argues nothing less; but since your lord
Is diversely reported for his parts,   65
What's your true censure of his general worth,
Virtue, and judgment?

Al. As of a picture wrought to optic reason,

That to all passers-by seems, as they move,
Now woman, now a monster, now a devil,   70
And till you stand and in a right line view it,
You cannot well judge what the main form is :
So men, that view him but in vulgar passes,
Casting but lateral or partial glances
At what he is, suppose him weak, unjust,   75
Bloody, and monstrous ; but stand free and fast
And judge him by no more than what you know
Ingenuously and by the right laid line
Of truth, he truly will all styles deserve
Of wise, just, good ; a man, both soul and nerve.   80
    As. Sir, I must join in just belief with you ;
But what's his rival, the Lord High Constable ?
    Al. As just, and well inclin'd, when he's himself
(Not wrought on with the counsels and opinions
Of other men), and the main difference is,   85
The Admiral is not flexible, nor won
To move one scruple, when he comprehends
The honest tract and justness of a cause :
The Constable explores not so sincerely
The course he runs, but takes the mind of others   90
(By name judicial), for what his own
Judgment and knowledge should conclude.
    As.   A fault,
In my apprehension : another's knowledge
Applied to my instruction cannot equal
My own soul's knowledge how to inform acts ;   95
The sun's rich radiance, shot through waves most fair,
Is but a shadow to his beams i' th' air ;
His beams, that in the air we so admire,
Is but a darkness to his flame in fire ;
In fire his fervour but as vapour flies,   100
To what his own pure bosom rarefies :
And the Almighty Wisdom, having given
Each man within himself an apter light
To guide his acts than any light without him
(Creating nothing not in all things equal)   105
It seems a fault in any that depend
On others' knowledge, and exile their own.
    Al. 'Tis nobly argued and exemplified ;
But now I hear my lord and his young rival
Are to be reconcil'd, and then one light   110

May serve to guide them both.

    As. I wish it may, the King being made first mover
To form their reconcilement and inflame it
With all the sweetness of his praise and honour.

    Al. See, 'tis dispatch'd, I hope ; the King doth grace it.   115

Loud Music, and enter Ushers *before the* Secretary, Treasurer,
    Chancellor ; Admiral, Constable, *hand in hand ; the*
    King *following, others attend.*

    King. This doth express the noblest fruit of peace.

    Chan. Which, when the great begin, the humble end
In joyful imitation, all combining
A Gordian beyond the Phrygian knot,
Past wit to loose it, or the sword ; be still so.   120

    Treas. 'Tis certain, sir, by concord least things grow
Most great and flourishing like trees, that wrap
Their forehead in the skies ; may these do so !

    King You hear, my lord, all that is spoke contends
To celebrate with pious vote the atonement   125
So lately and so nobly made between you.

    Chab. Which for itself sir, [I] resolve to keep
Pure and inviolable, needing none
To encourage or confirm it but my own
Love and allegiance to your sacred counsel.   130

    King. 'Tis good, and pleases, like my dearest health ;
Stand you firm on that sweet simplicity ? [*To the* Constable]

    Mont. Past all earth policy that would infringe it !

    King. 'Tis well, and answers all the doubts suspected.—

Enter one that whispers with the Admiral

And what moves this close message, Philip ?

    Chab.   My wife's   135
Father, sir, is closely come to court.

    King. Is he come to the court, whose aversation
So much affects him that he shuns and flies it ?
What's the strange reason that he will not rise
Above the middle region he was born in ?   140

    Chab. He saith, sir, 'tis because the extreme of height
Makes a man less seem to the imperfect eye
Than he is truly, his acts envied more ;
And though he nothing cares for seeming, so
His being just stand firm 'twixt heaven and him,

    45

Yet since in his soul's jealousy he fears
That he himself advanc'd would under-value
Men plac'd beneath him and their business with him,
Since height of place oft dazzles height of judgment,
He takes his top-sail down in such rough storms,   150
And apts his sails to airs more temperate.
    King. A most wise soul he has. How long shall kings
Raise men that are not wise till they be high ?
You have our leave ; but tell him, Philip, we
Would have him nearer.
    Mont.   Your desires attend you !   155
                               [*Exit* Chabot]

Enter another

    King. We know from whence you come ; say to the
       Queen,
We were coming to her. 'Tis a day of love,
And she seals all perfection.
                     Exit [*the* King *with* Attendants]
    Treas.   My lord,
We must beseech your stay.
    Mont.   My stay ?
    Chan.   Our counsels
Have led you thus far to your reconcilement,   160
And must remember you to observe the end
At which, in plain, I told you then we aim'd at :
You know we all urg'd the atonement, rather
To enforce the broader difference between you
Than to conclude your friendship ; which wise men   165
Know to be fashionable and privileg'd policy,
And will succeed betwixt you and the Admiral,
As sure as fate, if you please to get sign'd
A suit now to the King with all our hands,
Which will so much increase his precise justice   170
That, weighing not circumstances of politic state,
He will instantly oppose it and complain
And urge in passion what the King will sooner
Punish than yield to ; and so render you,
In the King's frown on him, the only darling   175
And mediate power of France.
    Mont.   My good Lord Chancellor,
Shall I, so late aton'd, and by the King's
Hearty and earnest motion, fall in pieces ?

Chan.   'Tis he, not you, that break.
Treas.   Ha' not you patience
To let him burn himself in the King's flame ?   180
   Chan.   Come, be not, sir, infected with a spice
Of that too servile equity, that renders
Men free-born slaves and rid with bits like horses,
When you must know, my lord, that even in nature
A man is *animal politicum* ;   185
So that when he informs his actions simply,
He does i[t] both gainst policy and nature :   •
And therefore our soul motion is affirm'd
To be, like heavenly natures', circular ;
And circles being call'd ambitious lines,   190
We must, like them, become ambitious ever,
And endless in our circumventions ;
No tough hides limiting our cheverel minds.
   Treas.   'Tis learnedly, and past all answer, argued ;
Y'are great, and must grow greater still, and greater,   195
And not be like a dull and standing lake,
That settles, putrefies, and chokes with mud ;
But, like a river gushing from the head,
That winds through the under-vales, what checks o'erflowing,
Gets strength still of his course,   200
Till, with the ocean meeting, even with him
In sway and title his brave billows move.
   Mont.   You speak a rare affection and high souls ;
But give me leave, great lords, still my just thanks
Remember'd to your counsels and direction,   205
I[n] seeking this way to confirm myself
I undermine the columns that support
My hopeful, glorious fortune, and at once
Provoke the tempest, though did drown my envy.
With what assurance shall the King expect   210
My faith to him that break it for another ?
He has engag'd our peace, and my revenge
Forfeits my trust with him, whose narrow sight
Will penetrate through all our mists, could we
Veil our design with clouds blacker than night ;   215
But grant this danger over, with what justice,
Or satisfaction to the inward judge,
Shall I be guilty of this good man's ruin ?
Though I may still the murmuring tongues without me,
Loud conscience has a voice to sh[u]dder greatness.   220

Sec. A name to fright, and terrify young statists.
There is necessity, my lord, that you
Must lose your light, if you eclipse not him ;
Two stars so lucid cannot shine at once
In such a firmament, and better you   225
Extinguish his fires than be made his fuel,
And in your ashes give his flame a trophy.
    Chan. My lord, the league that you have vow'd of friendship,
In a true understanding not confines you,
But makes you boundless ; turn not edge at such   230
A liberty, but look to your own fortune ;
Secure your honour : a precisian
In state is a ridiculous miracle ;
Friendship is but a visor, beneath which
A wise man laughs to see whole families   235
Ruin'd, upon whose miserable pile
He mounts to glory. Sir, you must resolve
To use any advantage.
    Mont.   Misery
Of rising statesmen ! I must on ; I see
That gainst the politic and privileg'd fashion,   240
All justice tastes but affectation.
    Chan. Why so ! We shall do good on him i' th' end.
                                                Exeunt

[SCENA II

Another Room in the Court]

Enter Father *and the* Admiral

    Chab. You are most welcome.
    Fath.   I wish your lordship's safety :
Which whilst I pray for, I must not forget
To urge again the ways to fix you where
No danger has access to threaten you.
    Chab. Still your old argument ; I owe your love for't.   5
    Fath. But, fortified with new and pregnant reasons,
That you should leave the court.
    Chab.   I dare not, sir.
    Fath. You dare be undone, then.
    Chab.   I should be ingrateful
To such a master, as no subject boasted.

To leave his service[s] when they exact   10
My chiefest duty and attendance, sir.
   Fath. Would thou wert less, degraded from thy titles
And swelling offices that will, i' th' end,
Engulf thee past a rescue ! I had not come
So far to trouble you at this time, but that   15
I do not like the loud tongues o' the world,
That say the King has ta'en another favourite,
The Constable, a gay man, and a great,
With a huge train of faction too ; the Queen,
Chancellor, Treasurer, Secretary, and   20
An army of state warriors, whose discipline
Is sure, and subtle to confusion.
I hope the rumour's false, thou art so calm.
   Chab. Report has not abus'd you, sir.
   Fath.   It has not !
And you are pleas'd ? Then you do mean to mix   25
With unjust courses, the great Constable
And you combining that no suit may pass
One of the grapples of your either's rape.
I that abhorr'd, must I now entertain
A thought that your so straight and simple custom   30
To render justice and the common good,
Should now be patch'd with policy, and wrested
From the ingenuous step you took, and hang
Upon the shoulders of your enemy,
To bear you out in what you shame to act ?   35
   Chab. Sir, we both are reconciled.
   Fath. It follows, then, that both the acts must bear
Like reconcilement ; and if he will now
Malign and malice you for crossing him
Or any of his faction in their suits,   40
Being now aton'd, you must be one in all,
One in corruption ; and 'twixt you two millstones,
New pick'd, and put together, must the grain
Of good men's needful means to live be ground
Into your choking superfluities ;   45
You both too rich, they ruin'd.
   Chab.   I conceive, sir,
We both may be enrich'd, and raise our fortunes
Even with our places in our Sovereign's favour,
Though past the height of others, yet within
The rules of law and justice, and approve   50

Our actions white and innocent.
 Fath.   I doubt it;
Whi[t]e in forc'd show, perhaps, which will, I fear,
Prove in true substance but a miller's whiteness,
More sticking in your clothes than conscience.
 Chab. Your censure herein tastes some passion, sir; 55
And I beseech you nourish better thoughts
Than to imagine that the King's mere grace
Sustains such prejudice by those it honours,
That of necessity we must pervert it
With passionate enemies, and ambitio[n]s boundless, 60
Avarice, and every licence incident
To fortunate greatness, and that all abuse it
For the most impious avarice of some.
 Fath. As if the total sum of favourites' frailties
Affected not the full rule of their kings 65
In their own partially dispos'd ambitions,
And that kings do no hazard infinitely
In their free realities of rights and honours.
Where they leave much for favourites' powers to order.
 Chab. But we have such a master of our King, 70
In the imperial art, that no power flies
Out of his favour, but his policy ties
A criance to it, to contain it still;
And for the reconcilement of us, sir,
Never were two in favour that were more 75
One in all love of justice and true honour,
Though in the act and prosecution
Perhaps we differ. Howsoever yet,
One beam us both creating, what should let
That both our souls should both one mettle bear, 80
And that one stamp, one word, one character?
 Fath. I could almost be won to be a courtier;
There's something more in's composition
Than ever yet was favourite's.—

Enter a Courtier

            What's he?
 Court. I bring your lordship a sign'd bill, to have 85
The addition of your honour'd hand; the Council
Have all before subscrib'd, and full prepar'd it.
 Chab. It seems then they have weigh'd the importance
  of it,
And know the grant is just.

Court.   No doubt, my lord ;
Or else they take therein the Constable's word,   90
It being his suit, and his power having wrought
The King already to appose his hand.

   Chab. I do not like his working of the King,
For, if it be a suit made known to him
And fit to pass, he wrought himself to it ;   95
However, my hand goes to no such grant,
But first I'll know, and censure it myself.

   Court. [*aside*]. [Até,] if thou beest goddess of contention,
That Jove took by the hair and hurl'd from heaven,
Assume in earth thy empire, and this bill   100
Thy firebrand make to turn his love, thus tempted,
Into a hate as horrid as thy furies.

   Chab. Does this bear title of his lordship's suit ?

   Court. It does, my lord, and therefore he beseech'd
The rather your dispatch.   105

   Chab.   No thought the rather !
But now the rather all powers against it,
The suit being most unjust, and he pretending
In all his actions justice, on the sudden
After his so late vow not to violate it,
Is strange and vile ; and if the King himself   110
Should own and urge it, I would stay and cross it ;
For 'tis within the free power of my office,
And I should strain his kingdom if I pass'd it.
I see their poor attempts and giddy malice ;
Is this the reconcilement that so lately   115
He vow'd in sacred witness of the King ?
Assuring me he never more would offer
To pass a suit unjust, which I well know
This is above all, and have often been urg'd
To give it passage.—Be you, sir, the judge.   120

   Fath. I wo' not meddle
With anything of state, you knew long since.

   Chab. Yet you may hear it, sir.

   Fath.   You wo' not urge
My opinion, then ? Go to !

   Chab.   An honest merchant,
Presuming on our league of France with Spain,   125
Brought into Spain a wealthy ship to vent
Her fit commodities to serve the country,
Which, in the place of suffering their sale,

Were seiz'd to recompense a Spanish ship
Priz'd by a Frenchman ere the league was made.   130
No suits, no letters of our King's could gain
Our merchant's first right in it ; but his letters
Unreverently receiv'd, the King's self scandal,
Beside the league's breach and the foul injustice
Done to our honest merchant, who endur'd all,   135
Till some small time since, (authoriz'd by our Council,
Though not in open court,) he made a ship out,
And took a Spaniard ; brings all home, and sues
To gain his full prov'd loss, full recompense
Of his just prize : his prize is stay'd and seiz'd   140
Yet for the King's disposure ; and the Spaniard
Makes suit to be restor'd her, which this bill
Would fain get granted, feigning, as they hop'd,
With my allowance, and way given to make
Our countryman's in Spain their absolute prize.   145

Fath. 'Twere absolute injustice.
Chab.   Should I pass it ?
Fath. Pass life and state before !
Chab.   If this would seem
His lordship's suit, his love to me and justice
Including plots upon me, while my simpleness
Is seriously vow'd to reconcilement,   150
Love him, good vulgars, and abhor me still ;
For if I court your flattery with my crimes,
Heaven's love before me fly, till in my tomb
I stick, pursuing it ; and for this bill,
Thus, say, 'twas shiver'd ; bless us, equal Heaven ! *Exit* 155
    Fath. This could I cherish now, above his loss.—
You may report as much, the bill discharg'd, sir. *Exeunt*

ACTUS SECUNDUS

[SCENA I

A Room in the Court]

Enter King *and* Queen, Secretary *with the torn bill*

King. Is it e'en so ?
Queen.   Good heaven, how tame you are !
Do Kings of France reward foul traitors thus ?
    King. No traitor, y'are too loud, Chabot's no traitor ;

He has the passions of a man about him,
And multiplicity of cares may make   5
Wise men forget themselves.   Come, be you patient.

   Queen.   Can you be so, and see yourself thus torn ?

   King.   Ourself ?

   Queen.   [*Showing the torn bill.*]   There is some left, if you
     dare own
Your royal character ; is not this your name ?

   King.   'Tis Francis, I confess.

   Queen.   Be but a name,   10
If this stain live upon't, affronted by
Your subject.   Shall the sacred name of King,
A word to make your nation bow and tremble,
Be thus profan'd ?   Are laws establish'd
To punish the defacers of your image   15
But dully set by the rude hand of others
Upon your coin, and shall the character
That doth include the blessing of all France,
Your name, thus written by your royal hand,
Design'd for justice and your kingdom's honour,   20
Not call up equal anger to reward it ?
Your Counsellors of state contemn'd and slighted,
As in [his] brain [were] circumscrib'd all wisdom
And policy of empire, and your power
Subordinate and subject to his passion.   25

   King.   Come, it concerns you not.

   Queen.   Is this the consequence
Of an atonement made so lately between
The hopeful Montmorency and his lordship,
Urge[d] by yourself with such a precious sanction ?
Come, he that dares do this, wants not a heart,   30
But opportunity—

   King.   To do what ?

   Queen.   To tear
Your crown off.

   King.   Come, your language doth taste more
Of rage and womanish flame, than solid reason,
Against the Admiral.   What commands of yours,
Not to your expectation obey'd   35
By him, is ground of your so keen displeasure ?

   Queen.   Commands of mine ?   He is too great and powerful
To stoop to my employment, a Colossus,
And can stride from one province to another

By the assistance of those offices   40
You have most confidently impos'd upon him.
'Tis he, not you, take up the people's eyes
And admiration, while his princely wife—
   King.   Nay, then I reach the spring of your distaste ;
He has a wife—

     Enter Chancellor, Treasurer, *and whisper with the* King

   Queen.   [*Aside*]   Whom for her pride I love not ;   45
And I but in her husband's ruin can
Triumph o'er her greatness.
   King.   [*To Chancellor*] Well, well ; I'll think on't.   *Exit*
   Chan.   He begins to incline.
Madam, you are the soul of our great work.
   Queen.   I'll follow, and employ my powers upon him.   50
   Treas.   We are confident you will prevail at last,
And for the pious work oblige the King to you.
   Chan.   And us your humblest creatures.
   Queen.   Press no further.   *Exit* Queen
   Chan.   Let's seek out my lord Constable.
   Treas.   And inflame him—
   Chan.   To expostulate with Chabot ; something may   55
Arise from thence, to pull more weight upon him.
                        Exeunt

[SCENA II

Another Room in the Court]

Enter Father *and* Allegre

   Fath.   How sorts the business ? How took the King
The tearing of his bill ?
   Al.   Exceeding well.
And seem'd to smile at all their grim complaints
Gainst all that outrage to his Highness' hand,
And said, in plain, he sign'd it but to try   5
My lord's firm justice.
   Fath.   What a sweet king 'tis !
   Al.   But how his rival, the Lord Constable,
Is labour'd by the Chancellor and others to retort
His wrong with ten parts more upon my lord,
Is monstrous.   10

 Fath. Need he their spurs ?

 Al.   Ay, sir, for he's afraid

To bear himself too boldly in his braves

Upon the King, being newly enter'd minion,

(Since 'tis but patience sometime [he] think[s]

Because, the favour spending in two streams,   15

One must run low at length) till when he dare

Take fire in such flame as his faction wishes ;

But with wise fear contains himself, and so,

Like a green faggot in his kindling, smokes ;

And where the Chancellor, his chief Cyclops, finds 20

The fire within him apt to take, he blows,

And then the faggot flames as never more

The bellows needed, till the too soft greenness

Of his state habit shows his sap still flows

Above the solid timber, with which, then,   25

His blaze shrinks head, he cools, and smokes again.

 Fath. Good man he would be, would the bad not spoil him.

 Al. True, sir ; but they still ply him with their arts ;

And, as I heard, have wrought him, personally

To question my lord with all the bitterness   30

The galls of all their faction can pour in ;

And such an expectation hangs upon't,

Th[r]ough all the Court, as 'twere with child and long'd

To make a mirror of my lord's clear blood,

And therein see the full ebb of his flood ;   35

And therefore, if you please to counsel him,

You shall perform a father's part.

 Fath.   Nay, since

He's gone so far, I would not have him fear,

But dare 'em ; and yet I'll not meddle in't.

Enter Admiral

He's here ; if he have wit to like his cause,   40

His spirit wo' not be asham'd to die in't.   *Exit*

 Al. My lord, retire ; y'are waylaid in your walks ;

Your friends are all fallen from you ; all your servants,

Suborn'd by all advantage to report

Each word you whisper out, and to serve you   45

With hat and knee, while others have their hearts.

 Chab. Much profit may my foes make of such servants !

I love no enemy I have so well,

To take so ill a bargain from his hands.

Al. Their other odds yet shun, all being combin'd,   50
And lodg'd in ambush, arriv'd to do you mischief
By any means, past fear of law or sovereign.
  Chab. I walk no desert, yet go arm'd with that
That would give wildest beasts instincts to rescue
Rather than offer any force to hurt me—   55
My innocence, which is a conquering justice
A[nd] wears a shield that both defends and fights.
  Al. One against all the world !
  Chab.   The more the odds,
The less the conquest ; or, if all the world
Be thought an army fit to employ gainst one,   60
That one is argued fit to fight gainst all :
If I fall under them, this breast shall bear
Their heap digested in my sepulchre.
Death is the life of good men : let 'em come.

Enter Constable, Chancellor, Treasurer, *and* Secretary

  Mont. I thought, my lord, our reconcilement perfect.   65
You have express'd what sea of gall flow'd in you,
In tearing of the bill I sent to allow.
  Chab. Dare you confess the sending of that bill ?
  Mont. Dare ? Why not ?
  Chab.   Because it brake your oath
Made in our reconcilement, and betrays   70
The honour and the chief life of the King,
Which is his justice.
  Mont. Betrays ?
  Chab.   No less, and that I'll prove to him.
  Omnes. You cannot !
  Treas. I would not wish you offer at an action   75
So most impossibly, and much against
The judgment and the favour of the King.
  Chab. His judgment nor his favour I respect,
So I preserve his justice.
  Chan.   'Tis not justice,
Which I'll prove by law, and absolute learning.   80
  Chab. All your great law and learning are but words,
When I plead plainly naked truth and deeds,
Which, though you seek to fray with state and glory,
I'll shoot a shaft at all your globe of light ;
If lightning split it, yet 'twas high and right.   *Exit* 85

Mont. Brave resolution ! So his acts be just,
He cares for gain no[r] honour.
    Chan.   How came he then
By all his infinite honour and his gain ?
    Treas. Well said, my lord !
    Sec.   Answer but only that.
    Mont. By doing justice still in all his actions.   90
    Sec. But if this action prove unjust, will you
Say all his other may be so as well,
And think your own course fitter far than his ?
    Mont. I will.   *Exit*
    Chan. He cools, we must not leave him ; we have no   95
Such engine to remove the Admiral.   *Exeunt*

[SCENA III

Another Room in the Court]

Enter King *and the* Admiral

King. I prithee, Philip, be not so severe
To him I favour ; 'tis an argument
That may serve one day to avail yourself,
Nor does it square with your so gentle nature,
To give such fires of envy to your blood ;   5
For howsoever out of love to justice
Your jealousy of that doth so incense you,
Yet they that censure it will say 'tis envy.
    Chab. I serve not you for them but for yourself,
And that good in your rule that justice does you ;   10
And care not this what others say, so you
Please but to do me right for what you know.
    King. You will not do yourself right. Why should I
Exceed you to yourself ?
    Chab.   Myself am nothing,
Compar'd to what I seek ; 'tis justice only,   15
The fount and flood both of your strength and kingdom's.
    King. But who knows not that extreme justice is
(By all rul'd laws) the extreme of injury,
And must to you be so ; the persons that
Your passionate heat calls into question   20
Are great and many, and may wrong in you
Your rights of kind, and dignities of fortune ;

And I advanc'd you not to heap on you
Honours and fortunes, that, by strong hand now
Held up and over you, when heaven takes off   25
That powerful hand, should thunder on your head,
And after you crush your surviving seeds.
   Chab.   Sir, your regards to both are great and sacred ;
But, if the innocence and right that rais'd me
And means for mine, can find no friend hereafter   30
Of Him that ever lives, and ever seconds
All kings' just bounties with defence and refuge
In just men's races, let my fabric ruin,
My stock want sap, my branches by the root
Be torn to death, and swept with whirlwinds out.   35
   King.   For my love no relenting ?
   Chab.   No, my Liege.
'Tis for your love and right that I stand out.
   King.   Be better yet advis'd.
   Chab.   I cannot, sir,
Should any oracle become my counsel ;
For that I stand not out thus of set will   40
Or pride of any singular conceit,
My enemies and the world may clearly know ;
I taste no sweets to drown in others' gall,
And to affect in that which makes me loathed,
To leave myself and mine expos'd to all   45
The dangers you propos'd, my purchas'd honours
And all my fortunes in an instant lost,
That m[a]ny cares, and pains, and years have gather'd
How mad were I to rave thus in my wounds,
Unless my known health, felt in these forc'd issues,   50
Were sound and fit ; and that I did not know
By most true proofs that to become sincere
With all men's hates doth far exceed their loves,
To be, as they are, mixtures of corruption ;
And that those envies that I see pursue me   55
Of all true actions are the natural consequents
Which being my object and my resolute choice,
Not for my good but yours, I will have justice,
   King.   You will have justice ? Is your will so strong
Now against mine, your power being so weak,   60
Before my favour gave them both their forces ?
Of all that ever shar'd in my free graces,
You, Philip Chabot, a mean gentleman,

Have not I rais'd you to a supremest lord,
And given you greater dignities than any ?   65
 Chab. You have so.
 King.   Well said ; and to spur your dulness
With the particulars to which I rais'd you,
Have not I made you first a knight of the Order,
Then Admiral of France, then Count Byzanges,
Lord and Lieutenant-General of all   70
My country and command of Burgundy ;
Lieutenant-General likewise of my son,
Dauphin and heir, and of all Normandy ;
And of my chiefly honour'd Privy Council
And cannot all these powers weigh down your will ?   75
 Chab. No, sir ; they were not given me to that end,
But to uphold my will, my will being just.
 King. And who shall judge that justice, you or I ?
 Chab. I, sir, in this case ; your royal thoughts are fitly
Exempt from every curious search of one,   80
You have the general charge with care of all.
 King. And do not generals include particulars ?
May not I judge of anything compris'd
In your particular, as well as you ?
 Chab. Far be the misery from you that you may !   85
My cares, pains, broken sleep, therein made more
Than yours, should make me see more, and my forces
Render of better judgment.
 King.   Well, sir, grant
Your force in this ; my odds in benefits,
Paid for your pains, put in the other scale,   90
And any equal holder of the balance
Will show my merits hoist up yours to air,
In rule of any doubt or deed betwixt us.
 Chab. You merit not of me for benefits,
More than myself of you for services.   95
 King. Is't possible ?
 Chab.   'Tis true.
 King.   Stand you on that ?
 Chab. Ay, to the death, and will approve to all men.
 King. I am deceiv'd but I shall find good judges
That will find difference.
 Chab.   Find them, being good.
 King. Still so ? What, if conferring   100
My bounties and your services to sound them,

We fall foul on some licences of yours ?
Nay, give me therein some advantage of you.
 Chab. They cannot.
 King. Not in sifting their severe discharges   105
Of all your offices ?
 Chab.   The more you sift,
The more you shall refine me.
 King.   What if I
Grant out against you a commission,
Join'd with an extraordinary process
To arrest and put you in law's hands for trial ?   110
 Chab. Not with law's uttermost!
 King.   I'll throw the dice.
 Chab. And I'll endure the chance, the dice being square,
Repos'd in dreadless confidence and conscience,
That all your most extremes shall never reach,
Or to my life, my goods, or honour's breach.   115
 King. Was ever heard so fine a confidence ?
Must it not prove presumption ? And can that
'Scape bracks and errors in your search of law ?
I prithee weigh yet with more soul the danger,
And some less passion.
 Chab.   Witness, heaven, I cannot, 120
Were I dissolv'd, and nothing else but soul.
 King [*aside*]. Beshrew my blood, but his resolves amaze
  me.—
Was ever such a justice in a subject
Of so much office left to his own swinge
That, left to law thus and his sovereign's wrath, 125
Could stand clear, spite of both ? Let reason rule it,
Before it come at law : a man so rare
In one thing cannot in the rest be vulgar ;
And who sees you not in the broad highway,
The common dust up in your own eyes beating, 130
In quest of riches, honours, offices,
As heartily in show as most believe ?
And he that can use actions with the vulgar,
Must needs embrace the same effects, and cannot (inform
  him),
Whatsoever he pretends, use them with such 135
Free equity, as fits one just and real,
Even in the eyes of men, nor stand at all parts
So truly circular, so sound, and solid,

But have his swellings-out, his cracks and crannies ;
And therefore, in this, reason, before law   140
Take you to her, lest you affect and flatter
Yourself with mad opinions.
   Chab.   I were mad
Directly, sir, if I were yet to know
Not the sure danger, but the certain ruin
Of men shot into law from kings' bent brow,   145
There being no dream from the most muddy brain
Upon the foulest fancy, that can forge
More horror in the shadows of mere fame,
Than can some lawyer in a man expos'd
To his interpretation by the king.   150
But these grave toys I shall despise in death ;
And while I live, will lay them open so
(My innocence laid by them), that, like foils,
They shall stick off my merits ten times more,
And make your bounties nothing ; for who gives   155
And hits i' th' teeth, himself pays with the glory
For which he gave, as being his end of giving,
Not to crown merits or do any good,
And so no thanks is due but to his glory.
   King. 'Tis brave, I swear !
   Chab.   No, sir, 'tis plain and rude, 160
But true and spotless ; and where you object
My hearty and gross vulgar love of riches,
Titles, and honours, I did never seek them
For any love to them, but to that justice
You ought to use in their due gift to merits,   165
To show you royal, and most open-handed,
Not using for hands, talons, pincers, grapples ;
In whose gripes, and upon whose gor'd point,
Deserts hang sprawling out their virtuous limbs.
   King. Better and better !
   Chab.   This your glory is,   170
My deserts wrought upon no wretched matter,
But show'd your royal palms as free and moist
As Ida, all enchas'd with silver springs,
And yet my merit still their equal sings.
   King. Sing till thou sigh thy soul out ; hence, and leave us ! 175
   Chab. My person shall, my love and faith shall never.
   King. Perish thy love and faith, and thee for ever !
                                     [Exit Chabot]

Who's there ?

Enter Asall

        Let one go for the Chancellor.
As. He's here in court, sir.
King.   Haste, and send him hither !
                                [*Exit* Asall]
This is an insolence I never met with.   180
Can one so high as his degrees ascend
Climb all so free and without stain ?

Enter Chancellor

                              My Lord
Chancellor, I send for you about a service
Of equal price to me, as if again
My ransom came to me from Pavian thraldom,   185
And more, as if from forth a subject's fetters,
The worst of servitudes, my life were rescued.
    Chan. You fright me with a prologue of much trouble.
    King. Methinks it might be. Tell me, out of all
Your famous learning, was there ever subject   190
Rais'd by his sovereign's free hand from the dust
Up to a height above air's upper region,
That might compare with him in any merit
That so advanc'd him, and not show, in that
Gross over-weening, worthy cause to think   195
There might be other over-sights excepted,
Of capital nature in his sifted greatness ?
    Chan. And past question, sir, for one absurd thing
      granted,
A thousand follow.
    King.   You must then employ
Your most exact and curious art to explore   200
A man in place of greatest trust and charge,
Whom I suspect to have abus'd them all,
And in whom you may give such proud veins vent,
As will bewray their boiling blood, corrupted
Both gainst my crown and life.   205
    Chan. And may my life be curs'd in every act,
If I explore him not to every fi[b]re.
    King. It is my Admiral.
    Chan.   Oh, my good Liege,
You tempt, not charge me, with such search of him.

 King. Doubt not my heartiest meaning : all the troubles 210
That ever mov'd in a distracted king,
Put in just fear of his assaulted life,
Are not above my sufferings for Chabot.
 Chan. Then I am glad and proud that I can cure you,
For he's a man that I am studied in,   215
And all his offices, and if you please
To give authority—
 King.   You shall not want it.
 Chan. If I discharge you not of that disease
About your neck grown, by your strange trust in him,
With full discovery of the foulest treasons— 220
 King. But I must have all prov'd with that free justice.
 Chan. Beseech your majesty, do not question it.
 King. About it instantly, and take me wholly
Upon yourself.
 Chan.   How much you grace your servant !
 King. Let it be fiery quick.
 Chan.   It shall have wings, 225
And every feather show the flight of kings.

             [Exeunt]

ACTUS TERTIUS

[SCENA I

A Gallery]

Enter Chancellor *attended, the* Proctor-General *whispering in
 his ear, two* Judges *following ; they past, enter* Chabot, *in
 his gown, a guard about him, his* Father *and his* Wife *on
 each side,* Allegre *[guarded]*

 Chab. And have they put my faithful servant to the rack ?
Heaven arm the honest man !
 Fath. Allegre feels the malice of the Chancellor.
 Chab. Many upon the torture have confess'd
Things against truth, and yet his pain sits nearer 5
Than all my other fears. *[To his* Wife] Come, don't weep.
 Wife. My lord, I do not grieve out of a thought
Or poor suspicion, they with all their malice
Can stain your honour ; but it troubles me

The King should grant this licence to your enemies,　　10
As he were willing to hear Chabot guilty.
　Chab.　No more ; the King is just ; and by exposing
Me to this trial, means to render me
More happy to his subjects and himself.
His sacred will be obey'd ; take thy own spirit,　　15
And let no thought infringe thy peace for me ;
I go to have my honours all confirm'd.
Farewell ; thy lip [*kisses her*] : my cause has so much inno-
　　cence,
It sha' not need thy prayer. [*To* Father] I leave her yours
Till my return. Oh, let me be a son　　20
Still in your thoughts. Now, gentlemen, set forward.
　　Exit [Chabot *with* Guards] *Manente* Father *and* Wife
　Fath.　See, you that trust in greatness, what sustains you ;
These hazards you must look for, you that thrust
Your heads into a cloud, where lie in ambush
The soldiers of state, in privy arms　　25
Of yellow fire, jealous, and mad at all
That shoot their foreheads up into their forges,
And pry into their gloomy cabinets ;
You, like vain citizens, that must go see
Those ever-burning furnaces wherein　　30
Your brittle glasses of estate are blown,
Who knows not you are all but puff and bubble,
Of breath and fume forg'd, your vile brittle natures
Cause of your dearness ? Were you tough and lasting,
You would be cheap, and not worth half your face.　　35
Now, daughter ; planet-struck ?
　Wife.　　　　　　　I am considering
What form I shall put on, as best agreeing
With my lord's fortune.
　Fath.　　　　　　Habit do you mean,
Of mind, or body ?
　Wife.　　　　　Both would be apparell'd.　　40
　Fath.　In neither you have reason yet to mourn.
　Wife.　I'll not accuse my heart of so much weakness ;
Twere a confession gainst my lord. The Queen !

　　Enter Queen, Constable, Treasurer, *and* Secretary

She has express'd gainst me some displeasure.
　Fath.　Let's this way through the gallery. [*They retire*]

Queen.   'Tis she.
Do you, my lord, say I would speak with her.   45
[*To the* Treasurer] And has Allegre, one of chiefest trust
    with him,
Suffer'd the rack ? The Chancellor is violent :
And what's confess'd ?
    Treas. Nothing ; he contemn'd all
That could with any cruell'st pain explore him,
As if his mind had robb'd his nerves of sense,   50
And through them diffus'd fiery spirits above
All flesh and blood ; for, as his limbs were stretch'd,
His contempts too extended.
    Queen.   A strange fortitude !
    Treas. But we shall lose th' arraignment.
    Queen.   The success
Will soon arrive.
    Treas.   You'll not appear, my lord, then ?   55
    Mont. I desire your lordship would excuse me.
    Treas. We are your servants.
                            Exeunt Treasurer *and* Secretary
    Mont.   She attends you, madam.
            [*Approaching with* Wife *who kneels*]
    Queen. This humbleness proceeds not from your heart.
Why, you are a queen yourself in your own thoughts,
The Admiral's wife of France cannot be less ;   60
You have not state enough ; you should not move
Without a train of friends and servants.
    Wife.   There is some mystery
Within your language, madam. I would hope
You have more charity than to imagine
My present condition worth your triumph,   65
In which I am not so lost, but I have
Some friends and servants with proportion
To my lord's fortune ; but none, within the list
Of those that obey me, can be more ready
To express their duties than my heart to serve   70
Your just commands.
    Queen.   Then pride will ebb, I see ;
There is no constant flood of state and greatness ;
The prodigy is ceasing when your lord
Comes to the balance ; he whose blazing fires
Shot wonders through the kingdom, will discover   75
What flying and corrupted matter fed him.

Wife.　My lord ?

Queen.　　　　　　　Your high and mighty justicer,
The man of conscience, the oracle
Of state, whose honourable titles
Would crack an elephant's back, is now turn'd mortal,　　80
Must pass examination and the test
Of law, have all his offices ripp'd up,
And his corrupt soul laid open to the subjects :
His bribes, oppressions, and close sins, that made
So many groan and curse him, now shall find　　85
Their just reward, and all that love their country,
Bless heaven and the King's justice, for removing
Such a devouring monster.

　　Fath.　[*To* Montmorency, *coming forward*] Sir, your pardon.
Madam, you are the Queen, she is my daughter,
And he that you have character'd so monstrous,　　90
My son-in-law, now gone to be arraign'd.
The King is just, and a good man ; but't does not
Add to the graces of your royal person
To tread upon a lady thus dejected
By her own grief.　Her lord's not yet found guilty,　　95
Much less condemn'd, though you have pleas'd to execute him.

　　Queen.　What saucy fellow's this ?

　　Fath.　　　　　　　I must confess
I am a man out of this element,
No courtier ; yet I am a gentleman
That dare speak honest truth to the Queen's ear　　100
(A duty every subject wo' not pay you),
And justify it to all the world.　There's nothing
Doth more eclipse the honours of our soul
Than an ill-grounded and ill-followed passion,
Let fly with noise and licence against those　　105
Whose hearts before are bleeding.

　　Mont.　　　　　　　Brave old man !

　　Fath.　Cause you are a queen, to trample o'er a woman
Whose tongue and faculties are all tied up !
Strike out a lion's teeth and pare his claws,
And then a dwarf may pluck him by the beard.　　110
'Tis a gay victory !

　　Queen.　[*To* Montmorency]　Did you hear, my lord ?

　　Fath.　I ha' done.

　　Wife [*rising*]　　And it concerns me to begin.
I have not made this pause through servile fear

Or guilty apprehension of your rage,
But with just wonder of the heats and wildness   115
Has prepossess'd your nature gainst our innocence.
You are my Queen ; unto that title bows
The humblest knee in France, my heart made lower
With my obedience and prostrate duty ;
Nor have I powers created for my use,   120
When just commands of you expect their service ;
But were you Queen of all the world, or something
To be thought greater, betwixt heaven and us,
That I could reach you with my eyes and voice,
I would shoot both up in defence of my   125
Abused honour, and stand all your lightning.
    Queen.   So brave !
    Wife.   So just, and boldly innocent,
I cannot fear, arm'd with a noble conscience,
The tempest of your frown, were it more frightful
Than ever fury made a woman's anger,   130
Prepar'd to kill with death's most horrid ceremony ;
Yet with what freedom of my soul I can
Forgive your accusation of my pride !
    Queen. ' Forgive ' ? What insolence is like this language ?
Can any action of ours be capable   135
Of thy forgiveness ? Dust, how I despise thee !
Can we sin to be object of thy mercy ?
    Wife.   Yes, and have done't already, and no stain
To your greatness, madam ; 'tis my charity,
I can remit. When sovereign princes dare   140
Do injury to those that live beneath them,
They turn worth pity and their pray'rs, and 'tis
In the free power of those whom they oppress
To pardon 'em ; each soul has a prerogative,
And privilege royal, that was sign'd by Heaven.   145
But, though i' th' knowledge of my disposition,
Stranger to pride, and what you charge me with,
I can forgive the injustice done to me,
And striking at my person, I have no
Commission from my lord to clear you for   150
The wrongs you have done him ; and till he pardon
The wounding of his loyalty, with which life
Can hold no balance, I must take just boldness
To say—
    Fath.   No more. Now I must tell you, daughter,

Lest you forget yourself, she is the Queen;   155
And it becomes not you to vie with her
Passion for passion: if your lord stand fast
To the full search of law, Heaven will revenge him,
And give him up precious to good men's loves.
If you attempt by these unruly ways   160
To vindicate his justice, I'm against you,
Dear as I wish your husband's life and fame:
[Subjects] are bound to suffer, not contest
With princes, since their will and acts must be
Accounted one day to a Judge supreme.   165
   Wife. I ha' done. If the devotion to my lord,
Or piety to his innocence, have led me
Beyond the awful limits to be observ'd
By one so much beneath your sacred person,
I thus low crave your royal pardon, madam.   [*Kneeling*]
I know you will remember in your goodness,   170
My life-blood is concern'd while his least vein
Shall run black and polluted, my heart fed
With what keeps him alive, nor can there be
A greater wound than that which strikes the life   175
Of our good name, so much above the bleeding
Of this rude pile we carry, as the soul
Hath excellence above this earth-born frailty.
My lord, by the King's will, is led already
To a severe arraignment, and to judges   180
Will make no tender search into his tract
Of life and state. Stay but a little while,
And France shall echo to his shame or innocence.
This suit I beg with tears; I shall have sorrow
Enough to hear him censur'd foul and monstrous,   185
Should you forbear to antedate my sufferings.
   Queen. Your conscience comes about, and you incline
To fear he may be worth the law's condemning.
   Wife. I sooner will suspect the stars may lose
Their way, and crystal heaven return to chaos;   190
Truth sits not on her square more firm than he:
Yet, let me tell you, madam, were his life
And action so foul as you have character'd
And the bad world expects, though as a wife
'Twere duty I should weep myself to death   195
To know him fall'n from virtue, yet so much
I, a frail woman, love my King and Country,

I should condemn him too, and think all honours,
The price of his lost faith, more fatal to me
Than Cleopatra's asps warm in my bosom,   200
And as much boast their killing.
    Queen [*aside*].   This declares
Another soul than was deliver'd me.
My anger melts, and I begin to pity her.
How much a prince's ear may be abus'd !—
Enjoy your happy confidence ; at more leisure   205
You may hear from us.
    Wife.   Heaven preserve the Queen,
And may her heart be charitable !
    Fath.   You bless and honour your unworthy servant.
                                        [*Exit* Wife *and* Father]
    Queen.   My lord, did you observe this ?
    Mont.   Yes, great madam,
And read a noble spirit, which becomes   210
The wife of Chabot ! Their great tie of marriage
Is not more strong upon 'em than their virtues.
    Queen.   That your opinion ? I thought your judgment
Against the Admiral. Do you think him honest ?
    Mont.   Religiously ; a true, most zealous patriot,   215
And worth all royal favour.
    Queen.   You amaze me.
Can you be just yourself then, and advance
Your powers against him ?
    Mont.   Such a will be far
From Montmorency. Pioneers of state
Have left no art to gain me to their faction,
And 'tis my misery to be plac'd in such   220
A sphere, where I am whirl'd by violence
Of a fierce raging motion, and not what
My own will would incline me. I shall make
This appear, madam, if you please to second   225
My free speech with the King.
    Queen.   Good heaven protect all !
Haste to the King ; Justice her swift wing needs ;
Tis high time to be good when virtue bleeds.   *Exeunt*

[SCENA II

A Court of Justice]

Enter Officers *before the* Chancellor, Judges, *the* Proctor-General *whispering with the* Chancellor ; *they take their places : to them enter* Treasurer *and* Secretary, *who take their places prepared on one side of the Court. To them the* Captain of the Guard, *the* Admiral *following, who is placed at the bar.*

Chan.   Good Master Proctor-General, begin.

Proc.   It is not unknown to you, my very good lords the Judges, and indeed to all the world, for I will make short work, since your honourable ears need not to be enlarged—I speak by a figure—with prolix enumeration, how infinitely the King hath favoured this ill-favoured traitor ; and yet I may worth-   5
ily too insist and prove that no grace hath been so large and voluminous as this, that he hath appointed such upright judges at this time, and the chief of this Triumvirie, our Chancellor, by name Poyet, which deriveth from the Greek his etymology, from ποιεῖν, which is, to make, to create, to in-   10
vent matter that was never extant in nature ; from whence also is the name and dignity of *Poeta*—which I will not insist upon in this place, although I am confident his lordship want-eth no faculty in making of verses.   But what addition, I say, is it to the honour of this delinquent, that he hath such a   15
judge, a man so learned, so full of equity, so noble, so notable, in the progress of his life so innocent, in the manage of his office so incorrupt, in the passages of state so wise, in affection to his country so religious, in all his services to the King so fortunate and exploring, as envy itself cannot accuse, or   20
malice vitiate, whom all lips will open to commend, but those of Philip, and in their hearts will erect altars and statues, columns and obelisks, pillars and pyramids, to the perpetuity of his name and memory.   What shall I say ? but conclude for his so great and sacred service, both to our King and king-   25
dom, and for their everlasting benefit, there may everlastingly be left here one of his loins ; one of his loins ever remain, I say, and stay upon this Bench, to be the example of all justice, even while the north and south star shall continue.

Chan.   You express your oratory, Master Proctor ; I pray   30
come presently to the matter.

Proc.   Thus, with your lordship's pardon, I proceed ; and the first thing I shall glance at will be worth your lordship's reflection—his ingratitude ; and to whom? To no less person than a king. And to what king ? His own, and our general Sovereign,   35
—*pro Deum atque hominum fidem*—a king and such a king, the health, life, and soul of us all, whose very mention draws

this salt water from my eyes ; for he, indeed, is our eye, who
wakes and watches for us when we sleep—and who will not
sleep for him ?   I mean not sleep, which the philosophers call   40
a natural cessation of the common, and, consequently, of all
the exterior senses, caused first and immediately by a deten-
tion of spirits, which can have no communication, since the
way is obstructed by which these spirits should commerce, by
vapours ascending from the stomach to the head ; by which   45
evaporation the roots of the nerves are filled, through which
the [animal] spirits [use] to be poured into the dwellings of the
external senses ;—but sleep, I take for death, which all know to
be *ultima linea*. Who will not sleep eternally for such a king
as we enjoy ?   If, therefore, in general, as he is King of us all,   50
all sharing and dividing the benefits of this our Sovereign,
none should be so ingrateful as once to murmur against him,
what shall be said of the ingratitude more monstrous in this
Chabot ? For our Francis hath loved, not in general, and in the
crowd with other subjects, but particularly, this Philip ; ad-   55
vanced him to the supreme dignity of a statesman, lodged him
in his very heart, yet—*monstrum horrendum*—even to this
Francis hath Philip been ingrateful.   Brutus, the loved son,
hath stabbed Cæsar with a bodkin.   Oh, what brute may be
compared to him, and in what particulars may this crime be   60
exemplified ? He hath, as we say, chopped logic with the king ;
nay, to the very teeth of his sovereign, advanced his own
guat-like merits, and justified with Luciferous pride that his
services have deserved more than all the bounty of our
munificent King hath paid him.   65
   Chan. Observe that, my lords.
   Proc. Nay, he hath gone further, and most traitorously
hath committed outrage and impiety to the King's own hand
and royal character, which, presented to him in a bill from
the whole council, he most violently did tear in pieces, and   70
will do the very body and person of our King, if your justice
make no timely prevention, and strike out the serpentine
teeth of this high and more than horrible monster.
   Treas. This was enforced home.
   Proc. In the next place, I will relate to your honours his   75
most cruel exactions upon the subject, the old vant-couriers
of rebellions. In the year 1536 and 37, this oppressor and this
extortioner under pretext of his due taxation, being Admiral,
imposed upon certain fishermen (observe, I beseech you, the
circumstance of their persons, fishermen), who, poor Johns,   80

were embarked upon the coast of Normandy and fishing there
for herrings (which some say is the king of fishes), he imposed,
I say, twenty sous, and upon every boat six livres.   O intoler-
able exaction ! Enough, not only to alienate the hearts of these
miserable people from their King, which, *ipso facto*, is high   85
treason, but an occasion of a greater inconvenience for want
of due provision of fish among the subjects ; for by this might
ensue a necessity of mortal sins, by breaking the religious
fast upon Vigils, Embers, and other days commanded by
sacred authority, besides the miserable rut that would follow,   90
and perhaps contagion, when feasting and flesh should be
licensed for every carnal appetite.—I could urge many more
particulars of his dangerous, insatiate, and boundless avarice ;
but the improvement of his estate in so few years, from a
private gentleman's fortune to a great duke's revenues, might   95
save our Sovereign therein an orator to enforce and prove
faulty, even to giantism against heaven.

Judge. This is but a noise of words.

Proc. To the foul outrages so violent, let us add his commis-
sions granted out of his own presumed authority—his Majesty   100
neither [informed] or respected—his disloyalties, infidelities,
contempts, oppressions, extortions, with innumerable abuses,
offences, and forfeits, both to his Majesty's most royal person,
crown, and dignity ; yet, notwithstanding all these injustices,
this unmatchable, unjust delinquent affecteth to be thought   105
inculpable and incomparable just ; but, alas ! my most learned
lord[s], none knows better than yourselves how easy the sincerity of justice is pretended, how hard it is to be performed,
and how common it is for him that hath least colour of title
to it, to be thought the very substance and soul of it ; he   110
that was never true scholar in the least degree, longs, as a
woman with child, to be great with scholar ; she that was never
with child longs, *omnibus viis et modis*, to be got with child,
and will wear a cushion to seem with child ; and he that was
never just, will fly in the King's face to be counted just,   115
though for all he be nothing but just a traitor.

Sec. The Admiral smiles.

Judge.   Answer yourself, my lord.

Chab. I shall, and briefly :
The furious eloquence of my accuser hath
Branch'd my offences heinous to the King,   120
And then his subject, a most vast indictment,
That to the king I have justified my merit

And services ; which conscience of that truth
That gave my actions life, when they are questioned,
I ought to urge again, and do without   125
The least part of injustice. For the bill,
A foul and most unjust one, and preferr'd
Gainst the King's honour and his subjects' privilege
And with a policy to betray my office
And faith to both, I do confess I tore it,   130
It being press'd immodestly, but without
A thought of disobedience to his name ;
To whose mention I bow, with humble reverence,
And dare appeal to the King's knowledge of me
How far I am in soul from such a rebel.   135
For the rest, my lord, and you, my honour'd Judges,
Since all this mountain, all this time in labour
With more than mortal fury 'gainst my life,
Hath brought forth nought but some ridiculous vermin,
I will not wrong my right and innocence   140
With any serious plea in my reply,
To frustrate breath and fight with terrible shadow[s,]
That have been forg'd and forc'd against my state,
But leave all, with my life, to your free censures,
Only beseeching all your learned judgments,   145
Equal and pious conscience, to weigh—
     Proc.   And how this great and mighty fortune has exalted
him to pride is apparent, not only in his braves and bearings
to the King, the fountain of all this increase, but in his contempt and scorn of the subject, his vast expenses in buildings, 150
his private bounties, above royal, to soldiers and scholars,
that he may be the general and patron and protector of arms
and arts ; the number of domestic attendants, an army of
grasshoppers and gay butterflies, able to devour the spring ;
his glorious wardrobes, his stable of horses, that are pricked 155
with provender, and will enforce us to weed up our vineyards,
to sow oats for supply of their provision ; his caroches shining with gold, and more bright than the chariot of the sun,
wearing out the pavements—nay, he is of late so transcen-
dently proud that men must be his mules and carry him up 160
and down, as it were in a procession for men to gaze at him, till
their chines crack with the weight of his insupportable pride,
and who knows but this may prove a fashion ? But who
groans for this ? The subject ! Who murmur, and are ready to
begin a rebellion, but the tumultuous sailors and water-rats, 165

who run up and down the city, like an overbearing tempest,
cursing the Admiral, who in duty ought to undo himself for
the general satisfaction of his countrymen ?

   Chab.   The variety and wonder now presented
To your most noble notice and the world's,   170
That all my life and actions and offices
Explor'd with all the hundred eyes of law,
Lighted with lightning, shot out of the wrath
Of an incens'd and commanding king,
And blown with foes with far more bitter winds   175
Than Winter from his Eastern cave exhales,
Yet nothing found, but what you all have heard ;
And then consider if a peer of state
Should be expos'd to such a wild arraignment
For poor complaints—his fame, faith, life, and honours   180
Rack'd for no more.

   Chan.   No more ?   Good Heaven !   What say
My learn'd assistants ?

   1st Judge.   My lord, the crimes urg'd here for us to censure
As capital and worth this high arraignment,
To me seem strange, because they do not fall   185
In force of law to arraign a Peer of state ;
For all that law can take into her power
To sentence is the exaction of the fishermen.

   2nd Judge.   Here is no majesty violated : I consent
To what my brother has express'd.

   Chan.   Break then in wonder, 190
My frighted words out of their forming powers,
That you no more collect from all these forfeits
That Master Proctor-General hath opened
With so apparent and impulsive learning
Against the rage and madness of the offender,   195
And violate majesty, my learned assistants,
When majesty's affronted and defied,
(It being compar'd with, and in such an onset
As leap'd into his throat, his life affrighting !)
Be justified in all insolence all subjects,   200
If this be so considered, and insult
Upon your privileg'd malice !   Is not majesty
Poison'd in this wonder, and no felony set
Where royalty is robb'd and [violate] ?
Fie, how it fights with law, and grates upon   205
Her brain and soul, and all the powers of reason !

Reporter of the process, show the schedule.

Notary. Here, my good lord.

1st *Judge.*   No altering it in us.

2nd *Judge.* Far be it from us, sir.

Chan.   Here's silken justice !

It might be altered ; mend your sentences.   210

Both. Not we, my lord !

Chan.   Not you ? The King shall know
You slight a duty to his will and safety.
Give me your pen ; it must be capital.

1st *Judge.* Make what you please, my lord ; our doom
    shall stand.

Chan. Thus, I subscribe : now, at your perils, follow.   215

Both. Perils, my lord ? Threats in the King's free justice ?

Treas. I am amaz'd they can be so remiss.

Sec. Merciful men, pitiful judges, certain !

1st *Judge* [*aside*]. Subscribe ; it matters nothing, being
    constrain'd.

On this side [*V*], and on this side this capital *I*,   220
Both which together put, import plain *Vi ;*
And witness we are forc'd.

2nd *Judge* [*aside*].   Enough ;
It will acquit us, when we make it known,
Our names are forc'd.

Chan.   If traitorous pride
Upon the royal person of a king   225
Were sentenc'd unfeloniously before,
I'll burn my books, and be a judge no more.

Both. Here are our hands subscrib'd.

Chan.   Why, so ! It joys me,
You have reform'd your justice and your judgment.
Now have you done like judges and learned lawyers ;   230
The King shall thank and honour you for this.
Notary, read.

Not. *We, by his sacred Majesty appointed judges, upon due
trial and examination of Philip Chabot, Admiral of France,
declare him guilty of high treasons, etc.*   235

Chan. Now, Captain of the guard, secure his person
Till the King signify
His pleasure for his death. This day is happy
To France, thus rescued from the vile devourer.

                                        A shout within

Hark, how the votes applaud their blest deliverance !   240

[*To* Chabot]   You that so late did right and conscience
    boast,
Heaven's mercy now implore, the King's is lost.   *Exeunt*

ACTUS QUARTUS
[SCENA I
A Room in the Court]
Enter King, Queen, *and* Constable

  King. You raise my thoughts to wonder, that you, madam,
And you, my lord, unite your force to plead
I' th' Admiral's behalf : this is not that
Language you did express, when the torn bill
Was late pretended to us ; it was then   5
Defiance to our high prerogative,
The act of him whose proud heart would rebel,
And, arm'd with faction, too soon attempt
To tear my crown off.
  Queen.   I was ignorant
Then of his worth, and heard but the report   10
Of his accusers and his enemies,
Who never mention in his character
Shadows of any virtue in those men
They would depress : like crows and carrion birds,
They fly o'er flowery meads, clear springs, fair gardens,   15
And stoop at carcases. For your own honour,
Pity poor Chabot.
  King.   Poor, and a Colossus
That could so lately straddle o'er a province ?
Can he be fallen so low and miserable,
To want my pity, who breaks forth like day,   20
Takes up all people's eyes and admiration ?
It cannot be. He hath a princely wife, too.
  Queen. I interpose not often, sir, or press you
With unbecoming importunity
To serve the profitable ends of others.   25
Conscience and duty to yourself enforce
My present mediation ; you have given
The health of your own state away, unless
Wisdom in time recover him.
  King.   If he prove
No adulterate gold, trial confirms his value.   30

Queen. Although it hold in metal, gracious sir,
Such fiery examination and the furnace
May waste a heart that's faithful, and together
With that you call the *fæces*, something of
The precious substance may be hazarded.   35
   King. [*To the* Constable] Why, you are the chief engine
      rais'd against him,
And in the world's creed labour most to sink him
That in his fall and absence every beam
May shine on you and only gild your fortune.
Your difference is the ground of his arraignment;   40
Nor were we unsolicited by you
To have your bill confirm'd; from that, that spring,
Came all these mighty and impetuous waves,
With which he now must wrestle; if the strength
Of his own innocence can break the storm,   45
Truth wo' not lose her servant, her wings cover him.
He must obey his fate.
   Mont.   I would not have
It lie upon my fame that I should be
Mentioned in story his unjust supplanter
For your whole kingdom. I have been abused,   50
And made believe my suit was just and necessary;
My walks have not been safe, my closet prayers,
But some plot has pursued me by some great ones
Against your noble Admiral; they have frighted
My fancy into my dreams with their close whispers   55
How to uncement your affections,
And render him the fable and the scorn
Of France.
   Queen. Brave Montmorency!
   King.   Are you serious?
   Mont. Have I a soul or gratitude to acknowledge
Myself your creature, dignified and honour'd   60
By your high favours? With an equal truth
I must declare the justice of your Admiral
(In what my thoughts are conscious), and will rather
Give up my claim to birth, title, and offices,
Be thrown from your warm smile, the top and crown   65
Of subjects' happiness, than be brib'd with all
Their glories to the guilt of Chabot's ruin.
   King. Come, come; you overact this passion,
And if it be not policy, it tastes

Too green, and wants some counsel to mature it;   70
His fall prepares your triumph.
 Mont.   It confirms
My shame alive, and, buried, will corrupt
My very dust, make our house-genius groan,
And fright the honest marble from my ashes.
His fall prepare my triumph! Turn me first   75
A naked exile to the world.
 King.   No more;
Take heed you banish not yourself; be wise,
And let not too much zeal devour your reason.

     Enter Asall

 As. Your Admiral is condemn'd, sir.
 King.   Ha, strange! No matter;
Leave us. [*Exit* Asall] A great man, I see, may be   80
As soon dispatch'd as a common subject.
 Queen. No mercy then for Chabot!

   Enter Wife *and* Father

 Wife.   From whence came
That sound of Chabot? Then we are all undone.
[*Kneeling*] Oh, do not hear the Queen, she is no friend
To my poor lord, but made against his life,   85
Which hath too many enemies already!
 Mont. [*To the* Father] Poor soul! She thinks the Queen
  is still against him,
Who employeth all her powers to preserve him.
 Fath. Say you so, my lord? Daughter, the Queen's our
  friend.
 Wife. Why do you mock my sorrow? Can you flatter   90
Your own grief so? [*To the* King] Be just and hear me,
  sir,
And do not sacrifice a subject's blood
To appease a wrathful Queen; let mercy shine
Upon your brow, and heaven will pay it back
Upon your soul: be deaf to all her prayers.   95
 King. Poor heart, she knows not what she has desir'd.
 Wife. I beg my Chabot's life; my sorrows yet
Have not destroy'd my reason.
 King.   He is in the power
Of my laws, not mine.
 Wife.   Then you have no power,

And are but the empty shadow of a king.   100
To whom is it resign'd.   Where shall I beg
The forfeit life of one condemn'd by law's
Too partial doom ?
    King.   You hear he is condemn'd then ?
    Fath. My son is condemn'd, sir.
    King.   You know for what too ?
    Fath. What the judges please to call it ;   105
But they have given 't a name—treason, they say.
    Queen. I must not be denied.
    King.   I must deny you.
    Wife. Be blest for ever for't !
    Queen.   Grant then to her.
    King. Chabot condemned by law !
    Fath.   But you have power
To change the rigour ; in your breast there is   110
A chancellor above it. [*Kneeling*] I ne'er had
A suit before ; but my knees join with hers
To implore your royal mercy to her lord,
And take his cause to your examination ;
It cannot wrong your judges, if they have   115
Been steer'd by conscience.
    Mont.   It will fame your justice.
    King. I cannot be prescrib'd ; you kneel in vain.
You labour to betray me with your tears
To a treason above his, gainst my own laws.

                        [*The Wife swoons*]
Look to the lady !

Enter Asall

    As.   Sir, the Chancellor !   120
    King. Admit him.—Leave us all.

                Exeunt [*all but the* King]

Enter Chancellor

                How now, my lord ?
You have lost no time ; and how thrive the proceedings ?
    Chan. 'Twas fit, my gracious Sovereign, Time should leave
His motion made in all affairs beside,
And spend his wings only in speed of this.   125
    King. You have show'd diligence ; and what's become
Of our most curious justicer, the Admiral ?

Chan. Condemn'd, sir, utterly, and all hands set
To his conviction.
 King.   And for faults most foul ?
 Chan. More than most impious : but the applausive
  issue,   130
Struck by the concourse of your ravish'd subjects
For joy of your free justice, if there were
No other cause to assure the sentence just,
Were proof convincing.
 King.   Now then he sees clearly
That men perceive how vain his justice was,   135
And scorn him for the foolish net he wore
To hide his nakedness. Is't not a wonder
That men's ambitions should so blind their reason
To affect shapes of honesty, and take pride
Rather in seeming than in being just ?   140
 Chan. Seeming has better fortune to attend it
Than being sound at heart, and virtuous.
 King. Profess all, nothing do, like those that live
By looking to the lamps of holy temples,
Who still are busy taking off their snuffs,   145
But for their profit sake will add no oil !
So these will check and sentence every f[l]ame,
The blaze of riotous blood doth cast in others,
And in themselves leave the fume most offensive.
But he to do this, more deceives my judgment   150
Than all the rest whose nature I have sounded.
 Chan. I know, sir, and have prov'd it.
 King.   Well, my lord,
To omit circumstance, I highly thank you
For this late service you have done me here,
Which is so great and meritorious   155
That with my ablest power I scarce can quit you.
 Chan. Your sole acceptance, my dread Sovereign,
I more rejoice in than in all the fortunes
That ever chanc'd me. But when may it please
Your Highness to order the execution ?   160
The haste thus far has spar'd no pinions.
 King. No, my lord, your care
Hath therein much deserv'd.
 Chan.   But where proportion
Is kept to th' end in things at start so happy,
That end set on the crown.

King.   I'll speed it therefore.   165
Chan. Your thoughts direct it ; they are wing'd.   *Exit*
King.   I joy
This boldness is condemn'd, that I may pardon,
And therein get some ground in his opinion,
By so much bounty as saves his life ;
And methinks that, weigh'd more, should sway the balance 170
'Twixt me and him, held by his own free justice ;
For I could never find him obstinate
In any mind he held, when once he saw
Th' error with which he laboured ; and since now
He needs must feel it, I admit no doubt   175
But that his alteration will beget
Another sense of things 'twixt him and me.
Who's there ?

Enter Asall

Go to the Captain of my guard, and will him
To attend his condemn'd prisoner to me instantly.   180
    As. I shall, sir.

Enter Treasurer *and* Secretary

King. My lords, you were spectators of our Admiral.
    Treas. And hearers too of his most just conviction,
In which we witness'd over-weight enough
In your great bounties, as they there were weigh'd,   185
With all the feathers of his boasted merits.
    King. Has felt a scorching trial ; and the test
That holds fire's utmost force we must give metals
That will not with the hammer and the melting
Confess their truth ; and this same sense of feeling   190
(Being ground to all the senses), hath one key
More than the rest to let in through them all
The mind's true apprehension, that thence takes
Her first convey'd intelligence.   I long
To see this man of confidence again.   195
How think you, lords, will Chabot look on me,
Now spoil'd of the integrity he boasted ?
    Sec. It were too much honour to vouchsafe your sight.
    Treas. No doubt, my Liege, but he that hath offended
In such a height against your crown and person,   200
Will want no impudence to look upon you.

Enter Asall, Captain, Admiral

Cap. Sir, I had charge given me by this gentleman
To bring your condemn'd prisoner to your presence.
King. You have done well ; and tell the Queen and our
Lord Constable we desire their presence ; bid   205
Our Admiral's lady, and her father too,
Attend us here : they are but new withdrawn.
As. I shall, sir.
Treas.   Do you observe this confidence ?
He stands as all his trial were a dream.
Sec. He'll find the horror waking. The King's troubled : 210
Now for a thunder-clap. The Queen and Constable !

Enter Queen, Constable, Wife, *and* Father

Treas. I do not like their mixture.
King.   My Lord Admiral,
You made it your desire to have this trial
That late hath pass'd upon you ;
And now you feel how vain is too much faith   215
And flattery of yourself, as if your breast
Were proof gainst all invasion ; 'tis so slight,
You see, it lets in death ; what's past hath been
To satisfy your insolence ; there remains
That now we serve our own free pleasure ; therefore,   220
By that most absolute power, with which all right
Puts in my hands these issues, turns, and changes,
I here, in ear of all these, pardon all
Your faults and forfeits, whatsoever censur'd,
Again advancing and establishing   225
Your person in all fulness of that state
That ever you enjoy'd before th' attainder.
Treas. Wonderful, pardon'd !
Wife.   Heaven preserve the King !
Queen. Who for this will deserve all time to honour him.
Mont. And live kings' best example.
Fath.   Son, y'are pardon'd ; 230
Be sure you look hereafter well about you.
Chab. Vouchsafe, great sir, to assure me what you said ;
You nam'd my pardon.
King.   And again declare it,
For all crimes past, of what nature soever.
Chab. You cannot pardon me, sir.
King.   How's that, Philip ? 235

Chab. It is a word carries too much relation
To an offence, of which I am not guilty.
And I must still be bold, where truth still arms,
In spite of all those frowns that would deject me,
To say I need no pardon.
 King.   Ha, how's this ?   240
 Fath. He's mad with over joy and answers nonsense.
 King. Why, tell me, Chabot, are not you condemn'd ?
 Chab. Yes, and that justifies me much the more ;
For whatsoever false report hath brought you,
I was condemn'd for nothing that could reach 245
To prejudice my life, my goods, or honour,
As first, in firmness of my conscience,
I confidently told you ; not, alas !
Presuming on your slender thread of favour,
Or pride of fortunate and courtly boldness, 250
But what my faith and justice bade me trust to ;
For none of all your learn'd assistant judges,
With all the malice of my crimes, could urge
Or felony or hurt of sacred power.
 King. Do any hear this but myself ? My lords, 255
This man still justifies his innocence.
What prodigies are these ? Have not our laws
Pass'd on his actions ; have not equal judges
Certified his arraignment and him guilty
Of capital treason ; and yet do I hear 260
Chabot accuse all these, and quit himself ?
 Treas. It does appear distraction, sir.
 King.   Did we
Seem so indulgent to propose our free
And royal pardon, without suit or prayer,
To meet with his contempt ?
 Sec.   Unheard-of impudence ! 265
 Chab. I were malicious to myself and desperate
To force untruths upon my soul, and, when
'Tis clear, to confess a shame to exercise
Your pardon, sir. Were I so foul and monstrous
As I am given to you, you would commit 270
A sin next mine by wronging your own mercy
To let me draw out impious breath : it will
Release your wonder if you give command
To see your process ; and if it prove other
Than I presume to inform, tear me in pieces. 275

King. Go for the process, and the Chancellor,
With the assistant Judges.

Exit Asall

I thank heaven

That with all these enforcements of distraction
My reason stays so clear to hear and answer
And to direct a message. This inversion   280
Of all the loyalties and true deserts
That I believ'd I govern'd with till now,
In my choice lawyers and chief counsellors,
Is able to shake all my frame of reason.

  Chab. I am much griev'd.

  King.   No more! [*Aside*] I do incline   285
To think I am abus'd, my laws betray'd
And wrested to the purpose of my judges.
This confidence in Chabot turns my judgment:
This was too wild a way to make his merits
Stoop and acknowledge my superior bounties,   290
That it doth raise and fix 'em past my art
To shadow ; all the shame and forfeit's mine.

Enter Asall, Chancellor, Judges

  As. The Chancellor and Judges, sir.

  Treas. [*aside*].   I like not
This passion in the King ; the Queen and Constable
Are of that side.

  King.   My lord, you dare appear, then ?   295

  Chan. Dare, sir ? I hope—

  King.   Well done ; hope still, and tell me,
Is not this man condemn'd ?

  Chan.   Strange question, sir !
The process will declare it, sign'd with all
These my assistant brothers' reverend hands,
To his conviction in a public trial.   300

  King. You said for foul and monstrous facts prov'd
          by him ?

  Chan. The very words are there, sir.

  King.   But the deeds
I look for, sir ; name me but one that's monstrous.

  Chan. His foul comparisons and affronts of you
To me seem'd monstrous.

  King.   I told you them, sir ;   305
Nor were they any that your so vast knowledge,
Being a man studied in him, could produce

And prove as clear as heaven ; you warranted
To make appear such treasons in the Admiral,
As never all law's volumes yet had sentenc'd,   310
And France should look on having scap'd with wonder.
What in this nature hath been clearly prov'd
In his arraignment ?

   1st Judge.   Nothing that we heard
In slend'rest touch urg'd by your advocate.

   King. Dare you affirm this too ?

   2nd Judge.   Most confidently.   315

   King. No base corruptions charg'd upon him ?

   1st Judge.   None, sir !

   Treas. [*aside*] This argues Chabot has corrupted him.

   Sec. [*aside*] I do not like this.

   1st Judge.   The sum of all
Was urg'd to prove your Admiral corrupt,
Was an exaction of his officers   320
Of twenty sous taken from the fishermen
For every boat that fish'd the Norman coast.

   King. And was this all
The mountains and the marvels promis'd me,
To be in clear proof made against the life   325
Of our so hated Admiral ?

   Judges.   All, sir,
Upon our lives and consciences !

   Chan. [*aside*]   I am blasted.

   King. How durst you then subscribe to his conviction ?

   1st Judge. For threats by my Lord Chancellor on the
      bench,
Affirming that your Majesty would have it   330
Made capital treason, or account us traitors.

   2nd Judge. Yet, sir, we did put to our names with this
Interposition of a note in secret
In these two letters, *V* and *I*, to show
We were enforc'd to what we did, which then   335
In law is nothing.

   Fath.   How do you feel, your lordship ?
Did you not find some stuffing in your head ?
Your brain should have been purg'd.

   Chan.   I fall to pieces.
Would they had rotted on the bench !

   King. And so you sav'd the peace of that high court, 340
Which otherwise his impious rage had broken ;

But thus am I by his malicious arts
A par[t]y render'd, and most tyrannous spur
To all the open course of his base envies,
A forcer of my judges, and a thirst   345
Of my nobility's blood, and all by one
I trusted to make clear my love of justice.
  Chan. I beseech your Majesty let all my zeal
To serve your virtues, with a sacred value
Made of your royal state to which each least   350
But shade of violence in any subject
Doth provoke certain death—
  King.   Death on thy name
And memory for ever! One command
Our Advocate attend us presently.
  As. He waits here.   355
  King. But single death shall not excuse thy skin
Torn o'er thine ears, and what else can be inflicted,
If thy life, with the same severity
Dissected, cannot stand so many fires.

  Sec. ⎫
  Treas. ⎬ Be merciful, great sir!   [*Kneeling.*]
       ⎭

  King.   Yet more amaze!   360
Is there a knee in all the world beside,
That any human conscience can let bow
For him. Y'are traitors all that pity him.
  Treas. [*Aside*] This is no time to move.
  King.   Yet 'twas my fault
To trust this wretch, whom I knew fierce and proud   365
With forms of tongue and learning. What a prisoner
Is pride of the whole flood of man! For as
A human seed is said to be a mixture
And fair contemperature extracted from
All our best faculties, so the seed of all   370
Man's sensual frailty may be said to abide,
And have their confluence in only pride;
It stupefies man's reason so, and dulls
True sense of anything but what may fall
In his own glory, quenches all the spirits   375
That light a man to honour and true goodness.
  As. Your advocate.

Enter Advocate

  King. Come hither.

Ad.   My most gracious Sovereign.
                        [King *talks with him aside*]
Chab.   Madam, you infinitely oblige our duty.
Queen.   I was too long ignorant of your worth, my lord, 380
And this sweet lady's virtue.
Wife.   Both your servants.
Chab.   I never had a fear of the King's justice,
And yet I know not what creeps o'er my heart,
And leaves an ice beneath it. My Lord Chancellor,
You have my forgiveness ; but implore Heaven's pardon 385
For wrongs to equal justice ; you shall want
No charity of mine to mediate
To the King for you.
Chan.   Horror of my soul
Confounds my gratitude.
Mont. [*To* Chabot]   To me now most welcome.
Ad. [*To the* King]   It was my allegiance, sir ; I did
enforce   390
But by directions of your Chancellor ;
It was my office to advance your cause
Gainst all the world, which when I leave to execute,
Flay me, and turn me out a most raw advocate.
King.   You see my Chancellor.
Ad.   He has an ill look with him. 395
King.   It shall be your province now, on our behalf,
To urge what can in justice be against him ;
His riot on our laws and corrupt actions
Will give you scope and field enough.
Ad.   And I
Will play my law prize ; never fear it, sir.   400
He shall be guilty of what you please. I am studied
In him, sir ; I will squeeze his villanies,
And urge his acts so home into his bowels,
The force of it shall make him hang himself,
And save the laws a labour.
King.   Judges, for all   405
The poisonous outrage that this viper spilt
On all my royal freedom and my empire,
As making all but servants to his malice,
I will have you revise the late arraignment ;
And for those worthy reasons that already   410
Affect you for my Admiral's acquittal,
Employ your justice on this Chancellor. Away with him !

Arrest him, Captain of my Guard, to answer
All that due course of law against him can
Charge both his acts and life.

   Cap.   I do arrest thee,   415
Poyet, Lord Chancellor, in his Highness' name,
To answer all that equal course of law
Can charge thy acts and life with.

   Chan.   I obey.
                     [*Exit* Chancellor *guarded*]

   King. How false a heart corruption has ! How base,
Without true worth, are all these earth-bred glories !   420
O, blessed justice, by which all things stand,
That stills the thunder, and makes lightning sink
'Twixt earth and heaven amaz'd, and cannot strike,
Being prov'd so now in wonder of this man,
The object of men's hate, and heaven's bright love ;   425
And as in cloudy days we see the sun
Glide over turrets, temples, richest fields,
All those left dark and slighted in his way,
And on the wretched plight of some poor shed,
Pours all the glories of his golden head :   430
So heavenly virtue on this envied lord
Points all his graces that I may distinguish
Him better from the world.

   Treas.   You do him right.

   King. But away, Judges, and pursue the arraignment
Of this polluted Chancellor with that swiftness   435
His fury wing'd against my Admiral ;
And be you all that sate on him compurgators
Of me against this false judge.

   Judges.   We are so.

   King. Be you two join'd in the commission,
And nothing urg'd but justly, of me learning   440
This one more lesson out of the events
Of these affairs now past : that whatsoever
Charge or commission judges have from us,
They ever make their aim ingenuous justice,
Not partial for reward or swelling favour ;   445
To which if your king steer you, spare to obey,
For when his troubled blood is clear and calm,
He will repent that he pursued his rage,
Before his pious law, and hold that judge
Unworthy of his place that lets his censure   450

Float in the waves of an imagin'd favour ;
This shipwrecks in the haven, and but wounds
Their consciences that soothe the soon-ebb'd humours
Of their incensed king.

Mont.⎱
Treas.⎰   Royal and sacred !

King. Come, Philip, shine thy honour now for ever,   455
For this short temporal eclipse it suffer'd
By th' interpos'd desire I had to try thee,
Nor let the thought of what is past afflict thee
For my unkindness ; live still circled here,
The bright intelligence of our royal sphere.   460

                                        Exeunt

ACTUS QUINTUS

[SCENA I

A Room in the Court]

Enter Queen, Constable, Father

Queen. The Admiral sick ?
Fath.   With danger at the heart ;
I came to tell the King.
Mont.   He never had
More reason in his soul to entertain
All the delights of health.
Fath.   I fear, my lord,
Some apprehension of the King's unkindness,   5
By giving up his person and his offices
To the law's gripe and search, is ground of his
Sad change ; the greatest souls are thus oft wounded ;
If he vouchsafe his presence, it may quicken
His fast decaying spirits, and prevent   10
The hasty ebb of life.
Queen.   The King is now
Fraught with the joy of his fresh preservation ;
The news so violent let into his ear,
May have some dangerous effect in him ;
I would not counsel, sir, to that.
Fath.   With greater reason   15
I may suspect they'll spread, my lord, and, as
A river, l[i]ft his curl'd and impetuous waves

Over the banks, by confluence of streams
That fill and swell [their] channel; for by this time
He has the addition of Allegre's suffering,   20
His honest servant, whom I met, though feeble
And worn with torture, going to congratulate
His master's safety.

   Queen.   It seems he much
Affected that Allegre.

   Mont.   There will be
But a sad interview and dialogue.   25

   Queen. Does he keep his bed?

   Fath.   In that alone
He shows a fortitude; he will move and walk,
He says, while his own strength or others' can
Support him, wishing he might stand and look
His destiny in the face at the last summons,   30
Not sluggishly exhale his soul in bed
With indulgence, and nice flattery of his limbs.

   Queen. Can he in this show spirit, and want force
To wrestle with a thought?

   Fath.   Oh, madam, madam!
We may have proof against the sword and tyranny   35
Of boisterous war that threatens us; but when
Kings frown, a cannon mounted in each eye,
Shoot death to apprehension ere their fire
And force approach us.

                   Enter King

   Mont.   Here's the King.

   Queen.   No words
To interrupt his quiet.

   Fath.   I'll begone, then.   40

   King. Our Admiral's father? Call him back.

   Queen. I wo' not stay to hear 'em.   *Exit*

   Mont.   Sir, be prudent,
And do not, for your son, fright the King's health. *Exit*

   King. What, ha' they left us?—How does my Admiral?

   Fath. I am forbid to tell you, sir.

   King.   By whom?   45

   Fath. The Queen and my Lord Constable.

   King.   Are there
Remaining seeds of faction? Have they souls
Not yet convinc'd i' th' truth of Chabot's honour,

Clear as the crystal heaven, and 'bove the reach
Of imitation ?
 Fath.   'Tis their care of you,   50
And no thought prejudicial to my son.
 King.   Their care of me ?
How can the knowledge of my Admiral's state
Concern their fears of me ? I see their envy
Of Chabot's happiness, whose joy to be
Render'd so pure and genuine to the world 55
Doth grate upon their conscience and affright 'em.
But let 'em vex, and bid my Chabot still
Exalt his heart, and triumph ; he shall have
The access of ours ; the kingdom shall put on
Such joys for him, as she would boast to celebrate 60
Her own escape from ruin.
 Fath. [*aside.*]   He is not
In state to hear my sad news, I perceive.
 King. That countenance is not right, it does not answer
What I expect ; say, how is my Admiral ?
The truth, upon thy life !
 Fath.   To secure his, 65
I would you had.
 King.   Ha ! Who durst oppose him ?
 Fath. One that hath power enough hath practis'd on him,
And made his great heart stoop.
 King.   I will revenge it
With crushing that rebellious power to nothing.
Name him.
 Fath. He was his friend.   70
 King. A friend to malice ; his own black imposthume
Burn his blood up ! What mischief hath engender'd
New storms ?
 Fath.   'Tis the old tempest.
 King.   Did not we
Appease all horrors that look'd wild upon him ?
 Fath. You dress'd his wounds, I must confess, but made 75
No cure ; they bleed afresh. Pardon me, sir ;
Although your conscience have clos'd too soon,
He is in danger, and doth want new surgery ;
Though he be right in fame and your opinion,
He thinks you were unkind.
 King.   Alas, poor Chabot ! 80
Doth that afflict him ?

Fath.   So much, though he strive
With most resolv'd and adamantine nerves,
As ever human fire in flesh and blood
Forg'd for example to bear all, so killing
The arrows that you shot were (still your pardon),   85
No centaur's blood could rankle so.
  King.   If this
Be all, I'll cure him ; kings retain
More balsam in their soul than hurt in anger.
  Fath. Far short, sir ; with one breath they uncreate ;
And kings, with only words, more wounds, can make   90
Than all their kingdom made in balm can heal ;
'Tis dangerous to play too wild a descant
On numerous virtue, though it become princes
To assure their adventures made in everything :
Goodness, confin'd within poor flesh and blood,   95
Hath but a queasy and still sickly state ;
A musical hand should only play on her,
Fluent as air, yet every touch command.
  King. No more !
Commend us to the Admiral, and say   100
The King will visit him, and bring [him] health.
  Fath. I will not doubt that blessing, and shall move
Nimbly with this command.   *Exeunt*

[SCENA II

A Court of Justice]

Enter Officers *before* ; Treasurer, Secretary, *and* Judges, *attended
  by* Petitioners, *the* Advocate *also, with many papers in his
  hand. They take their places : the* Chancellor, *with a* guard
  [*is led in*], *and placed at the bar.*

  Treas. [*aside*] Did you believe the Chancellor had been
So foul ?
  Sec. [*aside*]   He's lost to th' people ; what contempts
They throw upon him ! But we must be wise.
  1st Judge. Were there no other guilt, his malice show'd
Upon the Admiral in o'erbearing justice   5
Would well deserve a sentence.
  Treas.   And a deep one !
  2nd Judge. If please your lordships to remember, that

Was specially commended by the King,
As being most blemish to his royal person
And the free justice of his state.

Treas.   Already   10
He has confess'd upon his examinations
Enough for censure ; yet, to obey form—
Master Advocate, if you please—

Ad. I am ready for your lordships. It hath been said,
and will be said again, and may truly be justified, *omnia ex*   15
lite fieri. It was the position of philosophers, and now
proved by a more philosophical sect, the lawyers, that,
omnia ex lite fiant, we are all made by law—made, I say, and
worthily, if we be just ; if we be unjust, marred ; though in
marring some, there is necessity of making others, for if one   20
fall by the law, ten to one but another is exalted by the execution of the law, since the corruption of one must conclude the
generation of another, though not always in the same profession ; the corruption of an apothecary may be the generation
of a doctor of physic ; the corruption of a citizen may beget   25
a courtier, and a courtier may very well beget an alderman ;
the corruption of an alderman may be the generation of a
country justice, whose corrupt ignorance easily may beget a
tumult ; a tumult may beget a captain, and the corruption
of a captain may beget a gentleman-usher, and a gentleman-   30
usher may beget a lord, whose vit may beget a poet, and a
poet may get a thousand pound a year, but nothing without
corruption.

Treas. Good Master Advocate, be pleased to leave all
digressions, and speak of the Chancellor.   35

Ad. Your lordship doth very seasonably premonish ;
and I shall not need to leave my subject, corruption, while
I discourse of him, who is the very fen and Stygian abyss of
it : five thousand and odd hundred foul and impious corruptions, for I will be brief, have been found by several examina-   40
tions, and by oaths proved, against this odious and polluted
Chancellor ; a man of so tainted and contagious a life, that
it is a miracle any man enjoyeth his nostrils that hath lived
within the scent of his offices. He was born with teeth in
his head, by an affidavit of his midwife, to note his devouring,   45
and hath one toe on his left foot crooked, and in the form of
an eagle's talon, to foretell his rapacity—what shall I say ?—
branded, marked, and designed in his birth for shame and
obloquy, which appeareth further, by a mole under his

right ear, with only three witch's hairs in't; strange and 50
ominous predictions of nature !

Treas. You have acquainted yourself but very lately
with this intelligence, for, as I remember, your tongue was
guilty of no such character when he sat judge upon the
Admiral : a pious, incorrupt man, a faithful and fortunate 55
servant to his king ; and one of the greatest honours that ever
the Admiral received was, that he had so noble and just a
judge : this must imply a strange volubility in your tongue or
conscience. I speak not to discountenance any evidence for
the King, but to put you in mind, Master Advocate, that 60
you had then a better opinion of my Lord Chancellor.

Ad. Your lordship hath most aptly interposed, and with
a word I shall easily satisfy all your judgments. He was
then a judge, and *in cathedra*, in which he could not err—it
may be your lordships' cases. Out of the chair and seat of 65
justice he hath his frailties, is loosed and exposed to the
conditions of other human natures ; so every judge, your
lordships are not ignorant, hath a kind of privilege while he
is in his state, office, and being ; although he may, *quoad se*,
internally and privately be guilty of bribery of justice, yet, 70
quoad nos, and in public, he is an upright and innocent judge.
We are to take no notice, nay, we deserved to suffer, if we
should detect or stain him, for in that we disparage the office,
which is the King's, and may be our own ; but once removed
from his place by just dishonour of the King, he is no more 75
a judge, but a common person whom the law takes hold on,
and we are then to forget what he hath been, and without
partiality to strip and lay him open to the world, a counterfeit
and corrupt judge : as, for example, he may, and ought to
flourish in his greatness, and break any man's neck with as 80
much facility as a jest ; but the case being altered, and he
down, every subject shall be heard ; a wolf may be apparelled
in a lamb skin ; and if every man should be afraid to speak
truth nay, and more than truth, if the good of the subject,
which are clients, sometime require it, there would be no 85
remove of officers ; if no remove, no motions ; if no motion
in court, no heat, and, by consequence, but cold terms. Take
away this moving, this removing of judges, the law may
bury itself in buckram, and the kingdom suffer for want of a
due execution ; and, now, I hope, your lordships are satisfied. 90

Treas. Most learnedly concluded to acquit yourself.

1st Judge. Master Advocate, please you to urge, for

satisfaction of the world and clearing the King's honour, how
injustly he proceeded against the Admiral.

Ad. I shall obey your lordship.—So vast, so infinite hath   95
been the impudence of this Chancellor, not only toward the
subject, but even the sacred person of the King, that I
tremble, as with a palsy, to remember it. This man, or
rather this monster, having power and commission trusted
for the examination of the Lord Admiral, a man perfect in   100
all honour and justice, indeed, the very ornament and second
flower of France—for the flower-de-lis is sacred, and above
all flowers, and indeed the best flower in our garden—having
used all ways to circumvent his innocence, by suborning and
promising rewards to his betrayers, by compelling others by 105
the cruelty of tortures, as namely Monsieur Allegre, a most
honest and faithful servant to his lord, tearing and extending
his sinews upon the rack to force a confession to his purpose ;
and finding nothing prevail upon the invincible virtue of the
Admiral—   110

Sec. [*aside*] How he would flatter him !

Ad. Yet most maliciously proceeded to arraign him ; to be
short, against all colour of justice condemned him of high
treasons. Oh, think what the life of man is, that can never
be recompensed, but the life of a just man, a man that is 115
the vigour and glory of our life and nation, to be torn to death,
and sacrificed beyond the malice of common persecution !
What tiger of Hyrcanian breed could have been so cruel ?
But this is not all ! He was not guilty only of murder—guilty,
I may say, *in foro conscientiæ*, though our good Admiral was 120
miraculously preserved—but unto this he added a most prodigious and fearful rape, a rape even upon Justice itself, the
very soul of our state ; for the rest of the judges upon the
Bench, venerable images of [Astræa,] he most tyrannously
compelled to set their hands to his most unjust sentence. 125
Did ever story remember the like outrage and injustice ?
What forfeit, what penalty can be enough to satisfy this
transcendent offence ? And yet, my good lords, this is but
venial to the sacrilege which now follows, and by him committed : not content with this sentence, not satisfied with 130
horrid violence upon the sacred tribunal, but he proceeds
and blasphemes the very name and honour of the King himself,—observe that,—making him the author and impulsive
cause of all these rapines, justifying that he moved only by
his special command to the death, nay, the murder, of his   135

most faithful subject, translating all his own black and
damnable guilt upon the King. Here's a traitor to his
country ! First, he conspires the death of one whom the King
loves, and whom every subject ought to honour, and then
makes it no conscience to proclaim it the King's act, and, 140
by consequence, declares him a murderer of his own and
of his best subjects.

   [*Voices*] *within*. An advocate ! An advocate !
Tear him in pieces !   Tear the Chancellor in pieces !

   Treas. The people have deep sense of the Chancellor's
              injustice.   145

   Sec. We must be careful to prevent their mutiny.

   1*st Judge.* It will become our wisdoms to secure
The court and prisoner.

   Treas.   Captain of the Guard !

   2*nd Judge.* What can you say for yourself, Lord Chan-
      cellor ?

   Chan. Again, I confess all, and humbly fly to   150
The royal mercy of the King.

   Treas.   And this
Submission is the way to purchase it.

   Chan. Hear me, great judges : if you have not lost
For my sake all your charities, I beesech you
Let the King know my heart is full of penitence ;   155
Calm his high-going sea, or in that tempest
I ruin to eternity. Oh, my lords,
Consider your own places, and the helms
You sit at ; while with all your providence
You steer, look forth and see devouring quicksands !   160
My ambition now is punish'd, and my pride
Of state and greatness falling into nothing.
I, that had never time, through vast employments,
To think of Heaven, feel his revengeful wrath
Boiling my blood, and scorching up my entrails.   165
There doomsday is my conscience, black and horrid
For my abuse of justice ; but no stings
Prick with that terror as the wounds I made
Upon the pious Admiral. Some good man
Bear my repentance thither ; he is merciful,   170
And may incline the King to stay his lightning,
Which threatens my confusion. That my free
Resign of title, office, and what else
My pride look'd at, would buy my poor life's safety !

For ever banish me the court, and let   175
Me waste my life far off, in some village.
    Ad. How ! Did your lordships note his request to you ?
He would direct your sentence, to punish him with confining
him to live in the country ; like the mouse in the fable, that
having offended to deserve death, begged he might be banished 180
into a Parmesan. I hope your lordships will be more just to
the nature of his offences.
    Sec. I could have wish'd him fall on softer ground
For his good parts.
    Treas.   My lord, this is your sentence :
For you[r] high misdemeanours against his Majesty's judges, 185
for your unjust sentence of the most equal Lord Admiral, for
many and foul corruptions and abuse of your office, and that
infinite stain of the King's person and honour, we, in his
Majesty's name, deprive you of your estate of Chancellor, and
declare you uncapable of any judicial office ; and besides, con- 190
demn you in the sum of two hundred thousand crowns : whereof,
one hundred thousand to the King, and one hundred thousand to
the Lord Admiral ; and what remaineth of your estate, to go to
the restitution of those you have injured ; and to suffer per-
petual imprisonment in the castle.   195
So, take him to your custody.
Your lordships have been merciful in his sentence.
                                     Exit
   [*Chan.*] They have spar'd my life then ! That some cure
      may bring ;
I ['ll] spend it in my prayers for the King.   *Exeunt*

[SCENA III

A Room in Chabot's *House*]

Enter Admiral *in his gown and cap, his* Wife

    Chab. Allegre ! I am glad he hath so much strength ;
I prithee let me see him.
    Wife.   It will but
Enlarge a passion. My lord, he'll come
Another time, and tender you his service.
    Chab. Nay, then—
    Wife.   Although I like it not, I must obey.   5
                                       Exit

Enter Allegre, *supported*

Chab. Welcome, my injur'd servant, what a misery
Ha' they made on thee !
   Al.   Though some change appear
Upon my body, whose severe affliction
Hath brought it thus to be sustained by others,
My h[ea]rt is still the same in faith to you   10
Not broken with their rage.
   Chab.   Alas, poor man !
Were all my joys essential, and so mighty
As the affected world believes I taste,
This object were enough to unsweeten all.
Though in thy absence I had suffering,   15
And felt within me a strong sympathy,
While for my sake their cruelty did vex
And fright thy nerves with horror of thy sense,
Yet in this spectacle I apprehend
More grief than all my imagination   20
Could let before into me. Did'st not curse me
Upon the torture ?
   Al.   Good my lord, let not
The thought of what I suffer'd dwell upon
Your memory ; they could not punish more
Than what my duty did oblige to bear   25
For you and justice : but there's something in
Your looks presents more fear than all the malice
Of my tormentors could affect my soul with :
That paleness, and the other forms you wear,
Would well become a guilty admiral, and one   30
Lost to his hopes and honour, not the man
Upon whose life the fury of injustice,
Arm'd with fierce lightning, and the power of thunder,
Can make no breach. I was not rack'd till now :
There's more death in that falling eye than all   35
Rage ever yet brought forth. What accident, sir, can blast,
Can be so black and fatal, to distract
The calm, the triumph, that should sit upon
Your noble brow ? Misfortune could have no
Time to conspire with fate, since you were rescued   40
By the great arm of Providence ; nor can
Those garlands that now grow about your forehead,
With all the poison of the world be blasted.

Chab. Allegre, thou dost bear thy wounds upon thee
In wide and spacious characters ; but in   45
The volume of my sadness, thou dost want
An eye to read ; an open force hath torn
Thy manly sinews, which some time may cure ;
The engine is not seen that wounds thy master
Past all the remedy of art or time,   50
The flatteries of court, of fame, or honours :
Thus in the summer a tall flourishing tree,
Transplanted by strong hand, with all her leaves
And blooming pride upon her, makes a show
Of Spring, tempting the eye with wanton blossom ;   55
But not the sun, with all her amorous smiles,
The dews of morning, or the tears of night,
Can root her fibres in the earth again,
Or make her bosom kind to growth and bearing ;
But the tree withers ; and those very beams   60
That once were natural warmth to her soft verdure,
Dry up her sap, and shoot a fever through
The bark and rind, till she becomes a burthen
To that which gave her life ; so Chabot, Chabot—
Al. Wonder in apprehension ! I must   65
Suspect your health indeed.
Chab.   No, no, thou sha' not
Be troubled ; I but stirr'd thee with a moral,
That's empty, contains nothing. I am well ;
See, I can walk ; poor man, thou hast not strength yet !
                                                        [*Exit*]
Al. What accident is ground of this distraction ?   70

Enter Admiral

Chab. Thou hast not heard yet what's become o' th'
    Chancellor ?
Al. Not yet, my lord.
Chab.   Poor gentleman ! When I think
Upon the King, I've balm enough to cure
A thousand wounds ; have I not, Allegre ?
Was ever bounteous mercy read in story   75
Like his upon my life, condemn'd for sacrifice
By law, and snatch'd out of the flame unlooked for,
And unpetitioned ? But his justice then,
That would not spare whom his own love made great,
But give me up to the most cruel test   80

Of judges, for some boldness in defence
Of my own merits and my honest faith to him,
Was rare, past example.

Enter Father

Fath.   Sir, the King
Is coming hither.
Al.   It will
Become my duty, sir, to leave you now.   85
 Chab. Stay, by all means, Allegre, 't shall concern you.
I'm infinitely honour'd in his presence.

Enter King, Queen, Constable, and Wife

King. Madam, be comforted ; I'll be his physician.
Wife. Pray heaven you may !

[Chabot kneels. The King raises him]

 King.   No ceremonial knees ;
Give me thy heart, my dear, my honest Chabot ;   90
And yet in vain I challenge that ; 'tis here
Already in my own, and shall be cherish'd
With care of my best life ; [no] violence
Shall ravish it from my possession ;
Not those distempers that infirm my blood   95
And spirits shall betray it to a fear.
When time and nature join to dispossess
My body of a cold and languishing breath,
No stroke in all my arteries, but silence
In every faculty, yet dissect me then,   100
And in my heart the world shall read thee living,
And by the virtue of thy name writ there,
That part of me shall never putrefy,
When I am lost in all my other dust.
 Chab. You too much honour your poor servant, sir ; 105
My heart despairs so rich a monument ;
But when it dies—
 King.   I wo' not hear a sound
Of anything that trenche[th] upon death ;
He speaks the funeral of my crown that prophesies
So unkind a fate. We'll live and die together ;   110
And by that duty which hath taught you hitherto
All loyal and just services, I charge thee
Preserve thy heart for me and thy reward,
Which now shall crown thy merits.

Chab.   I have found
A glorious harvest in your favour, sir ;   115
And by this overflow of royal grace,
All my deserts are shadows, and fly from me.
I have not in the wealth of my desires
Enough to pay you now ; yet you encourage me
To make one suit.
 King.   So soon as nam'd, possess it.   120
 Chab.   You would be pleas'd take notice of this gentleman,
A secretary of mine.
 Mont.   Monsieur Allegre ;
He that was rack'd, sir, for your Admiral.
 Chab.   His limbs want strength to tender their full duty,
An honest man, that suffers for my sake.   125
 King.   He shall be dear to us. [*To* Allegre] For what has
  pass'd, sir,
By the unjustice of our Chancellor's power,
We'll study to recompense ; i' th' meantime, that office
You exercis'd for Chabot, we translate
To ourself ; you shall be our secretary.
 Al.   This is   130
An honour above my weak desert, and shall
Oblige the service of my life to satisfy it.
 Chab.   You are gracious, and in this act have put
All our complaints to silence.

 Enter Treasurer *and* Secretary, [*and give the* King *the sen-*
   tence of the Chancellor]

       You, Allegre,
Cherish your health and feeble limbs, which cannot,   135
Without much prejudice, be thus employ'd :
All my best wishes with thee.
 Al.   All my prayers
Are duties to your lordship.   *Exit*
 King.   'Tis too little !
Can forfeit of his place, wealth, and a lasting
Imprisonment, purge his offences to   140
Our honest Admiral ? had our person been
Exempted from his malice, he did persecute
The life of Chabot with an equal wrath ;
You should have pour'd death on his treacherous head.
I revoke all your sentences, and make   145

Him that was wrong'd full master of his destiny.

[*Turning to* Chabot]

Be thou his judge.

Chab.   Oh, far be such injustice !

I know his doom is heavy ; and I beg,

Where mercy may be let into his sentence,

For my sake, you would soften it ; I have   150

Glory enough to be set right in your's

And my dear country's thought, and by an act

With such apparent notice to the world.

King. Express it in some joy then.

Chab.   I will strive

To show that pious gratitude to you, but—   155

King. But what ?

Chab. My frame hath lately, sir, been ta'en a-pieces,

And but now put together ; the least force

Of mirth will shake and unjoint all my reason.

Your patience, royal sir.

King.   I'll have no patience,   160

If thou forget the courage of a man.

Chab. My strength would flatter me.

King.   Physicians !

Now I begin to fear his apprehension.

Why, how is Chabot's spirit fall'n !

Queen.   'Twere best

He were convey'd to his bed.

Wife.   How soon turn'd widow ! 165

Chab. Who would not wish to live to serve your goodness ?

Stand from me [*to those supporting him*], you betray me

     with your fears ;

The plummets may fall off that hang upon

My heart ; they were but thoughts at first : or if

They weigh me down to death, let not my eyes   170

Close with another object than the King ;

Let him be last I look on.

King. I would not have him lost for my whole kingdom.

Mont. He may recover, sir.

King.   I see it fall ;

For justice being the prop of every kingdom,   175

And mine broke, violating him that was

The knot and contract of it all in him ;

It [is] already falling in my ear.

Pompey could hear it thunder, when the Senate

And Capitol were deaf [t]o heaven's loud chiding.   180
I'll have another sentence for my Chancellor,
Unless my Chabot live.   In a prince
What a swift executioner is a frown !
Especially of great and noble souls.—
How is it with my Philip ?
    Chab.   I must beg   185
One other boon.
    King.   Upon condition
My Chabot will collect his scatter'd spirits,
And be himself again, he shall divide
My kingdom with me.
    Fath.   Sweet King !
    Chab.   I observe
A fierce and killing wrath engender'd in you ;   190
For my sake, as you wish me strength to serve you,
Forgive your Chancellor ; let not the story
Of Philip Chabot, read hereafter, draw
A tear from any family.   I beseech
Your royal mercy on his life and free   195
Remission of all seizure upon his state ;
I have no comfort else.
    King.   Endeavour but
Thy own health, and pronounce general pardon
To all through France.
    Chab.   Sir, I must kneel to thank you,
It is not seal'd else [*kneels*] ; your blest hand ; live happy.   200
May all you trust have no less faith than Chabot !
Oh !   [*Dies*]
    Wife.   His heart is broken.
    Fath.   And kneeling, sir,
As his ambition were in death to show
The truth of his obedience.
    Mont.   I fear'd this issue.
    Treas.   He's past hope.   205
    King. He has a victory in's death ; this world
Deserv'd him not.   How soon he was translated
To glorious eternity !   'Tis too late
To fright the air with words ; my tears embalm him !
    Wife.   What can become of me !   210
    [*King.*]   I'll be your husband, madam, and with care
Supply your children's father ; to your father
I'll be a son ; in what our love or power

Can serve his friends, Chabot shall ne'er be wanting.
The greatest loss is mine, past scale or recompence.　215
We will proceed no further gainst the Chancellor.
To the charity of our Admiral he owes`
His life, which, ever banish'd to a prison,
Shall not beget in us, or in the subject,
New fears of his injustice ; for his fortunes,　220
Great and acquir'd corruptly, 'tis our will
They make just restitution for all wrongs,
That shall within a year be prov'd aganst him.
Oh, Chabot, that shall boast as many monuments,
As there be hearts in France, which, as they grow,　225
Shall with more love enshrine thee ! Kings, they say,
Die not, or starve succession : Oh, why
Should that stand firm, and kings themselves despair
To find their subject still in the next heir ?　　*Exeunt*

FINIS